METROPOLITAN GOVERNANCE

American Governance and Public Policy series
Series Editor: Barry Rabe, University of Michigan

METROPOLITAN GOVERNANCE: CONFLICT, COMPETITION, AND COOPERATION

RICHARD C. FEIOCK, Editor

Georgetown University Press

WASHINGTON, D.C.

To my students, past and present

Georgetown University Press, Washington, D.C.

© 2004 by Georgetown University Press. All rights reserved.

Printed in the United States of America

The extracted text by J. Eric Oliver in chapter 2 is reprinted with the permission of Princeton University Press from *Democracy in Suburbia*, by J. Eric Oliver, © 2001.

10 9 8 7 6 5 4 3 2 1 2004

This book is printed on acid-free paper meeting the requirements of the American National Standard for Permanence in Paper for Printed Library Materials.

Library of Congress Cataloging-in-Publication Data

Metropolitan governance: conflict, competition, and cooperation / Richard, C. Feiock, editor.
    p. cm. — (American governance and public policy series)
  Includes bibliographical references and index.
  ISBN 1-58901-020-5 (pbk.: alk. paper)
  1. Metropolitan government.   I. Feiock, Richard C. II. American governance and public policy
  JS241.M48 2004
  320.8′5—dc22
                                                    2004005614

CONTENTS

LIST OF FIGURES AND TABLES

PREFACE

This book grew out of an October 2002 symposium on decentralized governance held at Florida State University in Tallahassee. This symposium was sponsored by the DeVoe Moore Center for the Study of Critical Issues in Economic Policy and Government at Florida State. All the contributors to this volume were participants in the symposium. This meeting was a watershed experience for some of us. More than just bringing together leading scholars of local government to report their research, it was an opportunity to take stock of the state of the urban politics field and critically evaluate its role within the discipline of political science.

The state of the field was seen as less than satisfactory, for reasons that are discussed in chapter 1 of the present volume. Nevertheless, considerable excitement was generated by the resurgence of interest in local government research outside the field and by the improvements in the theoretical and methodological rigor of new scholarship within the field. This enthusiasm and desire to speak to larger issues in political science provided the catalyst for the chapters presented here.

This book would not have been possible without the generous support of the DeVoe Moore Center and its director, David Rasmussen. A number of colleagues participated in the symposium and/or provided written comments to the authors on their work. They include Charles Barrilleaux, Robert Bradley, Tom Carsey, Timothy Chapin, Jim Gwartney, Carolyn Herrington, Keith Ihlanfeldt, David Rasmussen, John Scholz, and Christopher Stream. Some of the material in chapters 1 and 3 is based upon work supported by the National Science Foundation under Grant 0214174. Any opinions, findings, and conclusions or recommendations expressed in this material are those of the authors and do not necessarily reflect the views of the National Science Foundation.

Moon-Gi Jeong provided invaluable assistance in organizing, preparing, and editing the manuscript. Scott Lamothe carefully read the entire manuscript and provided detailed comments and suggestions. Sherry Rice and the staff of the DeVoe Moore Center provided great assistance in the final stages of production.

It is to my past and present doctoral students that I dedicate this work. I have had the good fortune of working with some very gifted students at Florida State and have had the pleasure of watching a number of them turn into productive young scholars.

PART ONE

THEORETICAL EXPLORATIONS

RICHARD C. FEIOCK

INTRODUCTION: REGIONALISM AND INSTITUTIONAL COLLECTIVE ACTION

The distinction between government and governance is emphasized in much of the contemporary work on local politics and public administration. At a local level, governance encompasses more than city or county governments; it includes voluntary, not-for-profit, and private organizations as well as intergovernmental linkages. By focusing on decentralized governance, this volume highlights issues of competition and cooperation within and across sectors. It also demonstrates the central role that municipal governments play in the governance of metropolitan areas. The organization and structure of city governments shape local governance by influencing the cost of accessing governmental authority. This volume explains how the configuration of local governments influences public and private policy decisions, the service provision choices available to citizens, and the ability of local units to act collectively to address regional problems.

Concerns about the organization of local government in metropolitan areas have produced some of the most important and enduring questions for the field of urban politics. Renewed interest in local institutions and the organization of governments in metropolitan areas has coincided with the rise of the "new regionalism" movement. The study of local government in political science, planning, and public administration has been taken with the concepts of regionalism in recent years (Wheeler 2002). There have been increased calls for a regional approach to the problems confronting America's urban areas (Downs 1994; Brookings Institution 2002).

To many, regionalism entails traditional prescriptions for metropolitan areas such as centralization and consolidation of governments and functions, or the creation of regional organizations (Stephens and Wikstrom 2000; Savitch and Vogel 2000). This first path to regional governance builds upon and extends arguments from the progressive reform tradition that emphasized the structural reform of local governments (Lowery 2000). The Progressive reform movement of the early twentieth century relied on the centralization of authority to wrest control of local governments from the political machines that had come to dominate municipal politics. The legacy of that movement has been continued support within public administration for centralization and consolidation of local governments as a means to promote efficiency, equity, and accountability (Carr and Feiock 2003).

This book outlines the contours of an alternative or second path to regional governance based on both cooperation and competition among decentralized governmental units in urban metropolitan areas. A decentralized approach to regionalism emphasizes self-governance through horizontally and vertically linked organizations. Although these linkages are primarily among governments, they can also include voluntary, not-for-profit, and private organizations and service producers—in other words, *decentralized governance*. Before exploring this second path, we take a few steps down the first path to survey the landscape.

THE NEOPROGRESSIVE PATH TO REGIONAL GOVERNANCE

Advocates of new regionalism correctly argue that the debate over centralized versus fragmented government should not be framed as merely a question of efficiency. The organization of governments in a metropolitan area has implications for democratic governance, economic growth, environmental externalities, and equality as well.

Recent work within the progressive reform tradition argues that the consolidation of existing government units or the creation of regional governments with significant powers to control land use and development can better promote economic development, reduce inequality, and address externalities. It is also argued that centralization enhances democratic control. The empirical record is incomplete, but the limited evidence available does not provide strong support for these prescriptions.

Several lines of inquiry provide the theoretical foundation for the neo-progressive case for regional government. The first focuses on the individual-level requisites for democratic politics. Meaningful democratic control of government requires citizens to have valid information about what government is doing and how well it is doing it. Lowery and his associates contend that a fragmented system of governments undercuts accountability and makes it difficult for citizens to identify units responsible for providing services (DeHoog, Lowery, and Lyons 1990; Lowery 2000). Recent work has countered this argument with evidence that a small set of informed citizen consumers can drive the public goods market, resulting in a stronger connection between policy decisions and citizens' preferences (Teske et al. 1993).

A second line of inquiry addresses the implications of government organization for social capital. Greater attachment to the community and engagement in civic issues is anticipated in consolidated settings along with higher levels of efficacy and political participation. Several recent studies have examined the implications of jurisdictional size and suburban separation for civic participation. Here, the findings indicate that "smaller is better," at least in terms of raw participation levels (Oliver 2001).

Arguments that governmental fragmentation is bad for economic development have also been employed in defense of regional government. Regional governments are expected to enhance economic development through coordinated regional planning, streamlined development approval, and the elimination of development subsidy competition among jurisdictions (Hawkins, Ward, and Becker 1991). On this issue, the empirical evidence is clearer; the consolidation of governments does not enhance economic development (Carr and Feiock 1999, 2003).

Regional governments can also provide a mechanism for intrametropolitan redistribution, particularly in light of evidence that suburbs and central cities are economically linked (Barnes and Ledebur 1998; Downs 1994; Gainsborough 2001). There is some evidence that jurisdictional fragmentation exacerbates the segregation of poor from rich people, or of minority groups from whites in metropolitan areas (Neiman 1976). Weiher (1991) suggests that political boundaries in a metropolitan area provide informational cues that reinforce residential and school segregation, but again, the evidence is incomplete.

The need to address pressing regional problems is at the heart of the resurgence of calls for regional government. Fragmented local governments are poorly positioned to address the housing, environmental, and transportation problems associated with urban sprawl (Rusk 1995; Downs 1994). The assumption that competition makes cooperation on regional issues close to impossible (Olberding 2002) leads to the conclusion that decentralized units of government will be unable to deal with regional externalities or spillovers that occur when the policy choices in one community impose costs on another. For example, if one community provides subsidies to attract industry, the new development could lead to increased traffic, overcrowded schools, or pollution problems in neighboring communities.

DECENTRALIZED GOVERNANCE AND INSTITUTIONAL COLLECTIVE ACTION

Institutional collective action (ICA) provides the theoretical framework for understanding a system of metropolitan governance without a metropolitan government. This theory posits that local governments can act collectively to create a civil society that integrates a region across multiple jurisdictions through a web of voluntary agreements and associations and collective choices by citizens.

To some, the argument that a decentralized system of governments can simultaneously produce the benefits of competition and cooperation sounds quite unrealistic—not unlike having your cake and eating it too. This reaction is in large part a response to a theoretical gap in arguments for decentralization. On the one hand, proponents of decentralization have a powerful body of economic theory, backed by formal models and empirical evidence, to explain competition in public good provision and its generally positive implications for efficiency. On the other hand, theoretical arguments to explain how decentralized systems of governments can effectively cooperate to address multijurisdictional or regional problems have not been clearly articulated and tested.

Theories of collective action provide the building blocks for such an approach. ICA is the mechanism by which cooperation is achieved among local governments, between levels of government, and between local government units and other actors in the community. ICA can provide the "glue" that holds an institutionally fragmented community together.

We begin with cooperation among local governments. ICA can be viewed as a form of collective action generalized to governmental institutions. Like individual collective action, ICA is motivated by a desire to achieve a collective benefit that could not be realized by solitary action (Feiock 2002). ICA emerges as the result of a dynamic political contracting process among local government units facing a collective action problem (North 1990; Libecap 1989). Local government policy actions to promote economic growth, reduce pollution, alleviate sprawl, or otherwise enhance the quality of urban life can produce positive externalities that spill across governmental jurisdictions. These externality or spillover benefits give communities in a metropolitan area a strong incentive to cooperate with each other to achieve joint or regional goals. Cooperative actions and institutions arise when potential benefits are high and the transaction costs of negotiating, monitoring, and enforcing the political contract are low (Hackathorn and Maser 1987). The scope of ICA can either be small, as in the case of two neighboring jurisdictions coordinating street repairs, or large, as in regional efforts to control urban sprawl or attract economic development.

Almost four decades of scholarship based on Mancur Olson's *The Logic of Collective Action* (1965) confirms that joint goals and common interests may be inadequate to motivate collective action. Internal or external forces help determine the benefits and transaction costs of institutional change (Alston 1996).

The role of policy entrepreneurs may be even more critical to ICA than it is to individual collective action. Collective action is advanced by individual leaders who have an incentive to overcome collective action costs (Schneider, Teske, and Mintrom 1995). Policy entrepreneurs have an incentive to promote ICA when they expect to receive a disproportionate benefit from the product of collective action.

Investigations of successful cooperation among decentralized actors faced with common-pool resource issues, such as managing watersheds or fisheries, provide a useful starting point for understanding how cooperative arrangements can be forged among local actors. Natural resources management is an area where externalities make cooperation difficult. Nevertheless, local cooperative institutions have emerged in some settings to resolve collective action problems involved in the management of these natural resources (Weber 1998). Lubell and others (2002) found that watershed partnerships emerged when the potential benefits of cooperation outweighed the transaction costs of forming new institutions.

Feiock and Carr (2001) framed the creation of municipalities and special districts in a similar manner. Their work highlights how contextual factors, such as economic conditions, local political culture, and state-level rules, shape institutional supply. Local jurisdictions seeking to realize gains from cooperation face collective action problems because each government unit would be better off if others took on the burden of forming the organization or crafting and carrying out an agreement. Furthermore, individual government units can often realize political or economic gains from being free riders. In the absence of confidence that other actors will abide by agreements and continue to cooperate, the anticipated payoffs from cooperation are low.

Voluntary collective action occurs in small groups because the transaction costs of coordinating actions among participants, monitoring their subsequent behavior, and identifying noncompliance with agreements is more difficult for large groups than for a small set of actors. Collective action among larger groups typically requires a third-party to absorb organization costs, apply coercion, or provide selective incentives to reduce the transaction costs of reaching agreements and enforcing them (Olson 1965).

The transaction cost of cooperation can be reduced to the extent that existing institutions, organizations, or groups can be used to pursue regional goals. Transaction costs are also reduced where state government or another actor plays the role of third-party enforcer or entrepreneur by building social capital or creating incentives for a single jurisdiction or sets of actors to shoulder a disproportionate share of the financial burden and mobilize diffuse regional interests.

ICA is possible even where third-party coercion and incentives are inadequate to overcome collective action problems. The work of Ostrom (1998) demonstrated that internal mechanisms are sometimes adequate to overcome barriers to collective action problems. For example, face-to-face communication can induce cooperation through the exchange of commitments among institutional actors. Increased trust among leaders of neighboring governments, the reinforcement of cooperative norms, and the development of a collective identity can reduce the transaction costs of exchange in ICA situations. Previous work has not combined the contextual elements of collective action frameworks with the internal explanations for overcoming social dilemmas, but both are necessary to understand cooperation among local governments.

The ICA framework can also be applied to cooperation between levels of government in a metropolitan area. Bickers and Stein (2002) identify instances of interlocal cooperation in which local governments form a coalition to jointly apply for federal grants. In instances such as these, the positive benefits from policy activities spill across the boundaries of neighboring jurisdictions. Members of Congress whose districts include these areas will have an incentive to encourage local cooperation, because success in bringing federal grants to their district may provide them with electoral advantages:

> The potential for spillovers creates an incentive for elected officials at all levels of government to cooperate to bring projects into an area. Cooperation among policymakers may involve formal, as well as informal, collective action by legislators and local government officials. Depending on the spatial overlap between congressional districts and local governments, and on the attributes of the policies under consideration, there may be strong incentives for congressional legislators to cooperate with city and local officials in their efforts to obtain federal outlays. (Bickers and Stein 2002, 5)

Elected officials play the role of third-party enforcers in brokering and monitoring cooperation among local government units. Where the political benefits to elected officials are high, they may be quite willing to play the role of third-party enforcer in promoting ICA.

ICA can also include private or nonprofit organizations in the community. A common example is public–private regional partnerships. In these contexts, private actors that have a selective interest in addressing interjurisdictional or regional goals can subsidize or facilitate cooperation, provide social capital as a policy entrepreneur, and play a third-party enforcer role to secure cooperation among units of government. For example, regional partnerships for economic development are often promoted by a chamber of commerce or national firm headquartered in the region. Typically, the entrepreneur provides start-up resources necessary for organizing the effort and eventually is able to attract other jurisdictions to join it.

THE IMPLICATIONS OF DECENTRALIZED GOVERNANCE

An enormous volume of pages has been written in the past three decades debating the policy implications of consolidated versus fragmented systems of government. Much of this literature falls into two categories. The first body of work is primarily normative in its approach and presents arguments favoring centralized or decentralized governments. This scholarship emphasizes the implications of governing structures for equity, representation, and democratic accountability in addition to efficiency, and it often has an advocacy tone. Many of the questions debated are empirical, but they are rarely subjected to rigorous test.

The second body of work builds upon the works of Charles Tiebout and his critics to explore the efficiency of fragmented and consolidated political systems. Although this literature has a stronger empirical foundation, it has directed its attention primarily to the explanation of local taxation and expenditure levels. The more general role of intergovernmental competition in urban areas also needs to be addressed. Competition and cooperation are evidenced through many mechanisms. In addition to tax competition, competitive forces shape the services communities choose to provide, the qualities of these services, and what organizations or actors are responsible for production. In communities with decentralized governance, markets and intergovernmental competition shape developmental decisions with regional effects—particularly in land use and economic development choices. Local governments' choices to cooperate or compete in response to external market forces reflect strategic interactions among local actors. Moreover, competition and cooperation can be complementary strategies.

Although the structure of governments has been included in studies of policy choices in areas such as economic development and school choice, they have usually not been systematically linked to theories of the organization of local governments. Understanding local policy requires attention to how choices in a variety of policy arenas are influenced by the configuration of government units and the extent of competition and cooperation among local governments.

POLITICAL SCIENCE AND THE STUDY OF LOCAL GOVERNMENTS

The work presented in the chapters that follow should be of interest to political scientists generally, not just scholars of urban politics. Regrettably, many potentially interested readers may never find this volume, because most of political science no longer pays great attention to research on urban politics. The field of urban politics no longer plays the prominent role in the discipline of political science that it once did. Its work is often ignored or dismissed by political scientists in other fields as not measuring up to their scholarly standards of theory and method.

This is somewhat ironic, because the study of local government played a leading role in political science until the past couple of decades. Recent neglect of the field could be seen to imply that the study of local government no longer has relevance to theories and explanations of politics and political systems in general. The work presented in this volume makes it clear that this proposition should be rejected. Instead, concerns of theory and method need to be taken seriously.

About ten years ago, James Clingermayer (1993) wrote an essay for the American Political Science Association's Urban Section newsletter titled "Confusion and Clarity in Urban Theory." Using examples taken from some of the leading work in the field, he argued that much of the theory in urban politics lacked conceptual clarity and logical rigor in its arguments. Although this essay probably did not win him many friends, it raised the issue of what constitutes good theory within the field. Formal and game-theoretic approaches have received a particularly hostile reception in the urban field.

Methodological practice in the study of local government has also been characterized by relatively unsophisticated designs and techniques. This criticism applies to qualitative as well as quantitative work. There have been tremendous advances in the methods and techniques of qualitative research in the past fifteen years. Although some subfields of political science have been quick to absorb and incorporate these advances, qualitative work in urban politics has not. The record of quantitative research has not been better. Unsophisticated design and modeling practices are endemic in quantitative urban research. For example, unrecognized and uncorrected endogeneity problems are common in empirical model estimations.

In the last two decades of the twentieth century, fewer good young scholars were being drawn into the field, and some of the best researchers in the field left to write primarily for other audiences in the discipline. Nevertheless, a resurgence of urban politics in political science is possible and appears to already be under way.

The larger political science discipline's recent focus on institutions, governance, and cooperation has positioned the urban politics field to make important contributions. Rather than continuing to lose good scholars to other fields, outstanding scholars who have built reputations in other areas of the discipline are now addressing questions about local politics in their work (see Maser 1998; Gerber 1999). Moreover, although their more recent work has been directed more to the public policy field, such senior scholars as Elaine Sharp and Mark Schneider never completely severed their connections to urban politics. Their strong ties to the field are evident in the chapters they have written for this volume (respectively, chapters 8 and 9).

There also seems to be renewed interest in the field among students and junior scholars. The next generation of urbanists is well on its way to making a mark not only in the field but also in the discipline as a whole.

The chapters in this volume by Annette Steinacker, Stephanie Post, and Jered Carr are exemplars (respectively, chapters 3, 4, and 10). The work of young scholars like Marschall (2001), Oliver (2001), Burns (Allard, Burns, and Gamm 1998), Ruhil (2003), and Lubell (Lubell et al. 2002) have been published in leading journals, and urban scholars are again contributing to a discipline-wide dialogue. This volume is one attempt to engage this dialogue and reinforce the linkages between urban politics and political science.

OVERVIEW OF THE BOOK

The chapters in this volume build upon the literatures described above and make a unique contribution to urban political science by providing a stronger theoretical foundation for explaining and evaluating local government organization. Governmental competition and cooperation are examined in a decentralized context. The chapters also provide original empirical analyses that link the organization of local governance to issues and services that have often been neglected in this debate, such as morality issues, land use decisions, and school choice.

The theoretical explorations in part one of the book provide a foundation linking governments to governance. Although each chapter in this part stands alone, together they also extend and modify the ICA framework described in this chapter. In chapter 2, Ronald Oakerson describes the institutional architecture of government organization in metropolitan areas and the government structures that emerge within the governmental framework provided by that institutional architecture. In chapter 3, Annette Steinacker demonstrates how game-theoretic approaches can contribute to our understanding of regional governance issues. She assesses a series of game-theoretic models and the likely conditions under which cooperation would evolve. In chapter 4, Stephanie Post explicitly builds a model of ICA. She addresses both formal and informal intergovernmental cooperation between local governments. The ICA model she presents emphasizes two attributes unique to local government: group size and the role of geography.

The empirical investigations in part two of the book examine the causes and consequences of decentralized governance and the factors that shape choices to cooperate or compete. In chapter 5, Paul Lewis attributes lack of progress in the study of metropolitan governance to the narrow focus on ideal types of consolidated or polycentric government that dominates the literature. In response, he constructs a more expansive typology of urban governmental arrangements and examines the land use and development consequences of whether the suburban portion of a metropolitan area is organized into numerous small municipalities or large suburbs.

Next, two studies of local economic development are presented. In chapter 6, Martin Johnson and Max Neiman focus on how the competitive forces in a decentralized system of government influence development policy choices. They report that competition—real and perceived—encourages cities to adopt policies that expand the scope of their development efforts. In sharp contrast, in chapter 7, Richard Feiock, Jill Tao, and Linda Johnson identify cooperation within the development arena and empirically test a theory of ICA. They report that decentralized governments that cooperate with each other through interlocal service agreements are better able to sustain cooperation in larger regional compacts that address regional economic development problems.

The long-standing debate within political science over the organization of governments is often waged over the somewhat abstract issues of efficiency and responsiveness in polycentric versus consolidated systems of government. Much less attention has been paid to the implications of government organization for specific policies of immediate importance to citizens. Morality policy issues in particular have been ignored in this literature. In chapter 8, Elaine Sharp reports that variation in the extent to which a metropolitan area is governmentally fragmented produces intergovernmental competition to exclude the sex industry and influences whether officials in the metropolitan core take aggressive action against it. Her examination of morality issues in metropolitan areas found little evidence of cooperative action among local actors.

The burgeoning literature on school reform has developed without recognition of the overlap of the concerns of the school reform movement and the polycentric metropolitan governance movement. In chapter 9, Mark Schneider and Jack Buckley argue that the concerns and the goals of these movements coincide. Their application of Oakerson's framework to education policy identifies how parents' satisfaction with, and participation in, their children's education is shaped by the way school systems are organized.

In chapter 10, Jered Carr provides a collective action framework for understanding why local government boundaries are changed, how the institutional framework erected by state legislatures shapes these changes, and the role played by local boundary entrepreneurs in creating the organization of local governments.

Chapter 11 draws out the implications of this work for regional governance and critically evaluates the role that the study of urban politics plays in political science. Before the urban subfield can make important contributions to political science, it must be willing to adopt the conceptual and theoretical tools developed by political scientists in other fields. New methodological tools are also needed. For example, models of strategic interaction can provide a bridge between formal models and empirical analysis. In addition, new approaches and techniques are necessary to identify the role of information and communication networks in building trust and facilitating institutional collective action.

REFERENCES

Allard, Scott, Nancy Burns, and Gerald Gamm. 1998. Representing Urban Interests: The Local Politics of State Legislatures. *Studies in American Political Development* 12, no. 2: 267–302.

Alston, L. J. 1996. Empirical Work in Institutional Economics. In *Empirical Studies in Institutional Change*, ed. L. J. Alston, T. Eggertsson, and D. C. North. Cambridge: Cambridge University Press.

Barnes, William R., and Lawrence C. Ledebur. 1998. *The New Regional Economics*. Thousand Oaks, Calif.: Sage Publishing.

Bickers, Kenneth N., and Robert M. Stein. 2002. Interlocal Cooperation and the Distribution of Federal Grant Awards. Paper presented at a Devoe L. Moore Center conference, Decentralized Governance: The Implications of Government Organization in Metropolitan Areas, Tallahassee, Fla., October 4–6.

Brookings Institution. 2002. *Beyond Merger: A Competitive Vision for the Regional City of Louisville*. Washington, D.C.: Brookings Institution Press.

Carr, Jered B., and Richard C. Feiock, eds. 1999. Metropolitan Government and Economic Development. *Urban Affairs Review* 34, no. 3: 476–88.

———. 2003. *Reshaping the Local Government Landscape: City-County Consolidation and Its Alternatives*. Armonk, N.Y.: M. E. Sharpe.

Clingermayer, James. 1993. Confusion and Clarity in Urban Theory. *Urban Politics Newsletter* 6, no. 1: 4–5.

DeHoog, Ruth H., David Lowery, and William Lyons. 1990. Citizen Satisfaction and Local Government: A Test of Individual, Jurisdictional, and City-Specific Explanations. *Journal of Politics* 52: 807–37.

Downs, Anthony. 1994. *New Visions for Metropolitan America*. Washington, D.C.: Brookings Institution Press.

Feiock, Richard C. 2002. A Quasi-Market Framework for Local Economic Development Competition. *Journal of Urban Affairs* 24: 123–42.

Feiock, Richard C., and Jered B. Carr. 2001. Incentives, Entrepreneurs, and Boundary Change: A Collective Action Framework. *Urban Affairs Review* 36: 382–405.

Gainsborough, Juliet F. 2001. *Fenced Off: The Suburbanization of American Politics*. Washington, D.C.: Georgetown University Press.

Gerber, Elisabeth R. 1999. *The Populist Paradox: Interest Group Influence and the Promise of Direct Legislation*. Princeton, N.J.: Princeton University Press.

Hackathorn, Douglas, and Steven Maser. 1987. Bargaining and the Sources of Transaction Costs: The Case of Government Regulation. *Journal of Law, Economics, and Organization* 3: 69–98.

Hawkins, Brett W., K. J. Ward, and M. P. Becker. 1991. Governmental Consolidation as a Strategy for Metropolitan Development. *Public Administration Quarterly*, summer, 253–67.

Libecap, Gary. 1989. *Contracting for Property Rights*. New York: Cambridge University Press.

Lowery, David. 2000. A Transaction Costs Model of Metropolitan Governance: Allocation vs. Redistribution in Urban America. *Journal of Public Administration Research and Theory* 10: 49–78.

Lubell, Mark, Mark Schneider, John Scholz, and Mihriye Mete. 2002. Watershed Partnerships and the Emergence of Collective Action Institutions. *American Journal of Political Science* 46, no. 1: 148–63.

Marschall, Melissa J. 2001. Does the Shoe Fit? Testing Models of Participation for African American and Latino Involvement in Local Politics. *Urban Affairs Review* 37, no. 2: 227–48.

Maser, Steven M. 1998. Constitutions as Relational Contracts: Explaining Procedural Safeguards in Municipal Charters. *Journal of Public Administration, Research, and Theory* 8, no. 4: 527–64.

Neiman, Max. 1976. Social Stratification and Government Inequality. *American Political Science Review* 53: 474–93.

North, Douglas. 1990. *Institutions, Institutional Change, and Economic Performance*. Cambridge: Cambridge University Press.

Olberding, Julie C. 2002. Does Regionalism Beget Regionalism? The Relationship between Norms and Regional Partnerships for Economic Development. *Public Administration Review* 62: 480–91.

Oliver, J. E. 2001. *Democracy in Suburbia*. Princeton, N.J.: Princeton University Press.

Olson, Mancur. 1965. *The Logic of Collective Action*. Cambridge, Mass.: Harvard University Press.

Ostrom, Elinor. 1998. A Behavioral Approach to the Rational Choice Theory of Collective Action. *American Political Science Review* 92, no. 1: 1–22.

Ruhil, Anirudh V. S. 2003. Structural Change and Fiscal Flows: A Framework for Analyzing the Effects of Urban Events. *Urban Affairs Review* 38, no. 3: 396–417.

Rusk, David. 1995. *Cities without Suburbs*. Washington, D.C.: Woodrow Wilson Center Press.

Savitch, H. V., and Ronald Vogel. 2000. Introduction: Paths to New Regionalism. *State and Local Government Review* 12: 158–68.

Schneider, Mark, Paul Teske, and Michael Mintrom. 1995. *Public Entrepreneurs: Agents for Change in American Government.* Princeton, N.J.: Princeton University Press.

Stephens, G. Ross, and Nelson Wikstrom. 2000. *Metropolitan Government and Governance: Theoretical Perspectives, Empirical Analysis, and the Future.* New York: Oxford University Press.

Teske, Paul, Mark Schneider, Michael Mintrom, and S. Best. 1993. Establishing the Micro Foundations of a Macro Theory: Information, Movers, and the Competitive Local Market for Public Goods. *American Political Science Review* 87: 702–13.

Weber, Edward P. 1998. *Pluralism by the Rules: Conflict and Cooperation in Environmental Regulation.* Washington, D.C.: Georgetown University Press.

Weiher, G. 1991. *The Fractured Metropolis: Political Fragmentation and Metropolitan Segregation.* Albany: State University of New York Press.

Wheeler, S. M. 2002. The New Regionalism: Key Characteristics of an Emerging Movement. *Journal of the American Planning Association* 68, no. 3: 267–78.

RONALD J. OAKERSON

THE STUDY OF METROPOLITAN GOVERNANCE

Metropolitan areas in the United States offer a fertile field for the study of effective governance. Not many years ago, such a statement would have been dismissed as preposterous—except for those few metropolitan areas with something approaching a consolidated metropolitan government. It is now more widely accepted—though far from universally understood—that metropolitan *governance* can and does occur without metropolitan *government*, and that it can be effective even when a metropolitan area is highly "fragmented" among a large number of small municipalities (Oakerson 1999; Parks and Oakerson 2000). The growing recognition of this phenomenon is associated in part with the development of the "new regionalism" (Savitch and Vogel 2000), which recognizes that metropolitan areas are able to create governance structures not tied to a single, dominant unit of metropolitan government. Without consolidated metropolitan-level governments, metropolitan areas manage to generate a rich world of governance activity carried out on a metropolitan scale and tailored to the specific metropolitan area.

Understanding the world of metropolitan governance, whether or not one appreciates its richness, is a research task of substantial importance for political scientists. It is important, primarily, for understanding how to practice effective local governance in rapidly growing and increasingly complex metropolitan regions. But that is not all. The study of metropolitan governance is equally important for gaining a better understanding of the governance structures that operate in *any complex environment*— whether a metropolitan area, computer network, financial market, ecosystem, nation, or community of nations.

Governance is increasingly of interest in political science. How we govern and how we can govern well are questions of both practical importance and keen theoretical interest; in the study of governance, there should be no great divide between the interests of the academy and of the public square. Although not disconnected from the struggle for power and influence that has dominated political science inquiry for the better part of a century, nor from the preoccupation with political obligation ("Why obey?") that has similarly dominated political philosophy, questions of governance go well beyond these concerns.

Moreover, the answers to these questions are not clear. Governance remains in many respects a mystery, one for which traditional concepts and theories often offer more puzzles than clues. For example, we equate "the state" with coercion, yet the most coercive states are in many ways the least effective instruments of governance. We focus on "the government," while understanding little about the role of "the governed" in governance. Is that role best understood as one of simple obedience to authority or one of civic engagement with one another? We advance solutions to problems based on relationships of command and control when we have little reason to expect that command and control will solve those problems. Yet, when we consider alternatives to the standard view of the state as a system of organized dominance, we often see no alternative other than anarchism. Most of us run home to the state like a frightened child to his mother.

For more than the past thirty years, however, social scientists have been crafting the conceptual tools needed to decode the process of governance. Of basic importance is theoretical and empirical work on collective action (Olson 1965). Although initially focused on the need for coercion, this line of research has increasingly led to an emphasis on reciprocity (Ostrom 1998). When applied to the study of the commons, collective action research has contributed significantly to our understanding of self-governing institutions (Ostrom 1990; Bromley et al. 1992). In related developments, social capital research (Putnam 2000) is exploring the productivity of nonmarket social relationships based on willing consent, and institutional economists (North 1990) are working out the implications of transaction costs for both market and nonmarket arrangements. Political scientists— reacting to the activities of predatory states in many parts of the world— have rediscovered the concept of "civil society" and begun to emphasize its importance as a counter to state coercion; and both historians and political scientists have rediscovered traditional republicanism, the primary way of thinking that informed the American founders (Wood 1991) and to a significant extent the design of governmental institutions in the United States (Ostrom 1989), which are highly dependent on civil society. In the midst of these developments, there occurred a "Tocqueville revival" among social scientists, which has brought the ideas of Alexis de Tocqueville, surely the keenest observer of American civil society in our history, into the center of political scholarship and discourse.

The term "governance," as distinct from "government," has come into widespread use in political science only during the past fifteen or twenty years. The standard presumption has long been that "governments govern" (Oakerson and Parks 1989, 279), supporting a myopic focus on "the government" that is less and less satisfactory as the world grows more and more complex. There is a great deal of conceptual work to be done before the distinction between government and governance will be sufficiently well established to guide research.

One possible conceptualization of governance is to define it as the process by which human beings regulate their interdependencies in the context of shared environments. Each environment is a source of values shared by the members of a community. Some of those communities are quite small; others are very large. Dahl (1990, 68) uses the imagery of Chinese boxes to convey the idea that smaller communities are nested within larger communities. The full set of values shared in any given community is what classical republicans called *res publica*—the public realm. Governance is focused on the protection and enhancement of the public realm. Included are both tangible and intangible values: streets and sidewalks, water resources and wildlife, markets and settlements, peace and prosperity. Sharing a common resource, we have learned from studies of collective action, is often problematic. The problems of sharing—from the scale of a household to the scale of the planet—constitute the agenda of governance.

A common environment supplies multiple values, subject to one major constraint: It is impossible to maximize all such values at once in a finite world. Trade-offs are required, about which community members will often disagree, requiring joint deliberation. Governance as a process is centrally concerned with making those trade-offs. To some degree, trade-offs are determined in nature, though modifiable by means of technology. Governance is focused on those trade-offs that are significantly affected by the working rules used to organize sharing, or by a deeper set of rules for making and sustaining those working rules. The process of governance includes the entire set of related processes—prescribing, invoking, applying, and enforcing rules (Oakerson and Walker 1997)—required to create and sustain a set of rules as "rules in use" (Ostrom 1992), rules that actually regulate behavior. Institutional design—which is the process of crafting a configuration of rules—is aimed at reducing the severity of the trade-offs among multiple values by shaping incentives in ways that encourage desirable behaviors.

Although governance depends on the availability of coercion, the actual use of coercion through command and control is a highly ineffective instrument for undertaking many of the activities on which governance depends. This is the basic point made by Michael Polanyi (1951) in *The Logic of Liberty*—and the basis for his introduction of the concept of "polycentricity." Transaction cost theory enables us to see more clearly why he was correct; the use of coercion, which imposes harm on others, is a very costly transaction, for others will take steps to avoid being coerced. To facilitate the process of governance, human beings create *governance structures* based on willing consent. These structures provide regularized means for identifying and diagnosing problems, elucidating information, arraying and assessing alternatives, and crafting rule-based solutions, as well as for monitoring those arrangements for both implementation and possible alteration.

Governance structures are more or less elaborate, depending on the complexity of the relevant environment, but even the simplest government tends to generate a structure (often called "informal") that facilitates the exercise of authority. These structures require *access* to governmental authority (to prescribe, invoke, apply, and enforce rules) but need not be confined to governmental institutions. Governments are a necessary condition of governance, but not a sufficient condition. Governance is the work of people both inside and outside governments—perhaps it is better conceived as cogovernance. Governance structures are not the products of government mandates; rather, they are the work of civil society and therefore are based on a rule of willing consent.

The need to access governmental authority means, however, that the *structure of government* will strongly affect the *structure of governance*.

The variable that connects governmental structure to governance structure is the cost of access to government—highlighting again the importance of transaction costs. We might anticipate that highly centralized governments, because they are more difficult to access, would engender very different governance structures than less centralized governments. Metropolitan areas that feature large numbers of small municipalities generate very different governance structures than consolidated city governments that encompass large and diverse populations. Different governance structures, in turn, can be expected to yield different processes of governance, as measured and evaluated on multiple dimensions, such as participation, representation, and accountability.

In what follows, I focus on the *relationship of government to governance* in highly fragmented metropolitan areas, examining the governance structures associated with metropolitan fragmentation and explaining those governance structures in terms of the design of governmental institutions. As originally argued by Ostrom, Tiebout, and Warren (1961), the model of the government–governance relationship that best fits a fragmented metropolitan area is polycentric—in Polanyi's sense. Polycentrism describes a process of decision making whereby multiple independent actors interact to produce an outcome that is commonly valued. It contrasts to monocentrism, a model in which a single actor (or cohesive set of actors) provides direction to others. Polycentrism describes a pattern of governance that emerges from the interactions of multiple independent centers of authority, whereas monocentrism describes a pattern of governance by a single center of authority (Ostrom 1989, 1999). The models are mutually exclusive: Polycentrism depends on the absence of dominance among various centers of authority, whereas monocentrism depends on a single center attaining dominance.

Intellectually, the monocentric model drives most efforts at metropolitan reform. The model posits that metropolitan governance can work only through the direction supplied by a single dominant unit of government. This holds even if subordinate governmental units also exist. The concentration of ultimate authority in the center enables the center to govern. In democratic terms, the public visibility and electoral connection of the center to voters enables voters to hold the center accountable. By contrast, a dispersion of authority among multiple governments, regarded from a monocentric perspective, enables no one to govern on a metropolitan scale. The proliferation of power centers is thought to overwhelm metropolitan voters, creating a fragmented system of government that is both ineffective and unaccountable.

Monocentric and polycentric systems of government engender very different governance structures. The argument I offer below is that polycentric systems of government allow for more open governance structures that include greater "civic space," defined as the set of opportunities for nongovernmental actors to enter *productively* into the governance process by producing general benefits for a community. By contrast, monocentric systems engender less open governance structures more apt to be dominated by "insiders," who compete to enjoy privileged access to governmental authority for the purpose of obtaining selective benefits.

Polycentric governance depends on two institutional conditions related to the design of governmental arrangements. The first is the existence of multiple independent centers of authority; the second is that their independence must not be absolute. All authority must be subject to limits, and it must be possible to introduce new limits. Such limits exist in recognition of interdependencies among clustered and nested communities and serve to qualify the independence of various centers of authority. Polycentrism thus describes a system of qualified independence among interdependent centers of authority. Maintaining (and modifying) the limits—and the qualified independence they permit—forms much of the agenda of a metropolitan governance structure.

TOCQUEVILLE'S MODEL OF LOCAL GOVERNANCE

Local governance, and, by extension, metropolitan governance, do not encompass the *whole* of governance in any society. We know this, but we often forget it when we are talking about what we expect local governance to accomplish. Local institutions can make a distinct contribution to the overall task of governance, but they are nonetheless limited in what they can do. The relationship between national and local institutions is reciprocal: The productivity of national institutions can be greatly truncated by an inability to reach effectively into local communities; and local communities can be sharply constrained by a lack of recognition from national governments (Ostrom 1992). It is worth bearing in mind that what the United States organizes as legitimate and lawful institutions of local governance are in many parts of the world organized outside the framework of the law (de Soto 1989).

Tocqueville's *Democracy in America* (1835) provides a classic statement of the potential contribution of local governance to the overall task of governance in a society. During the past quarter-century, Tocqueville has become one of the most popular figures in political theory—largely because he recognized the critical importance of civil society in the process of democratic governance. His emphasis on the importance of *local* governance is still not as well appreciated as it might be, I think, nor as well understood, for his appreciation of local governance is not simply a paean to participation of any sort. Rather, it is a recognition that civic engagement is productive:

> In no country in the world do the citizens make such exertions for the common weal. I know of no people who have established schools so numerous and efficacious, places of public worship better suited to the wants of the inhabitants, or roads kept in better repair. (Tocqueville 1835, vol. 1, 95)

Tocqueville was impressed not only with the extent of citizen participation but also with its contribution to the common good—to *res publica*. Tocqueville cited schools, churches, and roads—but the set is much larger, and it has grown larger over the years. Caring for the "public realm" within its local dimensions is no trivial undertaking—not even in the twenty-first century.

Besides its productivity, local civic engagement had the added advantage of teaching the arts of self-government and the virtues of citizenship (Tocqueville 1835, vol. 1, 63). Tocqueville argued that civic virtue—the willingness to serve the common good of the community—was tied to self-interest. He was convinced that the democratic movement away from aristocratic privilege and toward social equality would lead inevitably away from a sense of *duty* and toward a greater reliance on *self-interest* as a principle of social action. This did not mean, however, that democratic citizens would inevitably behave selfishly; instead, the outcome would depend on how individuals learned to understand or construe their self-interest. Americans, Tocqueville found, practiced "self-interest rightly understood"; that is, they construed their self-interest to include the well-being of their local communities (1835, vol. 2, 132).

Tocqueville also identified the institutional conditions under which productive citizen participation will tend to occur: local freedom coupled with local responsibility.[1] Local freedom, much like individual freedom, was predicated on the ability of townships to act independently of superior authority yet within the bounds of the law. The "independence and authority" of townships was a necessary condition of civic engagement (Tocqueville 1835, vol. 1, 69). Tocqueville's townships therefore satisfied the first condition of polycentricity: the existence of multiple, independent centers of authority.

Yet the authority of townships was not unlimited. Townships were independent in "all that concerns themselves alone" (Tocqueville 1835, vol. 1, 68), but municipal citizens nonetheless recognized the existence of social obligations in matters that affected others. A township could not, for example, decline to locate a state road within its boundaries; nor could it refuse to operate a school. Social duties such as these were specified by state law. Moreover, state legislation afforded a continuing opportunity to create social duties that municipalities would be required to observe. In this way, Tocqueville's townships also satisfied the second condition of polycentricity: the existence of limits on authority in recognition of interdependencies.

The social duties of townships were applied and enforced through the courts, not by state executive or administrative officers; this arrangement was a novelty of considerable interest to Tocqueville. One of the principal puzzles he wanted to solve during his visit to America was how a society might establish independent units of local government without dissolving into anarchy. In his native France and across the European continent, fear of anarchy was the great obstacle to municipal independence. The solution he discovered in America was the use of general legislation applied in the courts—in short, the rule of law. Instead of restricting the rule of law to relationships among individual citizens, Americans had extended the concept to include relationships between officials at different levels of government. For Tocqueville, this was a highly significant institutional innovation.

METROPOLITAN INSTITUTIONS OF GOVERNMENT

Even a cursory look at the prevailing practice of metropolitan governance in the United States reveals that, overwhelmingly, it is metropolitan governance *without* metropolitan government. Only a few of the 276 Metropolitan Areas (MAs) recognized by the U.S. government have established some form of metropolitan government. For my immediate purpose, I adopt a more restrictive definition of "metropolitan area": a *cluster* of relatively small, mostly adjacent municipalities that in the aggregate contain a relatively large population, one ordinarily measured in the hundreds of thousands or larger. The clustering of small municipalities (and often school districts) is one of the most important structural characteristics of metropolitan organization in the United States; the cooperation and mutual aid observed in such areas are among the advantages associated with clustering. Municipal clusters define the metropolitan areas of principal interest with regard to governance.

In the institutional analysis that follows, I examine two sets of governance-related variables: (1) the *institutional architecture* of governmental organization in metropolitan areas, and (2) the *governance structures* that emerge within the governmental framework provided by that institutional architecture. The government–governance relationship in metropolitan areas conforms well to the basic polycentric model and to Tocqueville's elaboration of it in the context of local governance.

Institutional Architecture

The governmental framework in metropolitan areas rests on an *institutional base* that consists of municipalities (and often school districts) that are (1) small enough to function in a highly participatory manner, and (2) in Tocqueville's phrase, exhibit "independence and authority." Consider:

- As Dahl (1990, 118) and many others have persuasively argued, the *size* of a democratic jurisdiction that can function on the basis of strong citizen participation is quite limited. In many MAs, clusters of municipalities each with 20,000 or fewer residents are common; outside central cities, municipalities with 50,000 or more residents are relatively rare.
- With Tocqueville, I posit that it is the *independence and authority* of a municipality that inspires the "loyalty" of its residents and prompts their exercise of "voice," to employ Hirschman's (1970) useful categories. Metropolitan municipalities are independent units of local government, not dependent subunits. Whatever the particular nomenclature (village, town, or city), municipalities by and large enjoy considerable autonomy or freedom of choice within the limits of the law; they exercise powers of government that do not require them to seek permission to act within an administrative hierarchy.

Because of the legally dependent nature of municipalities as so-called creatures of the state, there is some confusion on the second point (Oakerson and Parks 1989). Suffice it to say that authorizing statutes in most states endow local municipalities with ample authority to act, but not unlimited authority. They are self-governing but not sovereign.

Small municipalities (and small school districts) are not self-sufficient units of local government. They depend on supplementary units of government to carry out necessary functions that extend beyond the capabilities afforded by their limited size and jurisdiction. Tocqueville's discussion of New England counties addresses the same point: "The extent of the township was too small to contain a system of judicial institutions; the county, therefore, is the first center of judicial action" (Tocqueville 1835, vol. 1, 71). Eventually, in the metropolitan context, this consideration led to the creation of a variety of intermediate units between municipality and county. Municipalities or their citizens were given the authority to add incrementally to the institutional base by creating supplementary governments. These increments have been added over time as municipalities have encountered specific limits (usually of a technical sort, but sometimes of a legal sort) on what they can do. This led, beginning in the early twentieth century, to the creation of special-purpose districts, which now outnumber municipalities nationwide.

The diversity of special districts by purpose—fire protection, parks and recreation, water and sewer, libraries—indicates the pragmatic nature of their origins. Structurally, the result is that the institutional base provided by small municipalities is accompanied by an *institutional overlay* that consists of a variety of special-purpose districts, often overlapping one another. Because one of the advantages of district organization is that it need not follow municipal boundaries, a map showing local government boundaries begins to take on the appearance of the "crazy quilt" that has energized simplicity-seeking reform groups over the years.

The authority exercised by municipalities, school districts, and special-purpose districts is conferred through some combination of state constitutions and state legislation; local governments are also subject to legal obligations that stem from both state and federal law. This provides an *institutional framework* that operates through a rule of law to regulate the interdependencies among the various units of government that coexist in a metropolitan area. Municipal independence is therefore qualified and limited by legal duties and disabilities. As in Tocqueville's model, municipalities are not unfettered but are limited by the rule of law; at the same time, the rule of law protects municipalities from arbitrary supervision and control by state administrators, thus maintaining municipal independence (Tocqueville 1835, vol. 1, 67–68, 78–80). Ample opportunity exists to craft the authority and liability of tightly clustered municipalities so as to control for external effects, as these become relevant. Because all this is done by means of the rule of law, the maintenance of limits does not diminish the political and administrative autonomy of local officials, who remain accountable primarily to their own citizens.

Beyond the allocation of authority among existing units of government, the institutional framework extends to the creation and dissolution of local governments, the alteration of their boundaries, and the design of institutions internal to local governments. The prevailing mode of decision making is to assign basic constitutional authority to local voters. The specific configuration of local governments in a metropolitan area is thus usually a product of direct voter choices ascertained by means of local referenda. If to be a creature *of* X is to be created *by* X, most local governments are the creatures of local citizens, not of the state—legal fictions to the contrary notwithstanding (Oakerson and Parks 1989). State legislatures may also create new *types* of local governments, with powers and duties not heretofore specified, which local voters can subsequently establish as a means of addressing some new sort of problem.

The result is a trilevel framework for metropolitan decision making (Parks and Oakerson 1989). First, there are policy choices made by officials and citizens in the context of existing local governments. Second, there are local constitutional choices made by citizens as units of government are created, modified, or dissolved. Third, there are state statutory choices, which are formally made by state legislatures, which create and modify the repertoire of local institutions from which local citizens choose.

Each of these three levels provides added leverage for dealing with public problems as problems of interdependent decision making. Some problems can be dealt with adequately at the first level—on the basis of the existing governmental structure. Others may respond to modifications in the governmental structure, drawing on the existing repertoire of institutions. And still others may require modifications in the institutional repertoire, either creating new types of governmental units or modifying the design of units already included in the repertoire. Instead of reducing all choices to policy choices, policy choices are separated from institutional choices (Clingermayer and Feiock 2001), not just once but twice. In this way, if one set of decision-making arrangements becomes inadequate, it is possible to have recourse to a different set of arrangements capable of modifying the first. Building greater adaptability into the system, the trilevel structure makes possible a continuing process of incremental reform.

To sum up, the institutional architecture of government in metropolitan areas consists of (1) an institutional base that makes possible a broad functional base of citizen participation in local governance; (2) an institutional overlay of intermediate governmental units that supplements local municipalities and school districts, substituting for them in limited ways as needed; and (3) an institutional framework that (a) uses a rule of law to limit the authority of local governments without diminishing their administrative independence, (b) conveys to citizens the key constitutional decisions concerning the formation and dissolution of local governments, and (c) reserves to state legislatures the ability to modify the arrangements specified in (a) and (b).

Governance Structures

Fragmented metropolitan areas tend to generate elaborate governance structures that facilitate the process of metropolitan governance (Parks and Oakerson 1993). Specifying the institutional architecture of *governmental authority* in a metropolitan area does not describe its *governance structure* any more than the dimensions of a room communicate its contents. In particular, the institutional framework described above amounts to an open invitation to members of civil society to move in, occupy, and furnish the civic space it creates. "Civil society" refers to those aspects of human association based on the willing consent of participants, as contrasted to the necessarily coercive aspect of governments. Civil society contributes to metropolitan governance structures at two levels: municipal and intermunicipal.

To begin with, civil society occupies and animates the institutional base. Historically, many suburban villages began as homeowners' associations or as a league of associations—some began as garden clubs. Municipal incorporation does not usually lead to the dissolution of the parent association or to its inactivity. Rather, voluntary associations continue to function, carrying out community improvements, bringing concerns to the municipality, and recruiting local citizens to fill positions in local government (see Teaford 1997, 23). Elected officials usually serve in a part-time capacity: their official position is not a separate career but an extension of their local citizenship. At this level, government and civil society exhibit a high degree of *interpenetration*; there is no sharp boundary between the two because the same actors and leaders are involved in both.

In such a context, local governance comes as close as possible to governance by your friends and neighbors. The governance structure blends local government and civic association to such an extent that they become nearly indistinguishable. Most decisions can be made on the basis of willing consent, with governmental authority held in reserve. The search for agreement also entails transaction costs that, on occasion, can become excessive. These are the occasions when coercive authority is invoked more to override objections rather than to ratify an agreement.

Beyond the municipal level, the next level of general-purpose government is usually a county. County government, however, is only of modest importance as a coordinator of municipal service activity. Much more important are voluntary associations of municipal and special district officials, which are usually organized on a countywide basis—intergovernmental associations such as county leagues of municipalities and countywide organizations of police chiefs and fire chiefs. As civil, not governmental, organizations, intergovernmental associations exercise no formal powers; yet, along with countywide civic groups, they form a crucial part of the governance structure of metropolitan areas. Their principal role is to provide a forum in which municipalities can address common problems and resolve differences. From intergovernmental associations emerge plans for coordination in service delivery, joint facilities and projects, and occasionally new rules of service provision that require formal adoption—in effect, ratification—by the state legislature.

Although county *government* tends to make only a marginal contribution to municipal coordination, county *boundaries* are usually of substantial importance in defining metropolitan governance structures. Indeed, the structure of metropolitan civil society typically follows county lines—though in large counties there may be subcounty regional associations that conform to the local geography in some other respect. On other issues, multicounty governance structures also emerge. County boundaries are useful, as well, in crafting state legislation that applies to specific metropolitan areas.

Such state legislation is often used to prescribe rules proposed by countywide intergovernmental associations. Access to the state legislature—a governmental authority that can act on an areawide (or countywide) basis—is obtained through the local delegation that represents the metropolitan area or county in the legislature. This practice enables a metropolitan area to exercise areawide or intermunicipal governance capabilities without recourse to any single unit of local government, including county government. Because county government is frequently a party to interlocal conflict rather than a neutral arbiter, the intergovernmental governance structure creates a more level playing field for metropolitan decision making. At the same time, consensus does not imply unanimity. It remains possible to take action without obtaining unanimous agreement, thus inhibiting the use of blocking strategies by municipal holdouts.

The institutional architecture of government in metropolitan areas thus generates a governance structure that relies on civil society at two distinct levels. At one level, municipal governments are closely tied to civil society through patterns of voluntarism and civic association. At another level, municipal governments enter into relationships with one another through intergovernmental associations. As a result, local governance in metropolitan areas is strongly defined and shaped by its relationship to civil society. Indeed, governance occurs as much through civil society as it does through government.

CHARACTERISTICS OF METROPOLITAN GOVERNANCE

Just as different governmental arrangements yield different governance structures, so do different governance structures produce different *processes* of governance, as measured in multiple dimensions. The sort of governance structure that tends to be found in a polycentric metropolis is associated with a number of governance-process characteristics: (1) higher levels of citizen participation; (2) a less adversarial, more consensual, style of politics; (3) strong representation; (4) a pervasive pattern of public entrepreneurship; (5) community differentiation and the self-sorting of residents; and (6) patterns of accountability that greatly amplify the capabilities of individuals for self-governance. Many of the variables employed to measure the process dimensions of governance are suggested by traditional republicanism.

Citizen Participation

Tocqueville's account of the conditions of strong citizen engagement in local communities predicts stronger citizen participation in small suburban municipalities than in large central cities. Although, for some time, impressionistic evidence has suggested that this is true, the research of Oliver (2001) has recently confirmed its veracity. His work is of considerable importance, in part for showing that municipal size makes a substantial difference even in the midst of a large-scale metropolitan area. Participation is thus a function, not of social or psychological factors unconnected to municipal boundaries, but of the civic space created by small jurisdictions.

Oliver considers the standard dimensions of participation: (1) contacting local officials, (2) attending board meetings, (3) attending organization meetings, (4) engaging in informal civic activity, and (5) voting in local elections. He finds that for

> the first three civic activities, . . . steady declines occur as city size grows, although this effect is largely limited to residents of metropolitan areas. For example, 40 percent of residents of the smallest towns in a metropolis (under 5,000 in size) reported contacting locally elected officials, compared to only 30 percent in medium-size places (5,000 to 50,000 in size) and 25 percent in the biggest cities (over one million). Meeting attendance declines thirteen percentage points between the smallest and the largest metropolitan places for community boards and twelve percentage points for voluntary organizations. People in the smallest metropolitan places (under 5,000 in size) are also more likely to work informally with neighbors and report the highest rates of local voting. (Oliver 2001, 42)

Moreover, when controlling for individual and place-level characteristics, "the same negative relationship generally occurs between civic participation and city size" (Oliver 2001, 47). Perhaps most interesting of all, Oliver's research provides support for the *emphasis* that Tocqueville placed on the civic effects of municipal organization:

> Political scientists typically focus on the differences between individuals based on their age or education. . . . But these results show large differences occurring by a city's size as well. The predicted difference in civic participation between the smallest and largest places are larger than most differences across individual-level demographic traits, except for education and income. In other words, the differences in contacting or board meeting attendance between small towns and large places are greater than those between renters and homeowners, men and women, or whites and blacks. (Oliver 2001, 50)

Yes, institutions truly matter! Moreover, Oliver is also able to explain, empirically, the size differences he found, at least in substantial part. Consistent with Tocqueville's explanation, he concludes that "smaller municipalities make participation easier, make citizens feel more empowered and interested in their communities, and bring neighbors together" (Oliver 2001, 65).

Oliver also finds, however, that local citizen participation is negatively related to the economic homogeneity of municipalities (Oliver 2001, 87). This finding is not especially surprising either. "Participation" can be driven by two very different motivations: (1) a desire to contribute to one's community out of a sense of "self-interest rightly understood," or (2) a desire to protect one's interests from attack by others (or to gain at others' expense). Self-protection may often be a stronger incentive than civic virtue. To explain this finding in theoretical terms, Oliver relies on a "conflict model of civic participation" (2001, 87). Such a model, however, is the antithesis of Tocqueville's conception of civic engagement as a product of shared identities, reciprocity, and common interests. Participation may thus wear two very different faces; it is unclear whether both dimensions should be measured on the same scale.

In any event, the second finding with respect to homogeneity does not negate the first finding with respect to size. Size effects of most indicators of participation continue to be significantly negative when economic homogeneity or heterogeneity is controlled (Oliver 2001, 224). Of particular importance, the negative effect of homogeneity on participation does *not* overwhelm the positive effect of small size.

A Less Adversarial Politics

Most measures of "participation" miss the *character* of participation—its motivation and effects. Although the concept of participation has taken on an honorific quality, it is in fact a mixed bag. Northern Ireland, for example, ranks high among the nations of the world on some of the standard indicators of citizen participation.[2] Yet Northern Ireland, as we all know, has significant deficiencies as a *civil* society. It is important to consider not only the quantity of participation occurring in a metropolitan area but also its distinctive character and quality. Much that passes for participation would not qualify as civic engagement.

The institutional base supplied by small municipalities in metropolitan areas makes possible a distinctive style of democratic politics, which was identified by Mansbridge (1980) as nonadversarial politics or a politics of common interests. When interests are shared in common, collective decisions become more deliberative because they can be based on their technical merits. Thus, Mansbridge explained the *unanimous* adoption of the budget for the volunteer fire department in a Vermont town meeting in these terms:

> The homogeneity of the town's population meant that risk from fire did not vary enough among the individuals at town meeting to give them substantially different needs for fire protection. The implicit questions before the meeting became administrative: "What is the appropriate level of fire protection for everyone?" and "Is this level being delivered for the lowest cost?" (Mansbridge 1980, 72)

Reasonable people can still disagree over such issues, but new information and the open discussion of alternatives tend to reduce the level of disagreement without requiring some individuals to compromise their interests. Although Mansbridge based her conception on observations of a rural Vermont town, her characterization tends to fit small suburban municipalities quite well. She argues that such a style of politics carries with it some important advantages, including, in particular, the cultivation of civic virtue based on individual identification with the common good—in other words, "self-interest rightly understood." A less adversarial style also makes it possible for civil society to form a partnership with government in the process of governance—to be a coproducer of governance and problem solving—rather than to act mainly on the demand side as an advocate or special pleader. If small suburban municipalities contribute this ingredient to metropolitan governance, they make a unique contribution of considerable value to the broader polity.

A heavy reliance on civil society to provide the institutional facilities for addressing intermunicipal issues potentially extends the less adversarial style to a metropolitan level. Like New England town meetings and suburban municipalities, intergovernmental associations seek consensus on the issues they face, even though they may face more internal conflict, thus extending the civic pattern of politics characteristic of the institutional base to include problems and issues that cross municipal boundaries.

The argument can be carried still further. If small municipalities are constituted so as to define relatively coherent communities of interest, with each one conducting its politics in a less adversarial style, they increase the potential for the politics of more inclusive units of government to be conducted in a less adversarial style as well. By assigning territorially diverse interests to smaller units of government, more inclusive units are free to focus on limited interests shared in common on a wider scale. This is especially true of special-purpose districts, which are usually organized around a single problem or service. As small municipalities and their communities organize overlying units to address particular problems, the participants continue to operate in a nonadversarial style. In the absence of municipal organization on a small scale, larger-scale units of government necessarily become more adversarial. Large-scale governments without smaller nested governments *create* conflict by combining highly diverse interests in a single, comprehensive political jurisdiction.[3]

One of the keys to consensus politics as well as productive citizen participation is an institutional design that ties benefits and costs closely together, so that a community that receives benefits must also shoulder the burden of paying for those benefits.[4] Otherwise, various communities must compete with one another for access to a common treasury. Self-governance entails the acceptance of responsibility as well as the exercise of authority. The nested structure of service provision found in complex metropolitan areas links benefits and costs at multiple levels, increasing the productivity of governance throughout the public sector. This does not preclude larger, more inclusive levels of organization—such as a county—from investing in smaller, nested communities, in recognition of metro-politan interdependencies. Doing so may be entirely consistent with "self-interest rightly understood."

For these effects to occur, the primary unit of government must be sufficiently small and homogenous to generate a nonadversarial style. Once a size threshold is crossed, adversarial politics is almost certain to develop. Municipalities sufficiently large to obviate the need for most overlying units are likely to be too large to sustain a consensual style of politics. Efforts to determine an "optimal city size" ordinarily presume that a single unit of government ought to be expected to do all (or most) things local. Any possibility of sustaining a less adversarial politics would likely be lost in such an effort. Counties are usually too large as well, and it is the county in metropolitan areas (outside central cities) that often provides the first level of partisan political competition and ties the local arena into the larger political environment (Teaford 1997). Central cities, of course, are often the scene of fierce political rivalries. Although some political observers may consider this lively and entertaining, many citizens find it frustrating and unproductive. Those who *identify* politics with competition and conflict, rather than viewing conflict as simply one feature of politics among others, may be disappointed by less adversarial community styles; they may even seek to eliminate such political arenas, thinking perhaps that the only democratic politics worthy of the name is one dominated by competition and conflict.

Strong Representation

Higher levels of citizen participation in metropolitan areas coexist with what I would term "strong representation," the level and type of representation demanded by traditional republicans. Strong representation has two principal dimensions: (1) it is community based, and (2) it features low ratios of citizens to elected officials. Both were viewed by traditional republicans as necessary conditions for obtaining the "consent of the governed."[5] Among Saint Louis County's ninety municipalities in 1987, for example, the ratio of citizens to elected officials ranged from less than 500 to 1 in the smallest villages to 3,000 to 1 in all but the very largest suburban cities.

The aggregate result of this situation was startling: incorporated Saint Louis County elected more than 700 municipal officials to serve its 750,000 residents (Oakerson and Parks 1988). The contrast to central cities is stark: A central city of similar size may often elect only a dozen— or perhaps two dozen—city officials. The typical metropolitan–suburban pattern amounts to an extraordinary investment in representation. Without doubt, this investment increases citizen access to local officials; little wonder that "contacting officials" is considerably greater in the smallest municipalities, as Oliver reports. It also clearly reinforces the interpenetration of local government and civil society, linking civil society to government. Moreover, in this context, serving in elected office is itself a mode of citizen participation. When there is no sharp boundary between government and civil society, serving as an elected municipal official is little different from holding office in a civic association or local church.

Public Entrepreneurship

Strong representation, together with a highly organized civil society operating at multiple levels, provides an appropriate set of constraints for the conduct of public entrepreneurship. Public entrepreneurs are individuals—frequently elected or appointed public officials but often private citizens—who identify public problems and craft potential solutions, shouldering the burden of securing the consent needed to obtain adoption and implementation (Oakerson and Parks 1988). The process is one that depends on both *initiative* and *consent*.

Initiative depends on both opportunity and incentive. The opportunity to exercise initiative depends on a Tocquevillian independence among local officials, which is secured by the legal independence enjoyed by most units of local government. The potential for entrepreneurship is a function of the number of possible sources of entrepreneurial initiative. In a metropolitan area with a large number of small units of local government, this number is very high. Entrepreneurial incentive is increased by the stacking of units of government, which increases the probability that a problem will significantly affect the ability of some public official to perform well, thus creating an incentive to address the problem. Besides opportunity and incentive, entrepreneurship also depends on individual attributes such as creativity, imagination, energy, and persistence. Because these qualities are unequally distributed, the opportunities and incentives for public entrepreneurship must always exceed the actual amount of entrepreneurship. Not everyone is cut out to be an entrepreneur.

Consent is required from numerous sources. Ultimately, it may be required from elected representatives in a number of municipalities or in the county delegation to the state legislature. Along the way, it will likely be necessary to obtain consent from political or professional peers in the context of an intergovernmental association. Numerous opportunities will exist for others to enter objections and to help shape the solution being advanced. From the point of view of the citizens served, successful public entrepreneurship depends as much on the quality of the consent that must be obtained as on the opportunity to exercise initiative. Private entrepreneurs confront the marketplace; ultimately, they must attract consumers, although along the way they must attract support from bankers, shareholders, and employees. Public entrepreneurs confront a similar set of constraints; ultimately, they must please voters, but along the way they must attract an array of supporters—peers, other appointed officials, and elected representatives.

Civil society facilitates the process of public entrepreneurship by providing forums that connect entrepreneurs more easily to those from whom they need consent. Intergovernmental associations in particular function this way. The existence of such associations greatly reduces the transaction costs that could otherwise overwhelm the process. Imagine trying to negotiate a series of bilateral agreements with ninety municipalities. Intergovernmental associations facilitate negotiation in much the same way as a legislature. Indeed, county municipal leagues may frequently operate as *shadow legislatures* for dealing with the intergovernmental dimensions of metropolitan governance.

Community Differentiation

A multiplicity of primary local jurisdictions creates opportunities for differentiation among communities with respect to housing configurations, lifestyles, and concomitant public services. Residents, obviously, can choose among these communities, depending on housing availability and income constraints, among other factors. This leads, in turn, to greater diversity *among* communities in a metropolitan area as well as to greater homogeneity *within* communities. A significant degree of homogeneity within local municipalities is necessary to sustain the less adversarial politics discussed above. Note in particular that residential self-sorting predicts a *metropolitan or suburban area* that is diverse rather than homogeneous. Driving through a suburban area governed by a multiplicity of small local governments, one is struck, not by the dull and lifeless conformity of the area, but by the diversity of the communities clustered together.

The self-sorting of residents among local jurisdictions is often called "voting with your feet." The availability of such a choice set surely increases residents' satisfaction with their chosen communities. Many students of metropolitan areas have also assumed that residential choice contributes to metropolitan governance by engendering *competition* among local governments. The degree to which such an effect occurs is less clear. As Parks and I have pointed out (Oakerson and Parks 1988), the entry and exit of residents imposes only a weak form of market discipline in a world of homeownership and property taxes, at least when compared with the degree of market discipline experienced by the typical retailer. The difficulty is the lag time between municipal inattention or inefficiency and the consequent "cash drawer" effect on municipal revenues, which is prompted by falling real estate prices. The lag time is crucial, however, for responding effectively, leading to a conjecture that citizen "voice" rather than "exit," to use Hirschman's (1970) formulation, is the more critical ingredient in local governance. Clearly, the prospect of declining property values can motivate *both* local citizens and local officials to tend to municipal problems. The key is to have in place a political jurisdiction with ample incentive to respond to problems (Oakerson and Svorney 2002). This must be a jurisdiction closely tied to the interests of local residents.[6]

Accountability and How It Works

In suburban areas, metropolitan organization tends to get built from the ground up. As municipalities and school districts reach the limits of their service provision or production capabilities, they join together to organize overlying units—special-purpose districts, joint production facilities, and various other service agreements and partnerships. The result is the stacking or layering of jurisdictions. A single household may be subject to a number of such specialized units. Although this generally makes sense in provision or production terms (Oakerson 1999), it often is thought to be counterproductive for governance. The puzzle is this: how can an individual citizen keep track of and thus hold accountable such a large number of independent public officials? Fridley, Minnesota, once upon a time, made it into state and local government textbooks as an absurd example of piling governments on top of governments: Fridley had eleven. Overlapping jurisdictions, it is argued, simply confuse citizens and create insurmountable monitoring difficulties. Dahl (1990, 70–71), while arguing the case for nested governments, contends that the number should probably be limited well short of Fridley's eleven levels. Many analysts would recommend at most two (local) levels. The reason, of course, is the limited time and energy available to individuals.

Dahl's argument has a very sensible ring to it. If accountability is construed in individualistic terms, it is true that individuals face severe limits in the number of officials and units of government they can hold accountable. Viewed from this perspective, the number of units of government and government officials in highly complex (or fragmented) metropolitan areas surely does approach the absurd. If, however, accountability works more collectively, in some cases reciprocally, and frequently indirectly, individual citizens need not monitor everything. Complex metropolitan areas may then be workable. The key to their workability is the governance structure created by civil society. Individuals use the art of association, as Tocqueville expected, to *amplify* their capabilities, not only in accomplishing the discrete tasks associated with caring for their local communities but also in carrying out the work of accountability. If so, accountability far exceeds the capabilities of any single individual.

Consider again how public entrepreneurship works. Any given entrepreneur is subject to multiple sources of constraint—the need to obtain consent from various constituencies. The interests of multiple communities get represented—without individual citizens having to monitor the entire process. Instead of simply multiplying the number of officials that individual citizens must hold accountable, the complexity of a metropolitan area together with its civil society amplifies the capabilities of individuals, effectively enhancing accountability to citizens.[7] Polycentricity is thus able to achieve a degree of accountability that goes well beyond what can be achieved by individual citizens acting in relation to a monocentric system.

THE EFFECTS OF ALTERNATIVE PRESCRIPTIONS FOR REFORM

From the foregoing analysis, I conclude that large-scale metropolitan governments would lead to (1) greatly reduced citizen participation, (2) an exclusively adversarial style of politics, (3) dramatically lower levels of representation, (4) severely reduced levels of public entrepreneurship, and (5) sharply weakened democratic accountability. To compensate, in part, for these changes, it would be necessary to restructure metropolitan civil society from top to bottom. A much different governance structure would emerge. Self-governance on the part of local communities would of necessity be replaced by the special pleading of community groups. In more fragmented arrangements, civil society provides *partners* for governments at multiple levels. In a more consolidated structure, partners become lobbyists or, worse, adversaries. Civic associations would suffer from much more restricted access to governmental authority. The productivity of civil society would be sharply diminished, as the difficulties of obtaining collective action on public problems were magnified.

Before long, citizens would begin searching for ways to disaggregate metropolitan problems so that they might be dealt with more responsively and effectively in local communities. But they would find their efforts to obtain reform thwarted by the destruction of the trilevel system of metropolitan decision making that characterizes the polycentric metropolis and its replacement by a single, unified structure of authority. If all of this sounds familiar, it is: It describes the process of governance that characterizes many large, undifferentiated—unfragmented—cities.

Oliver's suggestion for a two-tier system with a base composed of municipalities of 50,000 to 100,000 residents (2001, 209–11) is less destructive in suburban areas and would make a positive contribution in central cities. In suburban areas, however, it also would (1) reduce citizen participation, (2) deprive citizens of a less adversarial politics, (3) lessen representation, (4) reduce public entrepreneurship, and (5) weaken accountability. The creation of a dominant metropolitan governmental unit would also weaken the intermunicipal governance structure that characterizes more fragmented areas.

In addition, to implement Oliver's preferred institutional design, it would be necessary to deprive citizens of their constitutional role in the formation of local governments. They would have to be forced into municipal consolidations against their will. This would destroy one whole level of metropolitan decision making, a level that contributes at present to a continuing process of institutional reform and adaptability. Instead, one must assume that an appropriate set of units can be devised by external observers and fixed in place until changed by equally knowledgeable outsiders. Who would actually do this and how they would obtain appropriate information are unanswered questions.

The principal difficulty with Oliver's argument is conceptual—referring to his concept of governance. "Local government," he contends, "is important primarily because it provides an accessible and small-scale arena for the resolution of social and economic conflict"(2001, 5). Note that *conflict* is central to this concept of local governance, not joint responsibility for a community in Tocqueville's sense. Of course, conflict resolution is one important dimension of governance, and metropolitan governance must be able to provide for it. In a federal system, conflict resolution is often facilitated by access to overlying jurisdictions. Nested governance structures are therefore often crucial to conflict resolution. Local residents and local communities need such access for metropolitan governance to work well.

The principal brief against the fragmented metropolis is that it has not solved the problem of racial division, as is manifest especially in housing. The metropolitan governance structures extolled above for their many positive attributes have failed to remedy the scourge of racial discrimination. Because suburbs tend to have white majorities and central cities African American majorities, the suburbs appear as bastions of white separation and the cities as black ghettos. The solution to many minds is straightforward: Tear down the boundaries that divide central city from suburb and thereby reintegrate the local polity.

Race-based inequities are one of America's most enduring and most serious problems. Local governance most likely cannot address this problem alone, but it surely can make a contribution. Localities are, after all, the places where people live. However, there is considerable reason and evidence to suggest that eradicating the local boundaries created by citizens would not be an effective way to find local remedies. Racial harmony will benefit from the characteristics of metropolitan governance associated with a polycentric model, provided that people of all races can claim its advantages. The benefits of polycentricity are color-blind—at least potentially. Racial harmony is likely to suffer from the less open governance structures associated with monocentric authority structures. Residents of central cities need the same civic space available to suburban residents. Government–governance relationships that reduce the capabilities of local citizens to care for their common concerns—to care for *res publica*—are unlikely to engender racial harmony or social harmony more generally. It is not a *consolidated unit of government* that urban and suburban residents need; it is a *common governance structure* in which both urban and suburban communities participate. What inhibits and usually forecloses the creation of a common governance structure embracing both urban and suburban communities is the concentration of political power in the central city. Metropolitan reform is indeed needed—desperately so. But instead of extending the monocentric arrangement of the central city into the suburbs, what is needed is the extension of the polycentric model into the central city.

Metropolitan reform, as usually envisioned, would have dramatic effects on governance. We generally do not understand these effects very well because we do not understand metropolitan governance under conditions of fragmentation. The initial steps needed are theoretical: to identify and conceptualize the dimensions of metropolitan governance and tie those dimensions to the institutional architecture that prevails, for the most part, outside central cities. As we do this, we will begin to discover a rich world of governance, one likely to be destroyed or crippled by reform efforts that would greatly reduce the complexity of metropolitan organization. A serious reduction in governance capabilities would surely have equally serious social consequences.

CONCLUSION

Fragmented metropolitan areas exhibit robust patterns of metropolitan governance—in the absence of metropolitan governments. The polycentric design of government in metropolitan areas is associated with the emergence of governance structures that draw heavily on civil society. This applies to both governance structures within small municipalities and intermunicipal governance structures that attend to metropolitan relationships and problems. Polycentricity creates civic space—opportunities for constructive engagement among citizens and officials. The specific design of governmental institutions in fragmented metropolitan areas— in particular, the absence of a local metropoliswide governmental jurisdiction with powers over subordinate units of government—allows local citizens and officials to create a metropolitan governance structure within civil society. Access to the state legislature via the local delegation provides the requisite access to coercive authority.

Such a governance structure enhances many important attributes of metropolitan decision making that contribute to effective governance. Metropolitan areas governed in this manner can be expected to be more participatory, to feature stronger representation, to engage in more effective problem solving related to the care of common goods (the maintenance of the public realm), to allow for more vigorous public entrepreneurship, and to strengthen the accountability of officials to the citizens they serve. Learning how to produce these effects is surely an important lesson in governance. If so, political scientists can ill afford to dismiss metropolitan governance or its careful study. Metropolitan areas are becoming more and more complex, not less. Civic engagement is diminishing, just as political scientists awake to its importance. If the study of governance as distinct from government becomes a theoretical and practical priority in political science, metropolitan governance will emerge as a key area of research.

NOTES

1. Tocqueville elaborates as follows: "Even while the centralized power, in its despair, invokes the assistance of the citizens, it says to them: 'You shall act just as I please, as much as I please, and in the direction which I please. You are to take charge of the details without aspiring to guide the system; you are to work in darkness, and afterwards you may judge the work by its results.' These are not the conditions on which the alliance of the human will is to be obtained; it must be free in its gait and responsible for its acts, or (such is the constitution of man) the citizen had rather remain a passive spectator than a dependent actor in schemes with which he is unacquainted" (Tocqueville 1835, vol. 1, 94).
2. The indicators are rates of membership in voluntary and religious associations as well as rates of volunteer work in those associations; see Verba, Schlozman, and Brady (1995, 80).
3. Such conflict can perhaps be mitigated if there is a strong, shared commitment to fiscal equivalence and the regular use of special tax districts to allow for the diverse expression of preferences. This pattern is characteristic of town (i.e., township) government in the metropolitan areas of upstate New York.
4. James Gwartney has emphasized this point to me in helpful comments on this chapter.
5. For excellent accounts of the traditional republican view of representation, see Wood (1969) and Rakove (1996).
6. The role of competition among municipalities is associated with the work of Charles M. Tiebout (1956). The effects of competition are often presumed to operate in market-like fashion on municipal officials. I would argue, however, that Tiebout effects operate most strongly on residents. The strongest incentives to maintain property values belong to property owners. Tiebout effects therefore motivate citizen participation—civic engagement. The effectiveness of participation depends, however, on the governance structure available to citizens. Tiebout effects cannot substitute for metropolitan governance carried out through nonmarket arrangements.

7. The argument is similar to that propounded by Berger and Neuhaus (1977) on the importance of "mediating institutions." The corollary offered here concerns the implications of mediating institutions for metropolitan governance structures.

REFERENCES

Berger, Peter L., and Richard John Neuhaus. 1977. *To Empower People: The Role of Mediating Structures in Public Policy.* Washington, D.C.: American Enterprise Institute.

Bromley, Daniel J., David Feeny, Margaret R. McKean, Pauline Peters, Jere L. Gilles, Ronald J. Oakerson, C. Ford Runge, and James T. Thomson, eds. 1992. *Making the Commons Work: Theory, Practice, and Policy.* San Francisco: ICS Press.

Clingermayer, James C., and Richard C. Feiock. 2001. *Institutional Constraints and Policy Choice: An Exploration of Local Governance.* Albany: State University of New York Press.

Dahl, Robert A. 1990. *After the Revolution? Authority in a Good Society.* Rev. ed. New Haven, Conn.: Yale University Press.

de Soto, Hernando. 1989. *The Other Path: The Invisible Revolution in the Third World.* New York: Harper & Row.

Hirschman, Albert O. 1970. *Exit, Voice, and Loyalty: Responses to Decline in Firms, Organizations, and States.* Cambridge, Mass.: Harvard University Press.

Mansbridge, Jane J. 1980. *Beyond Adversary Democracy.* New York: Basic Books.

North, Douglass C. 1990. *Institutions, Institutional Change and Economic Performance.* Cambridge: Cambridge University Press.

Oakerson, Ronald J. 1999. *Governing Local Public Economies: Creating the Civic Metropolis.* Oakland: ICS Press.

Oakerson, Ronald J., and Roger B. Parks. 1988. Citizen Voice and Public Entrepreneurship: The Organizational Dynamic of a Complex Metropolitan County. *Publius: The Journal of Federalism* 18: 91–112.

———. 1989. Local Government Constitutions: A Different View of Metropolitan Governance. *American Review of Public Administration* 19: 279–94.

Oakerson, Ronald J. and Shirley Svorny. 2002. Rightsizing Los Angeles Government. Paper prepared for presentation at the John Randolph Haynes and Dora Haynes Foundation Conference, "Reform, L.A. Style: The Theory and Practice of Urban Governance at Century's Turn," School of Policy, Planning, and Development, University of Southern California, Los Angeles, September 19–20.

Oakerson, Ronald J., and S. Tjip Walker. 1997. Analyzing Policy Reform and Reforming Policy Analysis: An Institutionalist Approach. In *Policy Analysis Concepts and Methods: An Institutional and Implementation Focus*, ed. Derick W. Brinkerhoff. Vol. 5 in *Policy Studies and Developing Nations*, ed. by Stuart S. Nagel. Greenwich, Conn.: JAI Press.

Oliver, J. Eric. 2001. *Democracy in Suburbia*. Princeton, N.J.: Princeton University Press.

Olson, Mancur. 1965. *The Logic of Collective Action*. Cambridge, Mass.: Harvard University Press.

Ostrom, Elinor. 1990. *Governing the Commons: The Evolution of Institutions for Collective Action*. New York: Cambridge University Press.

———. 1992. *Crafting Institutions for Self-Governing Irrigation Systems*. San Francisco: ICS Press.

———. 1998. A Behavioral Approach to the Rational Choice Theory of Collective Action. *American Political Science Review* 92: 1–22.

Ostrom, Vincent. 1989. *The Intellectual Crisis in American Public Administration*, 2d ed. Tuscaloosa: University of Alabama Press.

———. 1999. Polycentricity (Part 1) and Polycentricity (Part 2). In *Polycentricity and Local Public Economies*, ed. Michael D. McGinnis. Ann Arbor: University of Michigan Press.

Ostrom, Vincent, Charles M. Tiebout, and Robert Warren. 1961. The Organization of Government in Metropolitan Areas: A Theoretical Inquiry. *American Political Science Review* 55: 831–42.

Parks, Roger B., and Ronald J. Oakerson. 1989. Metropolitan Organization and Governance: A Local Public Economy Approach. *Urban Affairs Quarterly* 25: 18–29.

———. 1993. Comparative Metropolitan Organization: Service Production and Governance Structures in St. Louis (MO) and Allegheny County (PA), *Publius: The Journal of Federalism* 23: 19–39.

———. 2000. Regionalism, Localism, and Metropolitan Governance: Suggestions from the Research Program on Local Public Economies. *State and Local Government Review* 32: 169–79.

Polanyi, Michael. 1951. *The Logic of Liberty: Reflections and Rejoinders*. Chicago: University of Chicago Press.

Putnam, Robert D. 2000. *Bowling Alone: The Collapse and Revival of American Community*. New York: Simon & Schuster.

Rakove, Jack N. 1996. *Original Meanings: Politics and Ideas in the Making of the Constitution*. New York: Vintage Books.

Savitch, H. V., and Ronald K. Vogel. 2000. Introduction: Paths to New Regionalism. *State and Local Government Review* 12, no. 3: 158–68.

Teaford, Jon C. 1997. *Post-Suburbia: Government and Politics in the Edge Cities*. Baltimore: Johns Hopkins University Press.

Tiebout, Charles M. 1956. A Pure Theory of Local Expenditure. *Journal of Political Economy* 44: 416–24.

Tocqueville, Alexis de. 1835 (1945). *Democracy in America*. 2 vols. Henry Reeve text, ed. Phillips Bradley. New York: Vintage Books.

Verba, Sidney, Kay Lehman Schlozman, and Henry E. Brady. 1995. *Voice and Equality: Civic Voluntarism in American Politics*. Cambridge, Mass.: Harvard University Press.

Wood, Gordon S. 1969. *The Creation of the American Republic 1776–1787*. New York: W. W. Norton.

———. 1991. *The Radicalism of the American Revolution*. New York: Vintage Books.

ANNETTE STEINACKER

GAME-THEORETIC MODELS OF METROPOLITAN COOPERATION

3

In the mid-1990s, issues of metropolitan governance and the possibility of cooperative agreements among cities were raised by several journalists and public officials (Peirce, Johnson, and Hall 1993; Rusk 1993; Orfield 1997). Academics began writing on the topic as well, though more often to point out the limitations and political unfeasibility of achieving these changes on a wide scale (Downs 1994). Policy recommendations have evolved partly in response to those criticisms. Attention has shifted from metropolitan government efforts that would establish new areawide governmental units to metropolitan governance with an emphasis on informal or limited service arrangements—for example, intergovernmental compacts and special districts (Hamilton 1999; Wallis 1994). But for all the recent attention, we still have a limited understanding of the conditions under which cities are likely to cooperate (Feiock 2002).

Fostering cooperation among cities to provide services or share revenues is a type of collective action problem. But despite the prominence of this theoretical perspective in other areas of political science, it has not been a part of the metropolitan governance debate. A focus on collective action models highlights the conditions under which cooperation may evolve, even in a predominantly competitive environment. As Richard Feiock discussed in chapter 1, one consistent finding of the research on institutional collective action has been the importance of contextual factors. Ostrom demonstrated that cooperative solutions to common-property resource problems are possible if specific boundary and transaction cost conditions are met (Ostrom 1990). Lipecap and other new institutionalist researchers argue that the homogeneity of the actors involved will affect the resolution of certain competitive situations (Lipecap 1989, 1996).

This chapter focuses on two of the major contextual conditions emphasized in the collective action literature: the characteristics of the good or service provided, and the heterogeneity of the actors involved. The first section describes the impact of these factors on the likelihood of a cooperative outcome. The second section then reviews several commonly used models of cooperation to assess their appropriateness for modeling metropolitan relationships on the basis of their ability to incorporate the crucial features identified in the first section.

CHARACTERISTICS OF CITIES AND LOCAL ISSUES

Four characteristics of cities and local issues are significant in efforts to achieve cooperation. These are summarized in table 3.1. First, there must be joint gains from cooperation. This is a simple rationality claim, asserting that cities will not change service arrangements unless each benefits from doing so. The more serious the underlying problem, the larger the aggregate gains from resolving it, and the greater the likelihood of a cooperative arrangement to do so. This condition has most often been noted in the resolution of common-property resource problems. As losses from overconsumption increase, all the parties involved become more likely to seek an agreement to restrict use (Lipecap 1989; Lubell et al. 2002; Ostrom 1990; Ostrom, Gardner, and Walker 1994).

Work on the provision of public goods also notes the necessity for aggregate gains to exceed the aggregate costs of provision, with the greater the margin, the greater the ability of the collective to provide selective incentives or attract a political entrepreneur to organize the group (Olson 1971; Hardin 1982). Joint gains require that a Pareto-optimal outcome exists and is realizable—that an outcome can be achieved where no one is made worse off and at least one participant is made better off.

Table 3.1. City and Service Characteristics That Affect Cooperation

1. Joint gains from cooperation
   - The larger the aggregate gains, the more likely a cooperative solution.
   - Aggregate gains must exceed transaction costs.
   - Each participant must be at least as well off with the cooperative solution.
2. Preference diversity
   - Conflict over level and division of the policy.
   - Agreement over level but conflict over division.
   - Agreement over both level and division.
3. Asymmetry of players' positions and strengths
   - Alternative to the cooperative outcome.
   - Time preference or discount value.
   - Risk aversion.
4. Stability of game structure and parameters
   - Asset specificity or investment.
   - Preference drift.

However, even when the potential for aggregate gains are large, conflict over the distribution of the gains can prevent any change. The allocation of these joint gains will be affected by the level of asymmetry between players in their preferences and political strengths. The greater the heterogeneity of the participants and the more clear-cut which players win the most, the higher may be the political opposition to any cooperative solution. Joint gains are necessary but far from sufficient in establishing cooperative relationships (Lipecap 1989; Riker and Sened 1991).

This leads to the second critical feature affecting the probability of cooperation, the diversity in preferences among the participants. Diversity can exist at two levels. First, participants may disagree over the policy goal. Second, they may agree with the overall goal but then disagree over the division of the policy outcome. Disagreement over the goal itself is likely in zero-sum situations. Where one city's win means the other must lose, conflict and competition will define the situation. The participants' preferences diverge over the policy goal itself in that each prefers the outcome favorable to itself. Note that it is still possible that there are joint gains to be had in this case, but if the good is indivisible and rivalrous in consumption, then only one participant can receive the prize. The other participants benefit only by reducing their costs if they do not engage in competition for the good.

Economic development has often been treated as this type of policy. Cities are in competition with each other over the "good"—new businesses and the resulting tax base. If one wins, the others lose. The new firm location is both exclusive and rivalrous in consumption. Though less often characterized this way, debates over public "bads" or locally unwanted land uses, including affordable housing, also fall into this category. The community forced to accept the unwanted land use suffers a loss, while other communities benefit. Both these cases—competition to attract the good and to avoid the bad—suggest that land use decisions in general may fall into this "total conflict" category.

The second possibility is that all participants agree with the overall goal but disagree with the division of the outcome. "Club" goods—rivalrous in consumption but with limited exclusion—are likely to fall into this class. Participants may agree to jointly provide a service only for members of the coalition, establishing exclusion between those who join and those who do not. However, the indivisible nature of the good means that within the jurisdictions, exclusion is not complete. Police and fire services exhibit these characteristics. The participants may all agree that coordinated action will lead to a higher overall level of safety, but the rivalrous nature of the good and the lack of exclusion within the compact make it difficult to determine how that larger level of benefits will be divided or how new costs will be shared. Preferences are similar at the first level but then diverge at the second. Cooperation in these situations is dependent on the relationship between the value of the cooperative outcome and each player's ideal outcome. A player would choose to cooperate if the gain from the cooperative outcome (good provided but division less than ideal) over the status quo (good not provided) is greater than the forgone gain between this outcome and his ideal result.

Finally, participants could be in agreement on both the level and division of the service, so preference convergence is complete. This can occur for some system maintenance services, such as sewer and water or refuse collection. Because the amount of service received is divisible, easily measured, and rivalrous in consumption, the equivalent of a market within the regional compact can be created. Costs are allocated on the basis of benefits received through user fees. Total benefit levels may vary across jurisdictions, possibly due to differences in size, but the total fees paid also vary in accordance. Preferences on providing the service and then on its benefit/cost distribution are likely to be similar for all participants in the regional compact. Cooperation should be easiest to achieve with these types of services.

Besides differences in policy preferences, participants may also differ in their political power. The third critical characteristic that affects the likelihood of cooperation is the level of symmetry in this strength across the players. The power of each relative to the others is the result of three factors: the need for a cooperative agreement to provide the service (what will be the value of the alternative or status quo), their discount factor (how critical is it that the service be provided soon), and their level of risk aversion (willingness to trade off a sure thing vs. a chance at something better). If the asymmetry of the participants is too great, no cooperative outcome may be feasible. The power of some players may lead them to demand more than any joint gains that might result from a cooperative agreement, because they could do at least that well on their own or with another partnership arrangement. Where an agreement can be reached, the stronger player will be able to command more of the division of the spoils. Social norms regarding the fairness of these divisions may preclude some of the technically feasible outcomes from being reached.

Cities within a metropolitan area can differ from each other significantly in ways that could affect their relative power. This relationship will again depend on the type of good provided. For capital-intensive, physical-infrastructure goods, such as water and sewer treatment systems, the city with the largest population may command greater power, due to the declining average costs of such projects. Given their size, these cities capture most economies of scale in construction and operation, even if they pursue the project on their own. If they cooperate with other communities in providing an expanded service, they may be able to force the smaller cities to bear a disproportionate share of the cost, because that is still cheaper for them than constructing the project on their own. For labor-intensive services where economies of scale are less of an issue, the relative power across cities may be more equal. Fire and police protection compacts are more likely to reflect costs proportional to services provided, because any city can do nearly as well if they pull out of the compact and provide the service on their own.

Which situation is more likely to generate cooperative agreements is not certain a priori, because two factors push the results in different directions. The potential financial benefits leading to an agreement may clash with political costs and social norms. In an asymmetric power situation, the weaker player has fewer feasible alternatives and so may be more likely to accept the only deal available.

However, if the stronger player attempts to extract most of the financial gains that the other player could experience from the agreement, the fiscal benefit is pushed close to zero, and then fairness norms and political concerns over appearing to be "exploited" may come into play and prevent the weaker players from joining the agreement (Thaler 1988). With symmetric players, the cost division is more likely to be politically palatable but the fiscal benefits reaped from a cooperative agreement may be less. Joint action with other players that are similar rarely produces large payoffs, but participant homogeneity tends to reduce the political transaction costs so that the agreement may still be profitable (Deneckere and Davidson 1985). The probability of interlocal agreement will depend on both the fiscal benefits and the perceived fairness of the terms of the agreement.

The fourth characteristic that can affect a cooperative outcome is stability of the players' positions over time. The cooperative agreement itself may alter the strength of the participants, as well as outside forces. If the agreement requires players to make investments in specific assets or other long-term commitments, it can alter the outcomes that would be available to them if the agreement broke down in the future (Frieden 1994). A compact to forego construction of infrastructure or to refuse to compete for new businesses in return for current tax-base shares may reduce the growth opportunities available to a city in the future. For physical assets that are subject to congestion, such as shared use of a central library or landfill, both the party that provides it and the parties that contract for it are exposed to risk. The party providing the asset must make an investment greater than that necessary to cover its own needs, leaving it vulnerable to excessive costs if other participants later renege on the contract.

At the same time, if demand for the service increases, the party providing the good may prefer to terminate the interlocal compact to better serve its own constituency. The contracting participants are then forced to make an unplanned investment to develop their own asset. The greater the risk due to the size of the investment, the greater the need for the contract to include firm sanctions for reneging and generally the longer the time period it needs to cover. However, if at least some of the potential participants anticipate that their circumstances will change over time, they will be less willing to make a long-term, strongly enforceable commitment. And that willingness declines more rapidly as the size of the investment in the service increases.

The preferences of the participants may also diverge over time. Changes in population, political representatives, fiscal capacity, or other factors may lead cities' interests to drift apart. As conditions change, the value of the cooperative agreement can change, possibly increasing the incentive of some parties to pull out (Keohane and Martin 1995). Cities that are on different trajectories—a slowly declining central city or inner suburb versus rapid growth suburbs, for example—may anticipate that their preferences regarding services will eventually diverge. The higher the probability that their interests will drift apart, the less likely it is that a cooperative agreement will be made, especially if significant differences in asset investments would be required. If an agreement were made, it would require additional bonding or sanctioning commitments to protect the participants, which would raise the transaction costs of the agreement and reduce the feasibility of obtaining a contract.

Any model of cooperation must incorporate these four characteristics, which are summarized in table 3.1. Let us now consider several of the models used to explain metropolitan interactions and determine how they include these features, with an eye to assessing when each might be a good model of regional cooperation.

THE PRISONER'S DILEMMA GAME

The single-play Prisoner's Dilemma game has probably been the model most commonly used to study metropolitan relationships, especially in the area of economic development (Bowman 1988; Grady 1987; Green and Fleischman 1989; Rubin and Rubin 1987; Wolman 1988). A large part of its appeal is that the payoff structure does seem to capture the inherently competitive nature of relationships among cities. However, as is discussed below, this game depends on several very strong assumptions, which rarely hold among cities.

The standard payoff structure of the Prisoner's Dilemma game is shown in the first panel of figure 3.1. Each city must choose between a Cooperate or Defect strategy, such as refusing to offer location incentives or offering them. Because B is greater than A and D is greater than C, when each city considers what to do, it will always be better off with the returns from the Defect strategy, regardless of what the other city does. Because each player has a dominant strategy of defecting, there is only one possible outcome of the game (D, D). This outcome is a Nash Equilibrium, meaning that no player has an incentive to unilaterally switch to a different strategy because his or her payoff with the new outcome would be less.

But this is not a Pareto-optimal outcome. If all cities choose Cooperate, each would be made better off compared with the (D, D) outcome. The

Where A > D, D > C, B > A. Player One's payoff is first, Player Two's payoff second.

		City Two	
		Cooperate	Defect
City One	Cooperate	A, A	C, B
	Defect	B, C	D, D

Figure 3.1. Standard Prisoner's Dilemma Game

outcome mutual cooperation is not a Nash Equilibrium, however, because if Player One chose (C, C) to cooperate, Player Two could make himself or herself better off by defecting (B > A), and vice versa. In the case of cities competing for development, any city could improve its position if it defected and offered some incentives while its competitors did not. It would then attract more investment than it could have in the competitive market (when all cities refused to offer concessions). It even could reap these gains by offering a fairly low level of incentives because its competitors (who chose the Cooperate strategy) offered none. Because each city makes the same calculation, each defects to protect itself from the negative consequences of being the only one to cooperate. All cities would offer concessions, and the cooperative "no compete" agreement would collapse.

Though initially plausible, the Prisoner's Dilemma game does not stand up to scrutiny—even in the area of economic development. Considering the four characteristics defined in the first section, the Prisoner's Dilemma game is particularly limited in addressing divergence in preferences, asymmetry in player positions, and stability of the game over time. The model assumes that all players are interchangeable—they have the same preferences for development and the same political power. Neither is true. The existence of slow-growth and antigrowth movements in various parts of the country, plus strict zoning regulations that maintain wealthy, residential-only suburbs, belies the first claim. Equal positions imply that each city faces the same status quo without the cooperative development policy, that is, each would attract the same level and type of economic growth. Cities differ significantly in the other features they can offer new businesses—the quality of the workforce, wage rates, access to markets for inputs or the final product, and so forth. Cities that would attract considerable growth even without the regional agreement will be able to demand more of the benefits from an agreement, rather than accepting the symmetric division of the joint gains that the Prisoner's Dilemma model dictates.

Finally, the static nature of the model does not allow for the impact of repeated play or any changes over time that would make cooperation either more or less likely. As we will see below, repeated interactions with the same players can significantly change the dynamics of the game, providing implicit communication, permitting trade-offs of benefits in one interaction for higher costs in another, and incorporating safeguards for changes in the player's positions or preferences over time.

These limitations of the Prisoner's Dilemma have been addressed in three ways, each of which leads to a new model. First, the payoff structure was changed, leading to an Assurance Game. Second, repeated play was introduced, leading to the Iterated Prisoner's Dilemma Game. Third, variation in player preferences and political power was added, in Bargaining Games.

THE ASSURANCE GAME

In the Assurance game, the payoff structure is changed so that Defect is no longer a dominant strategy. This can be seen in figure 3.2. Each player would prefer to cooperate if the other player did as well (A > B, unlike in the Prisoner's Dilemma game), but prefer to defect if the other player did so (C > D, unchanged from the Prisoner's Dilemma). There is a clear Pareto-optimal outcome if both cooperate (A > D), which is also a Nash Equilibrium. All participants want to be at the mutual cooperation (C, C) Nash Equilibrium—if Player One knows that Player Two will cooperate, he or she has no incentive to defect, and the payoff is highest if he or she also cooperates. Conversely, if Player One knows that Player Two will defect, he or she also wants to defect. The payoff will be less than when both cooperate but greater than when cooperating while the other player defects. (C, C) is a Nash Equilibrium in this case, which it was not for the Prisoner's Dilemma.

Where A > D, D > C, B < A. Player One's payoff is given first, Player Two's payoff second. Nash Equilibrium outcomes are indicated with an asterisk.

		City Two	
		Cooperate	Defect
City One	Cooperate	A, A*	C, B
	Defect	B, C	D, D*

Figure 3.2. Standard Assurance Game

The difficulty is that there are two Nash Equilibria in this game: (C, C) and (D, D). If both players must choose simultaneously and without communication, it is not certain that each will play Cooperate. If one player is very risk averse and uses a "maximin" decision criterion that focuses on maximizing the value of his lowest possible payoff (which would occur when the other player defects), he or she would play Defect. If both use this strategy, there would be no incentive to change it in future play, because (D, D) is a Nash Equilibrium. Although one player may realize there is a better strategy available, he or she cannot be sure that the other player shares this realization. In the real world, communication between the players can allow them to determine what strategy each would play and to realize that matched strategies of (C, C) would be best.

In the case of metropolitan cooperation, because communication is possible, the question of whether players will be able to reach a cooperative agreement is not of particular interest. Of more importance is the likelihood that this payoff structure exists or could be created, for it would then lead to cooperative outcomes. The Assurance game corresponds to the case where preferences are in complete convergence. All players prefer the (C, C) outcome. The Prisoner's Dilemma structure, in contrast, corresponds to the case where preferences are in complete conflict. The only way for each player to get his or her own largest payoff is to take an action (defect) that will lower the other player's payoff. In cases where preferences have both features—convergence on the provision of the service, but conflict over the division of it—a nested model where the final payoffs combine the results from both the Assurance game (provide or not) and the Prisoner's Dilemma game (individual benefits greater than individual costs) is necessary. So the appropriate payoff structure will exist for some goods, but not all.

When the nature of the good dictates a Prisoner's Dilemma structure, policy recommendations have focused on recasting it as an Assurance game by lowering the Defect payoff through sanctions or increasing the Cooperate payoff through incentives (Sandler 1992). When the players are individuals, this may be done by appealing to solidarity incentives (Chong 1991). But for metropolitan politics, participants are political representatives (agents) whose utility function is more limited to effects on constituents (principals). Appeals to personal utility are less likely to be effective. Selective incentives for cooperation may require linking payoffs across games or different service provisions. For example, eligibility for state infrastructure funds has been linked to city economic development policies.

Although the Assurance game does increase the chances of a cooperative outcome, it still fails to capture several relevant characteristics of metropolitan politics. As a symmetric game, players continue to be interchangeable, with preferences and positions in convergence. The static nature of the game is not a concern if players are able to communicate, because the preferred outcome in repeated play is the same. However, a focus on only the static version obscures the possibilities of changes in the symmetric positions and preferences of the players over time.

THE ITERATED PRISONER'S DILEMMA GAME

While the Assurance game increases the chances of cooperation by linking the Prisoner's Dilemma payoffs to those in other areas, the Iterated Prisoner's Dilemma game (IPD) relies on the impact of repeated interactions to change the payoffs available to participants. Players attempt to maximize their payoffs over the entire course of interactions with each other. A strategy of Always Defect will provide the highest payoffs only if the other player also plays Always Defect. If there is any probability that Player Two might play Cooperate, then Player One could improve his or her total payoff by using a different strategy that includes cooperation.

Several parameters affect the optimal choice of strategy and therefore level of cooperation in this case. Uncertainty over the ending point of the game, discount rate of the players, and relative size of the payoffs can induce cooperation in early rounds because of the value of future payoffs. Credible sanctions imposed either internally or externally also work to maintain the Cooperate strategy. All are related to the possibility that future benefits from cooperation will be greater than current benefits from defection.

The relative size of the payoffs for Defect and Cooperate influences the possibility that sanctions can be imposed against a player who defects. Sanctions in this game are generally imposed by the other players through their decision to also defect in later rounds following one initial defection by a player. The cost to the sanctioning player cannot be so high that he or she would be better off not imposing the cost, while still high enough to prevent the other player from consistently using the Defect strategy.

Expectations about the number of rounds in the game affect the player decisions as well. The higher a player's expectation that the game is nearing its end, the more weight he or she attaches to current payoffs. Risk aversion is closely tied to these estimates when there is no natural stopping point. Risk aversion is the willingness of a participant to accept a lower amount that is a certainty (a payoff today) rather than the same or even higher amount that is the result of a gamble (a payoff in the next round, if the player is not certain there will be a next round). Greater risk aversion will lead to a greater probability of choosing to Defect in early rounds because the lower but certain payoff has greater value to the player than a higher but risky payoff in the future.

The same is true for a player's discount value. Even if future payoffs would occur with certainty, they are generally worth less because the benefits are not immediately available. The greater the impact that present conditions have on the player, the higher the discount rate, and again the more weight that is attached to getting the best possible payoff in the current round of play. The more important the current payoffs are to the player, the more likely he or she will choose Defect. He or she can reap the "sucker" payoff in that round if the other player uses a Cooperate strategy. Even with severe sanctions for playing Defect (e.g., the other player never cooperating again), if a player's discount rate is sufficiently high, the benefits of early defection can outweigh the losses in future rounds.

As an illustration of these relationships, if both players utilize a Tit-for-Tat strategy (where they play Cooperate on the first round and then match the other participant's move from the preceding round), neither player will play Defect as long as the common discount value (the percentage of the future payoff that would equal getting that payoff today) is greater than the larger of either $(C - A)/(A - B)$ or $(C - A)/(C - D)$ from the Prisoner's Dilemma payoff matrix in figure 3.1. Cooperation can be sustained if a specific set of relationships holds. Applying this model to metropolitan politics requires solving the game to determine the parameter values (payoffs and discount rates) that would sustain cooperation as done for the Tit-for-Tat strategy. These values establish "regimes"— ranges of values where the prediction from the model would be Cooperate and ranges where the prediction would be Defect. Assessing the range of values for these parameters in the real world then determines the probability of cooperation among cities.

One major difficulty with this approach is the multiplicity of solutions— both in the number of Nash Equilibria that exist and mathematically in the number of parameter estimates that must be solved for the system. Both features require simplifying assumptions to reduce the possible outcomes and mathematically restrict some of the parameter values. The most common of these simplifying assumptions has been to maintain symmetry among the players. Maintaining that assumption can limit the applicability of this approach to the metropolitan politics arena, where diversity among the players appears to be a major factor driving interactions.

The value of the IPD in studying metropolitan cooperation also depends on the assumption that the payoff structure in the single play adequately captures the participants' preferences and positions. If we believe some level of competition among cities is more likely than the agreement that underlies the Assurance game payoffs, the IPD framework is a more accurate approach. Club goods, where there is a mixture of agreement over provision of the good but conflict over its allocation, would require a different payoff structure.

Although the IPD game can incorporate more of the city and policy characteristics identified in table 3.1 than the two previous models, doing so does complicate the model and still requires strong simplifying assumptions to make the approach workable. Player diversity and change in players' positions over time are particularly difficult to add to this approach.

BARGAINING GAMES

The final model considered here is that of a bargaining game. This approach can explicitly take into account asymmetries of player preferences or political strengths. In addition, the impact of repeated play and change over time can be incorporated into the basic framework. This model is the most flexible of those considered, because it is capable of including several of the factors that not only determine if institutional cooperation will occur but also the terms of the cooperative agreement.

The basic bargaining game is the Nash model, which is similar to models of "splitting a pie" between two players. The size of the pie is the joint gains available from working together. Each player wants a piece of the pie, which requires working together to produce the good. But each also wants the largest piece, which means that the more one player gets, the less the other will receive. This captures both the incentives for cooperative behavior to provide the good and competitive behavior in its division.

Participants can vary on the three dimensions mentioned above: outside options, risk aversion, and time preference. The outside option is what the player receives if negotiations break down, typically the value of the status quo. For each player, this value implicitly reflects his or her need for the cooperative agreement. For example, if two communities are considering a tax-sharing or economic development pact, a residential community with slow-growth policies is likely already to place a high value on its current level of growth while a struggling central city places a low value on its growth rate. Each city's preference for more development is reflected in these numbers, with a higher outside option corresponding to a lower preference for the cooperative outcome.

In the negotiation process, each player will demand from any agreement at least the value of his outside option, or what he or she could get from going it alone. If the sum of both players' outside options is greater than the value of the pie being divided, then no agreement is possible. This captures the joint-gains requirement—each participant must achieve at least as much with the agreement as without, and when that is not possible (no joint gains), neither is a cooperative agreement.

Once each player receives the value of his outside option, the remainder of the joint gains is divided on the basis of the player's relative values of risk aversion and time preference. The division favors the player who is more risk accepting and who discounts the future at a lower rate. A risk-averse participant wants to finalize a deal, any deal, now because he or she places a high probability on the negotiations collapsing if he or she delays. His or her initial offer will demand little, because that is most likely to be accepted by the other participants. A risk-accepting player, conversely, will demand more initially with the expectation that the other player will counter rather than walk away if the level is too high. Consequently, he or she does better in the negotiations.

Similarly, the player who discounts the future at a high rate, so the deal is valuable only if it is achieved now, is in a weaker position. Intuitively, whichever player sees the value of the deal dropping faster if it is delayed would be more eager to get a deal now, even if that means taking a smaller portion of the value. Levels of fiscal stress, high unemployment or poverty rates, and politicians' concerns about upcoming elections are all factors that could affect cities and their representatives' attitudes toward finalizing an interlocal agreement quickly (Steinacker 2002).

These relationships are illustrated mathematically in figure 3.3. The solution of the bargaining game is the outcome or argument (x_1, x_2) that maximizes the Nash product. This product is the multiplication of factors that describe each participant and simply reflects the idea that how well each player does is contingent on the features of the other player as well. The solution equations at the bottom of the figure illustrate these interrelationships more clearly. M is the size of the pie, the total value of the item bargained for. The Nash solution assigns as a payoff (x_i) to each

$$\frac{Arg}{Max} (x_1 - \beta_1)^\alpha (x_2 - \beta_2)^{1-\alpha}$$

Where:

β_i = the breakdown point of player i

$$\alpha = \frac{\log \delta_1}{\log \delta_1 + \log \delta_2}$$

$$1 - \alpha = \frac{\log \delta_2}{\log \delta_1 + \log \delta_2}$$

$$\delta_i = \frac{1 - \theta_i}{1 + \rho_i} = \text{the discount factor of player } i$$

θ_i = risk aversion of player i = [0,1]

ρ_i = rate of time preference of player i = [0,1]

The solution for this game is:

Player One: $x_1 = \beta_1 + \alpha(M - \beta_1 - \beta_2)$

Player Two: $x_2 = \beta_2 + (1 - \alpha)(M - \beta_1 - \beta_2)$

where M is the value of the good being divided between the players.

Figure 3.3. Bilateral Bargaining Game

player the value of his or her outside option (β_i), plus some proportion (α or $1 - \alpha$) of what remains from M after both these values have been distributed. The size of this proportion is determined by the player's time preference and risk aversion (combined in the α ratio), which together determine the player's need to finalize a deal now.

The bargaining model predicts that a cooperative outcome can occur, provided both players are not highly advantaged. When both have very desirable alternatives to the deal (outside options), the total of these legitimate demands would be greater than any possible joint gains from the agreement. Even when joint gains are available, if both are risk accepting and have low discount rates, they may not find an acceptable division of the gains because both start with high demands and neither adjusts them significantly during the negotiations. However, in a large number of situations, a cooperative agreement is feasible, given the features of the cities involved. When both are only moderately strong or when one is strong but the other fairly weak, an agreement can be reached. The likelihood of cooperation depends on the context of the situation, both whether the type of good produces joint gains and whether the cities' features lead to compatible bargaining positions.

The model also suggests which player would receive the more advantageous deal in these negotiations, which introduces two important considerations. First, these disparities provide another reason for a potential breakdown of cooperation. Strict application of the bargaining model predicts that the weaker participant should accept any deal that makes him or her even slightly better off than previously. However, there is substantial experimental evidence that participants also respond to the perceived fairness of the deal, rejecting many offers where the stronger partner seems to benefit disproportionately (Roth 1995). In the world of metropolitan agreements, how unequal the terms of the deal can be before cooperation is abandoned is still an unanswered empirical question.

Second, differences in the outcome from a cooperative agreement have normative implications that rarely are a focus in the debate over metropolitan governance. Though cooperation will produce at least some benefits for all participants or no deal would be reached (the joint-gains requirement), the relative gains of the cities are not likely to be equal. Differences in preferences and bargaining strengths can cause the disparity between cities to widen under cooperation, with those having the greatest initial advantage receiving more from the agreement while the disadvantaged cities gain little. The benefits available from feasible agreements may do little to address the equity concerns that often have been the rationale for the pursuit of metropolitan governance.

Of the models described in this chapter, the bargaining model does the best job of incorporating the four critical features needed to generate cooperation. The possibility of joint gains is determined by the value of both players' outside options. Diversity in city preferences is reflected in these different option values, which also are dependent on the type of good. The allocation of the joint gains depends on both these preferences (as summarized in the outside options) and the players' other features (attitudes toward risk, time preferences, and norms of fairness). Asymmetry is easily incorporated by permitting each of the city characteristics to vary across communities. Changes over time in asset specificity can be included by changing the value of each player's outside option in later rounds—given the new investments, how well could that city then do in negotiations with other partners or by itself? Preference drift could be captured by using different trends in the evolution of each player's outside option over time. As a generic approach to assessing the feasibility of cooperative agreements among cities, the bargaining model provides a comprehensive framework of analysis, highlighting the important variables and their relationship with each other.

VALUE OF THE MODELS

Because the solutions to every formal model depend on their underlying assumptions, knowing which assumptions are critical to the model predictions and which are necessary to capture empirical reality are important in our decisions about how to study specific problems. All too often, models are applied without adequate consideration of whether they accurately capture the problem of interest. This chapter has laid out several models that could be appropriate for studying regional cooperation in a decentralized system of governance and more clearly specified the assumptions for each and their consequent strengths and weaknesses in studying this issue. The assumptions of each of the models reviewed here are summarized in table 3.2.

The Prisoner's Dilemma and Assurance games differ only in the assumptions about their payoffs. The Prisoner's Dilemma structure reflects the situation in which cities' preferences are completely divergent—services with a zero-sum nature, where what one participant wins, the other loses. The Assurance structure reflects the situation in which the preferences are completely convergent—cities agree on the amount of the service and its distribution among the participants. For all other cases, in which city preferences are convergent on the level but divergent in their distribution, neither payoff structure alone would be appropriate, and a different model would be needed. More important, even when the payoffs do correspond to preferences and the nature of the good, both models assume that all participants are identical and that the relationship is static, which limit their usefulness.

The next two models focus on relaxing these assumptions. The IPD removes the static assumption, which opens the possibility of cooperation as the effect of current actions on future payoffs are considered. Participants may defer some benefits available today to get a greater cumulative amount in the future. The possibility of cooperation will depend predominantly on the discount rate the players adopt toward the future and the cost of imposing sanctions on those who violate the agreement. The biggest limitation of the IPD is still the assumption of identical players, including that they share the same discount rate.

The bargaining model explicitly considers difference across participants, illustrating both the likelihood of cooperation and the division of

Table 3.2. Types of Models and Their Underlying Assumptions

PRISONER'S DILEMMA LIMITATIONS
1. Static
2. No communication between players; no learning over repeated plays
3. Competition in the payoffs, so (D, D) is dominant and a Nash Equilibrium
4. No credible sanctions or external enforcement
5. Symmetric players

ASSURANCE GAME
1. Static
2. Communication possible; permits coordination on one of the multiple Nash Equilibria that are possible
3. Cooperation increases payoffs, if other person cooperates. (C, C) is a Nash Equilibrium but so are other outcomes
4. No sanctions, but none needed
5. Symmetric players

ITERATED PRISONER'S DILEMMA
1. Repeated play with same participants
2. Possibility for implicit communication; learn other players' strategy or types
3. Cooperation is a possible Nash Equilibrium, but there are many others
4. Likelihood of (C, C) outcome depends on:
   • length of play (number of rounds)
   • risk aversion; affects beliefs about number of iterations
   • credible sanctions possible—either internal (achieved by other player's strategic choice to defect) or external (achieved by outside enforcement agent)
   • discount values; value of future (C, C) payoffs high enough to give up the difference between (D, C) and (C, C) today
5. Symmetric players

BARGAINING GAMES
1. Repeated play possible
2. Differences in players' preferences accommodated
   • size of joint gains determines if good provided or not (outside options)
   • strength of players determines division of the good (time preference and risk aversion)
3. Differences in players' strengths and positions accommodated
4. Cooperation is a possible Nash Equilibrium, dependent on parameter values

For clarity, all games are presented as two-person games, though each can be extended to N persons.

the benefits from it when the balance of power among cities is unequal. The importance of the future is summarized by risk aversion and time preferences. If the same game is repeated over time, specific asset investments or preference drift can be reflected with changes in the outside option values. That repetition also increases the importance of the participants' attitudes toward the future as well as the role of social norms. The knowledge that a city will continue to interact with the same other cities may lead the stronger player to accept less today, thereby complying with others' ideas of fairness and increasing the possibility of more cooperative interactions in the future. Future interactions may also lower the prospects of reneging on a current agreement because other cities will not form a partnership with the defector in the future. This can lower sanction and monitoring costs, in some cases reducing them sufficiently so that a previously infeasible cooperative arrangement becomes viable.

Work on metropolitan governance and regional cooperation has covered a broad range of issues—from establishing new general-purpose governments to single-purpose service contracts. The chapters in this volume demonstrate that these situations vary substantially in the characteristics of both the policies and the cities involved. The extent of these variations suggests that not all situations can be completely analyzed or understood with one simple model and that past generalizations across cases may be misleading. More careful matching of the model to the specifics of each case should improve our understanding of the prospects for metropolitan cooperation.

REFERENCES

Bowman, Ann O'M. 1988. Competition for Economic Development among Southeastern Cities. *Urban Affairs Quarterly* 23: 511–27.
Chong, Dennis. 1991. *Collective Action and the Civil Rights Movement.* Chicago: University of Chicago Press.
Deneckere, Raymond, and Carl Davidson. 1985. Incentives to Form Coalitions with Bertrand Competition. *RAND Journal of Economics* 16, no. 4: 473–86.
Downs, Anthony. 1994. *New Visions for Metropolitan America.* Washington, D.C.: Brookings Institution Press.
Feiock, Richard C. 2002. A Quasi-Market Framework for Local Economic Development Competition. *Journal of Urban Affairs* 24: 123–42.
Frieden, Jeffrey. 1994. International Investment and Colonial Control: A New Interpretation. *International Organization* 48, no. 4: 559–93.

Grady, D. 1987. State Economic Development Incentives: Why Do States Compete? *State and Local Government Review* 19, no. 3: 86–94.

Green, G. and A. Fleischman. 1989. Analyzing Local Strategies for Promoting Economic Growth. *Policy Studies Journal* 17: 557–73.

Hamilton, David. 1999. *Governing Metropolitan Areas: Responses to Growth and Change*. New York: Garland.

Hardin, Russell. 1982. *Collective Action*. Baltimore: Johns Hopkins University Press.

Keohane, Robert, and Lisa Martin. 1995. The Promise of Institutionalist Theory. *International Security* 20, no. 1: 29–51.

Lipecap, Gary. 1989. *Contracting for Property Rights*. New York: Cambridge University Press.

———. 1996. Economic Variables and the Development of the Law: The Case of Western Mineral Rights. In *Empirical Studies in Institutional Change*, ed. Lee J. Alston, Thrainn Eggertsson, and Douglas North. New York: Cambridge University Press.

Lubell, Mark, Mark Schneider, John Scholz, and Mihriye Mete. 2002. Watershed Partnerships and the Emergence of Collective Action Institutions. *American Journal of Political Science* 46, no. 1: 148–63.

Olson, Mancur. 1971. *The Logic of Collective Action*. Cambridge, Mass.: Harvard University Press.

Orfield, Myron. 1997. *Metropolitics: A Regional Agenda for Community and Stability*. Washington, D.C.: Brookings Institution Press.

Ostrom, Elinor. 1990. *Governing the Commons*. New York: Cambridge University Press.

Ostrom, Elinor, Roy Gardner, and James Walker. 1994. *Rules, Games, and Common-Pool Resources*. Ann Arbor: University of Michigan Press.

Peirce, Neal, Curtis Johnson, and John Hall. 1993. *Citistates: How Urban America Can Prosper in a Competitive World*. Washington, D.C.: Seven Locks Press.

Riker, William, and Itai Sened. 1991. A Political Theory of the Origin of Property Rights: Airport Slots. *American Journal of Political Science* 35, no. 4: 951–69.

Roth, A. 1995. Bargaining Experiments. In *Handbook of Experimental Economics*, ed. J. Kogel and A. Roth. Princeton, N.J.: Princeton University Press.

Rubin, I., and H. Rubin. 1987. Economic Development Incentives: The Poor Pay More. *Urban Affairs Quarterly* 22: 32–62.

Rusk, David. 1993. *Cities without Suburbs*. Washington, D.C.: Woodrow Wilson Center Press.

Sandler, Todd. 1992. *Collective Action*. Ann Arbor: University of Michigan Press.

Steinacker, Annette. 2002. The Use of Bargaining Games in Local Development Policy. *Review of Policy Research* 19, no. 4: 120–53.

Thaler, Richard. 1988. Anomalies: The Ultimatum Game. *Journal of Economic Perspectives* 2, no. 4: 95–206.

Wallis, Allan. 1994. The Third Wave: Current Trends in Regional Governance. *National Civic Review* 83 (summer–fall): 290.

Wolman, H. 1988. Local Economic Development Policy: What Explains the Divergence between Policy Analysis and Political Behavior? *Journal of Urban Affairs* 10: 19–28.

STEPHANIE S. POST

METROPOLITAN AREA GOVERNANCE AND INSTITUTIONAL COLLECTIVE ACTION

4

A great deal of recent urban research examines the social and economic relationships among metropolitan area local governments. This research has caused numerous scholars and practitioners to call for increased regional cooperation among local governments. Local government cooperation is believed to be the key to reducing social inequalities as well as improving local government economic efficiencies.

The appropriate mechanism to encourage metropolitan area government cooperation, however, is the subject of considerable debate. At one extreme are those who advocate formally consolidating the political powers of existing local governments into one large super–metropolitan area government, and at the other extreme are those who promote cooperation among existing local governments on a policy-by-policy basis. Between these two extremes are those who advocate creating a new tier of local government—regional government. This solution often preserves existing political units yet allows for a more centralized authority to have responsibility for regional issues such as pollution, transportation, and economic development.

Savitch and Vogel (2000a, 198) term this group of policy recommendations the "new regionalism," which encompasses recent metropolitan area reforms that try to "reduce disparities between the cities and their suburbs and enhance the ability of the city-region to compete in the global economy" (Savitch and Vogel 2000b, 198). The new regionalism is a combination of *local government*—the "formal institutions and elections and established decision-making processes and administrative structures"—and *local governance*—"the voluntary and fluid cooperation among localities" (Savitch and Vogel 2000b, 161). "Regional government" refers to the formal institutions of local government, whereas "regional governance" refers to the policy decisions made by existing governments.

The distinction between regional *government* and regional *governance* becomes especially significant when one considers changing the status quo. Changing regional government often requires a significant change in the existing political structure of local government, whereas changing regional governance maintains existing local governments and simply requires a shift in the behavior of these governments. Historically, altering the structure of metropolitan area government is a difficult process. There are significant collective action costs associated with establishing general-purpose local governments (Burns 1994; Feiock and Carr 2001), and once they are established, they are difficult to abolish.

For these reasons, the number of U.S. general-purpose local governments has been relatively constant. The U.S. Census Bureau (2000) reports that between 1967 and 1997, the number of U.S. county governments decreased by 6, the number of municipal governments grew 1,324, and the number of townships decreased by 476. When one considers the total number of U.S. general-purpose governments, these changes in the structure of local government are relatively insignificant.[1] Further evidence of the difficulty in altering the structures of metropolitan area government is the large number of failed city–county consolidation attempts. Savitch and Vogel (2000b, 162) note "only 20 percent of referenda on consolidations are approved by the electorate."

The difficulty of establishing and abolishing local governments indicates that regional government solutions may be politically challenging at best and impossible at worst. Regional governance, however, does not face the same political hurdles. Regional governance merely requires cooperation among existing local governments. Almost by definition, it promotes local intergovernmental cooperation. Given that most scholars today agree that some form of regional governance is in the social and economic interest of a metropolitan area, it is important to identify the conditions that promote cooperation among local governments.

This chapter identifies the conditions that promote or hinder local intergovernmental cooperation using a collective action framework. The first section defines local intergovernmental cooperation. The second section develops a theory of institutional collective action, and the third section applies that theory to metropolitan area local governments. The fourth section summarizes the conclusions drawn from this theory, and the fifth section provides a brief review of some of the relevant empirical literature. The sixth section identifies an agenda for future research.

LOCAL INTERGOVERNMENTAL COOPERATION

Local intergovernmental cooperation, broadly defined, includes all policy activities that require some level of policy coordination between local governments. These efforts may include formal or informal agreements among local jurisdictions, and they may (or may not) require the exchange of revenue. Formal intergovernmental cooperation often includes written agreements among local governments.

In some cases, these formal intergovernmental agreements are codified by one or all of the participating local governments. These agreements may dictate a division of labor among local governments, which may (or may not) require the transfer of funds between those governments. For example, a city and county may formally agree that the city will provide bus service to both city and county residents, and in return the county will maintain the roads in both areas. Alternatively, the county may simply contract with the city to provide bus service to its residents. This service arrangement would likely require a fee-for-service contract between the two governments, because the county is not providing a service benefit to the city in exchange for the bus service.

Not all local intergovernmental cooperation is formal. Informal intergovernmental cooperation is defined as unwritten agreements among city officials. These agreements are often the result of "handshake" deals among local officials, where the division of service responsibility is understood but never formalized. For example, a city may maintain the county parks within its jurisdiction, based on a mutual understanding between the directors of the city and county parks and recreation departments. Informal agreements often have the effect of functionally coordinating service activities without a written agreement or the exchange of revenue.

The existence of personal as well as professional relationships among local officials increases the likelihood that local governments will enter into informal intergovernmental agreements (Thurmaier and Wood 2002). These types of agreements are most likely to occur when local government officials have worked with each other over and over for a number of years or when local government officials know each other through professional and educational networks such as professional associations or graduate or professional schools (Bingham et al. 1981). Repeated interactions and previous relationships among local officials can generate significant reservoirs of trust and performance expectations that can facilitate local government cooperation.

INSTITUTIONAL COLLECTIVE ACTION

All local intergovernmental cooperation, both formal and informal, is in effect institutional collective action—a group of institutions working collectively to achieve shared policy objectives. A theory of institutional collective action can be derived from theories of individual collective action. Olson (1965) argues that collective action occurs when individuals find it in their self-interest to join a group and engage in collective behavior. Individuals join groups for a variety of reasons, but the two most dominant motivations are (1) to receive benefits they could not otherwise receive (Olson 1965), and (2) to advance common policy goals and preferences (Rothenberg 1992). Group formation is often facilitated by the presence of a strong leader and/or an entrepreneur who is willing to overcome the costs of collective action (Salisbury 1969; Wilson 1995; Schneider, Teske, and Mintrom 1995). Entrepreneurs have an incentive to form groups when they expect to receive a disproportionate benefit from the group. The benefit may be in the form of a job with the organization, access to the institutional powers and resources of the group, economic gain, or the satisfaction of seeing a specific issue addressed.

Individual collective action is most likely to occur in small groups because the transaction costs of cooperation are dramatically reduced. Small groups increase the likelihood that members will realize direct benefits from group membership and participation. They also make it easier to monitor the behavior of members, minimizing shirking and noncompliance among group members. Collective action in large groups, by contrast, is much more difficult. Large groups diminish the ability of members to realize direct benefits from group membership. They also make it difficult to monitor the behavior of group members. This makes it easier for members to shirk their responsibilities and free ride on the efforts of others.

In some cases, if a group is too large, individuals may be able to receive the benefits of the group's efforts without formally joining it (Olson 1965). Olson argues that the best way for large groups to overcome the costs of collective action is through some form of coercion and/or selective incentives for individual members (Olson 1965; also see Wilson 1995). Coercion occurs when group membership is necessary to avoid some type of sanction. For example, in many states, it is necessary for some workers to join a union before obtaining employment. In this case, the threat of unemployment is the incentive for group membership. Selective incentives for group membership are positive individual benefits that can only be obtained through group membership. For example, everyone with a television has access to public television programming, but only public television members receive benefits such as coffee mugs, compact discs, videocassettes, and gala invitations. These selective benefits are used to encourage individuals to financially support public television programming.

Institutional collective action can be explained using the basic principles of individual group formation. The conditions for institutional collective action are similar to those for individual cooperation: group size, common policy objectives, coercion and/or selective incentives, and the presence of a strong leader or policy entrepreneur. The application of these traditional explanations of individual collective action to institutional collective action requires further analysis and explanation.

Two attributes unique to local governments must be accounted for when explaining institutional collective action. These are group size and the role of geography. Group size in institutional collective action has two dimensions—the number of institutions seeking to cooperate, and the size and heterogeneity of the institution's constituencies. Local governments are an aggregation of individual preferences. Because local government leaders are elected, they must account for the policy preferences of their constituents when considering any type of intergovernmental agreement. The need to accommodate the preferences of their individual constituents may hinder the ability of local governments to cooperate. In addition, an increase in the number of local governments seeking to cooperate may impose significant monitoring and transaction costs on the cooperating governments. The geographic proximity among institutions may also influence their ability to cooperate. Local governments' inability to move, their limited ability to alter their board-ers, and the spatial relationships among them all influence their ability to work collectively.

INSTITUTIONAL COLLECTIVE ACTION AND LOCAL GOVERNMENT COOPERATION

The theoretical framework of institutional collective action can be used to explain local government cooperation. Geography, group size, common policy objectives, leader or policy entrepreneurs, and coercion and/or se-lective incentives are all important determinants of local government cooperation.

The Geographic Density of Metropolitan Area Governments

The role of geography in explaining local government cooperation is largely ignored in the literature, yet geography affects local government cooperation in a variety of ways. Local governments are place-bound; they may be able to expand their boundaries by annexation or consolidation, but they are not mobile. This lack of mobility limits the number of poten-tial collaboration partners. Local governments generally cooperate with geographically proximate governments. Theoretically, a city could con-tract with another city located in another part of the state or even the country, but the distance may significantly reduce the cost/benefit ratio often associated with contracting. For example, piping clean water from a county's well into a city located within that county is not as expensive as piping clean water across the state.

The geographic limitation on potential contracting partners means that an increase in the number of metropolitan area governments signals an increase in the number of opportunities for intergovernmental coopera-tion. A large number of local governments in a metropolitan area signals a large number of potential service providers. The number of available service providers is a key determinant of local government contracting. Morgan and Hirlinger (1991) recognize the importance of geography in their analysis of intergovernmental service contracts. Their study of local intergovernmental agreements includes a dummy variable to indicate if a city was located in a metropolitan statistical area (MSA). They reason that cities of all sizes located in MSAs are more likely to have intergovern-

mental contracts than cities not located in MSAs due to access to a large
number of potential suppliers (i.e., other governments). Their empirical
analysis confirmed this hypothesis.

It is also possible, however, that a large number of local governments
could decrease the likelihood of local government cooperation. Morgan
and Hirlinger's analysis does not account for differences in the number of
local governments within a metropolitan area. Consequently, their findings are far from definitive. Tiebout (1956) and Peterson (1981) argue that
an increase in the number of local governments generates market-like
competition among those governments for productive capital and labor.
This competition may hinder local government cooperation.

The potential negative impact of local government competition on the
likelihood of institutional collective action may be reduced by the geographic distribution of metropolitan area governments, if an increase in
the geographic concentration of local governments increases the probability that local governments will find it in their interest to cooperate. A geographic concentration of local governments will increase the likelihood
of contact and repeated interaction among local officials in multiple jurisdictions; increase the likelihood that residents will live, work, and recreate
across multiple jurisdictions, which creates political incentives for cooperation; and increase the likelihood of policy spillovers across local governments in a metropolitan area.

Government officials in adjoining governments will have personal as
well as professional relationships that can facilitate local government cooperation. Stone's (1989) study of Atlanta finds that norms of reciprocity
and trust generated by informal relationships among elected officials and
the business community are key elements in a stable governing coalition.
These same norms and informal relationships are important for local government cooperation. Thurmaier and Wood (2002) argue that personal
relationships among local government officials across jurisdictions, and
repeated interactions among those individuals, act as a catalyst for interlocal agreements.

The geographic density of metropolitan area governments also influences the ability of metropolitan area residents to live, work, and recreate
in multiple communities. Increases in the geographic density of metropolitan area governments promote the fluid movement of residents across
government borders, which create strong economic and social ties between these areas. These ties create political incentives for local elected officials to work together. Specifically, elected officials in multiple jurisdictions are able to take credit for policies that positively impact the entire

metropolitan area—not just their own community. Each local official who takes credit for the benefits derived from local government cooperation should receive an electoral boost (Mayhew 1974).

The geographic density of metropolitan area governments increases the likelihood that policy spillovers will affect multiple local governments, creating incentives for cooperation. Netzer argues this point:

> It is inevitable that, if there are numerous local government units with substantial decision-making authority within a metropolitan area . . . the tax and expenditure decisions of individual units will have effects, positive and negative, that spill over the boundaries of that unit and affect households, firms and governmental entities elsewhere in the metropolitan area. (Netzer 1997, 204)

All local governments in geographically dense metropolitan areas face similar possibilities of externalities. The desire to minimize positive and negative externalities should encourage local government cooperation.

Group Size

Group size is perhaps the most important determinant of collective action. The size of the group dictates the ease with which groups can distribute benefits and monitor member behavior. The smaller the group, the easier it is to form. Small groups have fewer problems determining how to allocate benefits among their members. In addition, the relative benefit from being a group member increases as the number of members decreases. Furthermore, small groups generally have lower monitoring costs and less shirking.

The number of governments seeking to cooperate directly relates to Olson's (1965) notion of group size. The greater the number of governments, the greater the organization costs, the smaller the distribution of benefits, and the easier it is to free ride. In particular, transaction costs increase with the number of organizations included in the group (Williamson 1975). Ugboro, Obeng, and Talley define the transaction costs associated with local intergovernmental cooperation as

> the costs of extensive decision making for negotiating, operating, and enforcing the provisions of the system. The negotiation cost, in particular, may be high because it is time intensive. Enforcement costs are those ensuring compliance with system arrangements or arrangements by the merged or cooperating agencies. (Ugboro, Obeng, and Talley 2001, 83)

As the number of local governments seeking to cooperate increases, the costs of negotiation and enforcement also increase. Furthermore, local governments will only cooperate as long as they receive a direct benefit from the group's activity. Stein's (1980) examination of the impact of the federal grant-in-aid programs of the 1970s and 1980s (i.e., Federal Management Circular A-95) demonstrates that as soon as the benefits of group membership subside, local governments will leave the group. Most of these federal programs required federal grant applications by local governments to be reviewed and approved by some type of regional authority. In many cases, the only way for local governments to apply for and receive federal grant monies was to join a regional government. Consequently, many new regional governments were formed in response to these federal mandates. These regional governments, however, were short-lived. Once the federal mandates ended, many local governments were eager to cut ties with these regional governments, because they no longer received a direct benefit from group membership.

The size and homogeneity of the affected constituencies also influence the transaction costs of government collective action. Each government represents constituent populations of varying sizes and policy preferences. Local governments must aggregate the policy preferences of their citizens before they can even begin negotiations with other local governments. Consequently, institutions seeking to cooperate must simultaneously accommodate a variety of internal and external policy preferences. As the diversity of policy goals and objectives that must be accommodated increases, so does the cost of collective action. For this reason, large local governments with heterogeneous populations may find it more difficult to cooperate with other local governments than small local governments with homogeneous populations. Governments representing homogeneous populations are presumed to have constituents with similar policy preferences.

Thus, these institutions must expend fewer resources to ensure cooperation and unity of preferences among their constituents. This in turn facilitates their participation in intergovernmental cooperation. Ferris and Graddy (1988, 276) also reach this conclusion when they "expect governments with homogenous local populations to be more likely to contract out for services in general" because "disputes over service outputs are less likely to arise when there is relatively small variation in citizen demands." Intergovernmental cooperation is most likely when a small number of local governments with homogeneous populations seek to cooperate and least likely when a large number of local governments with heterogeneous populations seek to cooperate.[2]

Common Policy Objectives

One of the strongest incentives for local government cooperation is common policy objectives. Local governments will cooperate only if it is in their self-interest to do so. Several factors affect the likelihood that local governments will believe that cooperation is beneficial. These include potential cost savings, the desire for service continuity across districts, the heterogeneity (or homogeneity) of constituent preferences for specific goods and services, and the attributes of the goods and services being provided.

Promises of cost savings are often cited as the dominant reason local governments contract with private firms, nonprofit firms, and other governments for service provision and production (Stein 1990). The potential savings from service contracts are derived from three primary sources: sector differences in labor practices, competition among suppliers, and economies of scale (Ferris and Graddy 1986). The savings derived from economies of scale is the primary economic motivation for local intergovernmental contracting. This is because the other two factors are inapposite; labor costs are roughly equivalent across local governments, and local governments are unlikely to enter into a competitive bidding war to provide services (Ferris and Graddy 1986). Economies of scale are realized when larger producers can obtain equipment and materials at a lower cost, and when goods and services are used to capacity.

The start-up costs of many capital-intensive projects often result in larger burdens and increasing tax rates. The costs are more difficult to justify for smaller local governments than for larger local governments. Larger local governments have the tax base and the access to capital markets necessary to raise the funds to provide capital-intensive goods and services themselves. They can also spread the costs over a larger population, which drives down the average cost of these goods and services. In contrast, smaller local governments have neither the tax base nor the access to capital markets necessary to fund the high start-up costs of many capital-intensive projects without incurring a large per capita tax burden. They also lack the population to make the average costs of these goods and services affordable. If smaller local governments want to provide their residents these goods and services, they must either pool their resources or contract with larger local governments (or private service vendors) for their production.

The desire for service continuity across local jurisdictions is another incentive for local intergovernmental agreements (Ugboro, Obeng, and Talley 2001). Metropolitan area governments often strive to ensure that the provision of certain goods and services is seamless. For example, roads do not end at city boundaries, because cities cooperate to ensure a consistent transportation system across jurisdictions. In addition, many local government policies produce spillover benefits and costs to surrounding local governments, especially if the costs are magnified when the quality of some services is allowed to vary across jurisdictions:

> In the Los Angeles area, for example, city managers cited "standardization of minimum service level" as the primary effect of contracting with the county. As Sonenblum, Kirlin, and Ries (1977, 42) pointed out, inadequate maintenance of storm drains in one place can cause flooding in other communities, or less desirable recreational facilities in one city can lead to overloaded facilities in other places. (Morgan and Hirlinger 1991, 132)

These "extralocal spillovers" provide a strong incentive for intergovernmental agreements.

The likelihood that local governments will identify common policy objectives is often influenced by the relative diversity of constituent preferences for specific goods and services. Local governments with homogeneous constituencies are in a better position to cooperate with other local governments for service production. When citizen preferences vary dramatically regarding the cost, amount, and types of services local governments should provide, it is difficult for local governments to identify common policy objectives within their own constituencies, much less identify common policy objectives across multiple local governments.

One important factor that influences the probability that local governments will identify common policy objectives is the attributes of the good or service being provided. Publicly provided goods and services that require a significant capital commitment, that benefit from economies of scale, and that have easily monitored outputs are more likely to be collectively produced and/or provided. These goods and services meet the criteria identified by Lubell and others for voluntary local government cooperation:

> Partnership contracts are most likely to emerge when potential benefits are high and the transaction costs of developing, negotiating, monitoring, and enforcing the political contract are low. (Lubell et al. 2002, 149)

Capital-intensive projects should promote local intergovernmental cooperation, because they meet most of the criteria outlined above. They require significant capital commitments, benefit from economies of scale, have easily monitored outputs, have relatively invariant citizen preferences for how they are produced, and have low negotiation costs. Savings from economies of scale are realized when the mass production of a good or service reduces its average cost. Capital-intensive goods and services generally require large amounts of equipment and materials that are cheaper when purchased en masse.

The high input costs associated with capital-intensive goods and services create a barrier to entry for many small governments. Small local governments have neither the tax base nor the access to capital markets necessary to fund the high start-up costs of many capital-intensive projects. Consequently, smaller local governments are often unable to produce them alone (Ostrom, Tiebout, and Warren 1961; Stein 1990; Ferris and Graddy 1986, 1988). If they want to provide these types of goods and services to their residents, they must either work collectively with each other or they must contract with larger governments or private vendors (Stein 1990). For example, Miller (1981) argues that many Los Angeles bedroom communities would never have been established without the ability to contract with the county for the provision of basic services, such as police and fire protection and water and sewer services. Contracting for service production is often the only way small local governments survive.

Capital-intensive goods and services also lend themselves to monitoring service outputs, which makes them good candidates for local government contracting. Ferris and Graddy (1986) argue that it is difficult to write a contract for the production of services whose outputs are not tangible or whose production is complex. Services such as a wastewater treatment plant have tangible outputs that are relatively easy to monitor. There is often lack of diversity in constituent policy preferences for capital-intensive goods and services. Metropolitan area residents are generally uniform in their expectation that clean water will come from their faucets and that solid waste and sewage will be removed from their home, all at a reasonable price. There is generally little concern over how local governments choose to make these services available to their residents.

In contrast, labor-intensive goods and services do not have high start-up costs, nor does their average cost dramatically decrease with an increase in the amount of goods and services being produced. Consequently, smaller local governments may not realize economic benefits from collectively providing or producing labor-intensive goods and services. Altshuler and others confirm this conclusion:

> The preponderance of the evidence indicates that small local governments (and thus metropolitan areas characterized by fragmentation) are more efficient for labor-intensive services, whereas larger units

are more efficient for capital-intensive services (because of economies of scale) and for certain overhead functions. (Altshuler et al. 1999, 106)[3]

The lack of cost savings associated with collectively producing labor-intensive goods and services indicates that local governments should not rush to cooperate in producing them.

Leaders and Entrepreneurs

Intergovernmental cooperation does not occur without some individual initiative. Local government cooperation is often the result of innovative leaders who are willing to take advantage of specific opportunities. Schneider, Teske, and Mintrom (1995) term these individuals "political entrepreneurs." These leaders "perceive opportunities for political and policy change, they advocate innovative ideas, and they transform political arenas (or 'markets')" (Schneider, Teske, and Mintrom 1995, 3). Schneider and his colleagues argue that these entrepreneurs are motivated by personal gain, much like their private-sector counterparts. But the personal gain comes from power, prestige, and policy influence, rather than personal wealth. It is the promise of personal gain that motivates these individuals to overcome the transaction costs associated with group formation, policy development, and policy implementation. These researchers identify two groups of political entrepreneurs: "*political* entrepreneurs, such as mayors and city council members who operate in the world of electoral politics; and *managerial* entrepreneurs, such as city managers or high-level managers of public bureaucracies who control the resources of established agencies" (Schneider, Teske, and Mintrom 1995, 11–12). Both these groups are influential in promoting local intergovernmental cooperation.

Strong policy leaders can be instrumental in overcoming opposition to local intergovernmental cooperation. Political pressure from local residents, as well as municipal employees and unions, often influences the decision whether to contract for the production of a particular good or service (Morgan and Hirlinger 1991; Ferris and Graddy 1986). Resident populations may vary in their support of intergovernmental contracting. Heterogeneous populations may be so diverse in their policy preferences that it is more efficient for local governments to produce most of their goods and services rather than contracting with other local governments.

In addition, local government employees and union members often resist local government contracting, due to potential layoffs and shrinking budgets. A strong leader, however, may be able to unify heterogeneous populations and persuade local government employees and unions that cooperating with other local governments is in their best interest. The absence of a strong political leader may make intergovernmental cooperation especially difficult if a significant number of residents, government employees, or union members do not agree with the decision to contract with other local governments. Cooperation with other local governments may be difficult even in the presence of a strong leader if opposition from one or more of these groups is high. Even politically strong elected officials will not promote policies that jeopardize their own electoral security (Mayhew 1974; Bledsoe 1993).

In some cases, the promise of cost savings from local intergovernmental cooperation generates electoral benefits to elected representatives. These benefits often spill over to other elected officials from the same area, creating an incentive for cooperation. For example, if multiple jurisdictions work together to obtain a federal grant to build a new wastewater treatment plant, all the local elected officials from those jurisdictions can take credit for the new facility. In addition, members of Congress and state legislators can also take electoral credit for the new facility. Mayhew (1974) argues that credit claiming is an important element of an incumbent's reelection bid. Elected officials try to give the impression that they are personally responsible for policy decisions that benefit their districts. When a project promises to generate political goodwill for multiple elected officials simultaneously, the likelihood of intergovernmental cooperation increases, because all elected officials involved in the agreement can claim credit for its success.

Coercion and/or Selective Incentives

Local government collective action may be facilitated by selective incentives and regulations from the state and federal governments. Historically, the federal government has provided financial incentives for local government cooperation through grant monies, while state governments have encouraged (and discouraged) local government cooperation through regulation.

Federal grant-in-aid requirements (i.e., Federal Management Circular A-95) that local governments submit grant applications to regional review boards led to the formation of numerous regional governments, coercing local government cooperation. Many of these regional governments, however, were short-lived, because the A-95 programs were terminated in

1982. As a result, most cities withdrew from the newly formed regional governments because they received little benefit from participation (Stein 1980). This exodus dramatically limited the regional governments' power and effectiveness. In many cases, they ceased to exist. The fact that only a few of these governments remain demonstrates that federal policies can temporarily foster local government cooperation, but unless each government receives some direct benefit from that cooperation (i.e., grant monies), they will cease to cooperate.

State laws have a similar influence on local government cooperation. They influence the number of governments available for cooperation by regulating local government formation and the expansion or contraction of existing local government boundaries (Burns 1994; Miller 1981; Foster 1997; Feiock and Carr 2001). State laws also influence the costs of intergovernmental collective action, through regulation of intergovernmental agreements. The Advisory Commission on Intergovernmental Relations (ACIR 1992) reports that a majority of states have laws allowing interlocal service agreements. Unfortunately, the study does not elaborate on the nature and scope of these state laws. It is likely, however, that states that have laws permitting intergovernmental agreements are regulating the terms and conditions of those agreements. They may even be regulating the types of policies eligible for local intergovernmental cooperation. Each constraint the state places on local governments increases the costs of collective action and decreases the likelihood that they will choose to cooperate. Local governments may be more likely to cooperate when the state does not regulate their behavior.

SUMMARY OF CONDITIONS INFLUENCING INSTITUTIONAL COLLECTIVE ACTION

Table 4.1 provides a summary of the factors influencing collective action and the direction of their hypothesized relationship with local intergovernmental cooperation. This table and the discussion above identify several conditions that influence local intergovernmental cooperation. Because each condition will exert a different influence on the likelihood of institutional collective action, it is important to consider how interactions among these variables influence intergovernmental cooperation. Three conditions negatively influence the likelihood of local government cooperation: (1) increasing numbers of local governments seeking to cooperate, (2) increasing heterogeneity of the populations served by the local

Table 4.1. Institutional Collective Action: Determinants of Local
Government Cooperation

Geography	*Leadership/Entrepreneurs*
• Increase in the number of local governments (+) • Increase in the number of local governments per square mile (+)	• Presence of strong leader or entrepreneur (+)
Group Size	*Coercion and/or Selective Incentives*
• Increase in the number of local governments seeking to cooperate (−) • Heterogeneous constituency (−)	• Federal grant programs mandating or providing financial incentives for local government cooperation (+) • State laws governing intergovernmental agreements (−)
Common Policy Objectives	

• Potential cost savings (+)
 • Service continuity (+)
 • Attributes of goods and services:
    Capital intensive (+)
    Labor intensive (neutral or −)	

governments, and (3) increasing regulation of local government behavior by state laws. Five conditions positively influence the likelihood of local government cooperation: (1) increasing geographic density of local governments, (2) increasing homogeneity of the populations served by local governments, (3) common policy objectives among the local governments seeking to cooperate (i.e. potential cost savings, service continuity, capital-intensive goods and services), (4) presence of strong leaders and entrepreneurs, and (5) federal incentives for local government cooperation.

The relative strength of each of these five factors (positive and negative) influencing local government cooperation will ultimately determine if local governments will cooperate. For example, a highly fragmented metropolitan area in which each government governs a heterogeneous population would not be a strong candidate for high levels of local intergovernmental cooperation. These negative conditions, however, could be mitigated by the presence of a strong political leader or policy entrepreneur who promotes institutional collective action in policy areas where cities share common objectives, such as capital-intensive goods and services. The exact nature of the interaction among these determinants of institutional collective action should be the subject of future empirical research.

PREVIOUS EMPIRICAL RESEARCH

Previous empirical research provides some insight into the impact of each of these variables on local government cooperation. To date, relatively few studies have directly addressed questions of local intergovernmental cooperation, and no single study has incorporated all the relevant variables. Most of the relevant research attempts to explain why local governments choose alternative service providers. This research examines the conditions that promote contracts with private for-profit and nonprofit suppliers, as well as with other units of government.

The Geographic Density of Metropolitan Area Governments

An increase in the number of local governments per square mile increases the possibility of policy spillovers. It is also easier for local residents to work, live, and recreate across multiple local jurisdictions. These two conditions create electoral incentives for local officials to work together. Morgan and Hirlinger (1991) and Post (2002) provide some empirical evidence that the geographic relationship among local governments influences the probability that they will cooperate.

Morgan and Hirlinger (1991) examine the conditions that foster local government cooperation. Among the factors they consider is a city's location in an MSA. They find cities located in an MSA are more likely to engage in intergovernmental agreements than cities located outside a metropolitan area. They argue: "If a community lies within a metropolitan area, it is much more likely to have found other jurisdictions with which to contract" (Morgan and Hirlinger 1991, 141). Although their findings indicate that geographic proximity to other local governments influences local government cooperation, their analysis was not intended to test the relationship between the geographic distribution of local governments and the probability of cooperation. Post (2002) directly examines this relationship and finds a positive and significant relationship between the two variables. Her analysis concludes that, as the geographic density of metropolitan area general-purpose local governments increases, so does the likelihood of local intergovernmental cooperation. Consequently, the geographic relationship of local governments is an important determinant of local government cooperation.

Morgan and Hirlinger (1991) and Post (2002) each demonstrate that geography influences the likelihood of local government cooperation. Their findings are significant because few studies consider the importance of geography when explaining local government policy behavior. Future studies of local government cooperation should account for the geographic relationship among local governments. Studies that include measures of the distance between local governments would greatly contribute to our understanding of local government cooperation.

Group Size

An increase in the number of local governments seeking to cooperate and an increase in the heterogeneity of the populations served by those local governments are expected to be negatively related to local government cooperation. In contrast, a decrease in the number of local governments seeking to cooperate and a decrease in the heterogeneity of the populations served by those local governments are expected to be positively related to local government collective action. Surprisingly, little empirical research examines these two components of group size together, and no research to date examines their impact on local government cooperation.

A great deal of urban research focuses on the impact of metropolitan area government fragmentation (i.e., a large number of smaller-sized local governments). Research has linked metropolitan area fragmentation to everything from residential location decisions (Lowery and Lyons 1989; Lyons, Lowery, and DeHoog 1992; Sharp 1984, 1986; Percy and Hawkins 1992; Teske et al. 1993; Stein 1987) to political participation (Oliver 2001). There is considerable debate regarding the positive or negative impact of metropolitan area government fragmentation on local government behavior, but most researchers agree that fragmentation generates market-like competition among those governments for productive capital and labor. Consequently, most research in this area argues that an increase in metropolitan area government fragmentation produces greater competition rather than intergovernmental cooperation.

Most research focusing on local intergovernmental cooperation suffers from one of two limitations: Either the research is limited to specific geographic areas, or it uses the city as the unit of analysis. Consequently, this research is unable to fully evaluate the role of metropolitan area fragmentation in explaining local government cooperation. By contrast, Post (2002) uses the MSA as the unit of analysis. Consequently, she is able to evaluate the impact of local government fragmentation on local government cooperation. A negative relationship between fragmentation and cooperation confirms her expectation that metropolitan area fragmentation generates competition among local governments.

Post's model, however, also includes a measure of the geographic density of local governments. She finds that an increase in the geographic concentration of local governments leads to an increase in the incidence of local government cooperation. This positive relationship is significantly stronger than the negative relationship between fragmentation and local government cooperation. More research is necessary to adequately explain the relationship between metropolitan area fragmentation and local government cooperation.

The impact of population heterogeneity on local government cooperation is largely ignored in the literature. Most studies only include proportional measures of the local population. For example, Morgan and Hirlinger (1991) include two proportional measures in their explanatory models (the proportion of a city's population that is over sixty-five years of age and the proportion that is black). Although these measures provide some indication of the relative homogeneity of the population, they do not provide an adequate picture of the relative diversity of the local government population. Consequently, the finding that "cities with larger proportions of elderly are less inclined to use intergovernmental service arrangements" (Morgan and Hirlinger 1991, 138) may indicate that cities with older populations are less likely to cooperate, or it may indicate that some other factors associated with older populations influence local government cooperation. Future research should pay attention to the role of heterogeneity in local government cooperation.

Common Policy Objectives

Cities are most likely to work together when cooperation is in their mutual interest; consequently, identifying common policy objectives is an important determinant of local government collective action. Common policy objectives may come in the form of cost savings, service continuity, or the attributes of the goods and services being provided. Potential cost savings is one of the most common reasons cited for service contracting (Stein 1990; Ferris and Grady 1986, 1988; Morgan and Hirlinger 1991).

Hodge (2000) provides an extensive review of the literature on local government service contracting, and he concludes that cost savings are an important determinant of service contracting. Local governments seek alternative service providers when they believe doing so will save money. Cost savings are often realized when local governments cooperate in the provision and/or production of capital-intensive goods and services. These goods and services often generate economies of scale and constituent preferences for the manner of service provision are often invariant. For example, small local governments may contract with other local governments for wastewater treatment, because these governments lack the tax base to build their own treatment facility and their residents are not concerned with who performs this service—simply that it is performed.

In addition to cost savings, service contracting often allows local governments to provide their citizens with higher-quality goods or services. Stein (1990) provides extensive empirical analysis regarding the determinants of local government service contracting. He concludes that promised cost savings are not always realized with service contracts, but improvements in service quality are often realized.

Previous research demonstrates that local government's decision to seek alternative service providers is driven by self-interested policy objectives. Future research should identify those policy areas that promote or hinder local government cooperation.

Leaders and Entrepreneurs

Schneider, Teske, and Mintrom (1995) argue that most political entrepreneurs emerge in response to growth-related issues. Entrepreneurs may be progrowth or antigrowth. In both cases, once the individuals seeking to change local government obtain office, they often attempt to streamline existing government functions. This process is often difficult, due to the many external constraints imposed on local government by higher levels of government and the mobility of capital and labor (Peterson 1981; Schneider, Teske, and Mintrom 1995). One obvious avenue for promoting local government efficiency is to utilize alternative service providers. These providers may be private for-profit or nonprofit vendors as well as other local governments. Some local policy entrepreneurs may be more likely than others to use other local governments as alternative service providers. For example, city managers who become political entrepreneurs are likely to have existing relationships with other local officials that could facilitate local intergovernmental cooperation.

Thurmaier and Wood (2002) examine the relationship between the social networks of local elected officials and professional bureaucrats and the incidence of interlocal agreements in the Kansas City metropolitan area. They interviewed the chief administrative officer and the chief financial officer for one county and two cities from Kansas and Missouri. On the basis of these interviews, they conclude

> that the astounding volume of interlocal agreements in [the Kansas City metropolitan area] can be explained only partly by direct economizing in negatively connected exchange networks. Instead interlocal agreements are more likely the products of positively connected exchange relationships facilitated by a regional *norm of reciprocity* and a brokering role that synergistically augments local resources into the provision of effective government services in a metropolitan area. (Thurmaier and Wood 2002, 590)

Thurmaier and Wood's analysis indicates that repeat interactions among local officials build reservoirs of trust and norms of reciprocity that facilitate local government cooperation. Many of these agreements hinge on the presence of a broker (either an individual or an institution). The Mid-America Regional Council plays this role in the Kansas City metropolitan area. This organization (more specifically, a few key leaders) facilitated many of the interlocal agreements in the metropolitan area.

State Laws and Federal Grant Programs

Finally, the actions of the state and federal governments may influence local government cooperation in a variety of ways. Morgan and Hirlinger (1991) argue that state laws can restrict the likelihood of intergovernmental agreements. They examine the impact of state-imposed tax limits on the incidence of local government agreements. They argue that cities that operate under an externally imposed tax limit may have to deal with "unusual pressures to find cost savings" (Morgan and Hirlinger 1991, 134). Their empirical findings, however, fail to find a significant relationship between state laws and local government agreements. This nonfinding, however, is far from definitive. State laws governing local governments often influence their behavior and more research is needed to evaluate the impact of such laws on local government cooperation.

Morgan and Hirlinger also examine the impact of state and federal grant monies on local government cooperation. They argue that "cities more dependent on outside funding are those most likely to suffer fiscal stress" once these grant monies dry up (Morgan and Hirlinger 1991, 134). Consequently, these cities should be more likely to utilize intergovernmental agreements. Their empirical analysis provides some evidence that cities that are more dependent on state and federal grant monies are more likely to use intergovernmental agreements. Their findings demonstrate that state and federal laws and programs can influence local government behavior. But once again, more research is needed regarding this series of relationships.

RECOMMENDATIONS FOR FUTURE RESEARCH AND CONCLUSION

This chapter has outlined one theory of institutional collective action. Drawing on theories of individual collective action and group formation, it has identified five factors that influence institutional collective action—*geography, group size, common policy objectives, leaders and policy entrepreneurs,* and *coercion and/or selective incentives.* Each of these factors may facilitate or hinder local government cooperation in a variety of ways.

This theory of institutional collective action is applied to local government cooperation. Previous research on local government service contracting and intergovernmental agreements provides some insights into the motivations for local government cooperation, but no single study addresses all the theoretical explanations outlined in this chapter. This omission in the literature is significant, given the many recent calls for increased regional governance. A more complete understanding of the factors that contribute to local government cooperation may help policymakers develop more effective policies aimed at regional cooperation.

Future research should provide a more in-depth examination of the role of geography in local government cooperation. Post (2002) provides some preliminary analysis regarding the relationship between the geographic density of local governments and local government cooperation. In addition, more research is needed regarding the interaction and impact of the two elements of group size—heterogeneous constituencies, and the number of local governments seeking to cooperate. A great deal of urban research emphasizes the impact of metropolitan area fragmentation, but to date few researchers have examined its impact on local intergovernmental cooperation. A more complete understanding of how and when local leaders are able to aggregate constituent preferences would help us determine when local intergovernmental agreements are possible.

The research dedicated to questions of local government cooperation is relatively limited. Most of it focuses on limited geographic areas or a few local governments, and none of it accounts for the impact of geography, group size, common policy objectives, leaders and policy entrepreneurs, and coercion and/or selective incentives in one model. It appears that future research is necessary to fully evaluate the determinant of institutional collective action among local governments.

NOTES

1. The number of single-function governments—i.e., special districts—has not been stable over time. The number of special districts increased from 21,264 in 1967 to 34,683 in 1997. This dramatic increase in special districts may be attributable to their unique characteristics. They generally address a single policy area, and they often have boundaries that overlap multiple local governments. For example, a water district may encompass several cities and the county. In addition, special districts are typically not very democratic. Although many have elected governing boards, the overall participation rate in these elections is low and often the mandates of the voting rights act do not apply. E.g., there can be a property ownership requirement for voting in special district elections (Burns 1994; Foster 1997). This combination of unique features often allows special districts to be used as a unique form of regional governance. Local governments seeking to circumvent state imposed taxing and spending limits or ease fiscal pressure on existing programs may turn to special districts (MacManus 1981). This combination of unique attributes explains why it is easier to alter the number of special districts than the number of general-purpose governments.
2. There is a subtle distinction between the impact of the number of local governments in a metropolitan area and the number of local governments seeking to cooperate. As was discussed in the preceding section, an increase in the number of metropolitan area governments may signal an increase in the incidence of local government cooperation due to an increase in the number of potential suppliers. It may also signal a decrease in the likelihood of intergovernmental cooperation due to competition among those local governments and increase in the number of local governments seeking to cooperate.
3. The quotation is cited by Savitch and Vogel (2000a, 204).

REFERENCES

ACIR (Advisory Commission on Intergovernmental Relations). 1992. *State Laws Governing Local Government Structure and Administration: A Comparison of the Laws in 1978 and 1990.* Washington, D.C.: ACIR.

Altshuler, Alan, William Morrill, Harold Wolman, and Faith Mitchell, eds. 1999. *Governance and Opportunity in Metropolitan America.* Washington, D.C.: National Academy Press.

Bingham, Richard D., Bret W. Hawkins, John P. Frendreis, and Mary P. Le Blanc. 1981. *Professional Associations and Municipal Innovation.* Madison: University of Wisconsin Press.

Bledsoe, Timothy. 1993. *Careers in City Politics: The Case for Urban Democracy.* Pittsburgh: University of Pittsburgh Press.

Burns, Nancy. 1994. *The Formation of American Local Governments: Private Values in Public Institutions.* New York: Oxford University Press.

Feiock, Richard C., and Jered B. Carr. 2001. Incentives, Entrepreneurs, and Boundary Change: A Collective Action Framework. *Urban Affairs Review* 36: 382–405.

Ferris, James, and Elizabeth Graddy. 1986. Contracting Out: For What? With Whom? *Public Administration Review* 46: 332–44.

———. 1988. Production Choices for Local Government Services. *Journal of Urban Affairs* 10: 273–89.

Foster, Kathryn. 1997. *The Political Economy of Special-Purpose Government.* Washington, D.C.: Georgetown University Press.

Hodge, Graeme. 2000. *Privatization: An International Review of Performance.* Boulder, Colo.: Westview Press.

Lowery, David, and William E. Lyons. 1989. The Impact of Jurisdictional Boundaries: An Individual-Level Test of the Tiebout Model. *Journal of Politics* 51: 73–97.

Lubell, Mark, Mark Schneider, John Scholz, and Mihriye Mete. 2002. Watershed Partnerships and the Emergence of Collective Action Institutions. *American Journal of Political Science* 46, no. 1: 148–63.

Lyons, William E., David Lowery, and R. Hoogland DeHoog. 1992. *The Politics of Dissatisfaction: Citizens, Services, and Urban Institutions.* Armonk, N.Y.: M. E. Sharp.

MacManus, Susan. 1981. Special District Governments: A Note on Their Use as Property Tax Relief Mechanisms in the 1970s. *Journal of Politics* 43, no. 4: 1207–14.

Mayhew, David. 1974. *Congress: The Electoral Connection.* New Haven, Conn.: Yale University Press.

Miller, Gary. 1981. *Cities by Contract: The Politics of Municipal Incorporation.* Cambridge, Mass.: MIT Press.

Morgan, David, and Michael Hirlinger. 1991. Intergovernmental Service Agreements: A Multivariate Explanation. *Urban Affairs Quarterly* 27: 128–44.

Netzer, Dick. 1997. Metropolitan-Area Fiscal Issues. In *Intergovernmental Fiscal Relations*, ed. Ronald Fischer. Boston: Kluwer Academic Publishers.

Oliver, J. Eric. 2001. *Democracy in Suburbia*. Princeton, N.J.: Princeton University Press.

Olson, Mancur. 1965. *The Logic of Collective Action*. Cambridge, Mass.: Harvard University Press.

Ostrom, Vincent, Charles Tiebout, and Robert Warren. 1961. The Organization of Governance in Metropolitan Areas. *America Political Science Review* 55: 831–42.

Percy, Stephen, and Brette Hawkins. 1992. Further Test of Individual-Level Propositions from the Tiebout Model. *Journal of Politics* 54, no. 4: 1149–57.

Peterson, Paul. 1981. *City Limits*. Chicago: University of Chicago Press.

Post, Stephanie. 2002. Local Government Cooperation: The Relationship between Metropolitan Area Government Geography and Service Provision. Paper presented at the 2002 annual meeting of the American Political Science Association, Boston, August 29–September 1.

Rothenberg, Lawrence. 1992. *Linking Citizens to Government: Interest Group Politics at Common Cause*. New York: Cambridge University Press.

Salisbury, Robert. 1969. An Exchange Theory of Interest Groups. *Midwest Journal of Political Science* 13: 1–32.

Savitch, H. V., and Ronald K. Vogel. 2000a. Metropolitan Consolidation versus Metropolitan Governance in Louisville. *State and Local Government Review* 32, no. 3: 198–212.

———. 2000b. Paths to New Regionalism. *State and Local Government Review* 32: 169–79.

Schneider, Mark, Paul Teske, and Michael Mintrom. 1995. *Public Entrepreneurs: Agents for Change in American Government*. Princeton, N.J.: Princeton University Press.

Sharp, Elaine. 1984. Exit, Voice, and Loyalty in the Context of Local Government Problems. *Western Political Quarterly* 37: 67–83.

———. 1986. *Citizen Demand-Making in the Urban Context*. Birmingham: University of Alabama Press.

Sonenblum, Sidney, John Kirlin, and John Ries. 1977. *How Cities Provide Services: An Evaluation of Alternative Delivery Structures*. Cambridge, Mass.: Ballinger.

Stein, Robert. 1980. Federally Mandated Substate Regional Government: The Maintenance of Governmental Structures. *Urban Interest* 1: 74–82.

———. 1987. Tiebout's Sorting Hypothesis. *Urban Affairs Quarterly* 23: 140–60.

———. 1990. *Urban Alternatives: Public and Private Markets in the Provision of Local Services*. Pittsburgh: University of Pittsburgh Press.

Stone, Clarence. 1989. *Regime Politics: Governing Atlanta 1946–1988*. Lawrence: University Press of Kansas.

Teske, Paul, Mark Schneider, Michael Mintrom, and Samuel Best. 1993. Establishing the Micro Foundations of a Macro Theory: Information, Movers, and the Competitive Local Market for Public Goods. *American Political Science Review* 87, no. 3: 702–13.

Thurmaier, Kurt, and Curtis Wood. 2002. Interlocal Agreements as Overlapping Social Networks: Picket Fence Regionalism in Metropolitan Kansas city. *Public Administration Review* 62, no. 5: 585–98.

Tiebout, Charles. 1956. A Pure Theory of Local Expenditures. *Journal of Political Economy* 64: 416–24.

Ugboro, Isaiah, Kofi Obeng, and Wayne Talley. 2001. Motivations and Impediments to Service Contracting: Consolidations and Strategic Alliances in Public Transit Organizations. *Administration and Society* 33, no. 1: 79–103.

U.S. Census Bureau. 2000. *Statistical Abstract of the United States: 2000.* Washington, D.C.: Economics and Statistics Administration, Bureau of the Census, U.S. Department of Commerce.

Williamson, Oliver. 1975. *Market and Hierarchies.* New York: Free Press.

Wilson, James. 1995. *Political Organizations.* Princeton, N.J.: Princeton University Press.

PART TWO

EMPIRICAL INVESTIGATIONS

PAUL G. LEWIS

AN OLD DEBATE CONFRONTS NEW REALITIES: LARGE SUBURBS AND ECONOMIC DEVELOPMENT IN THE METROPOLIS

5

More than four decades of debate on metropolitan political structure have passed since the landmark works of Charles Tiebout and Robert Wood (Tiebout 1956; Wood 1958; see also Ostrom, Tiebout, and Warren 1961; Wood 1961). At this point, however, a fair judgment would be that the intellectual battle between advocates of political centralization and decentralization in metropolitan areas has essentially reached a stalemate. Although skirmishes still periodically flare up over such issues as school choice, regional tax-sharing schemes, and occasional proposals for city–county consolidations, metropolitan reformers and public choice advocates have been largely content with remaining within their own intellectual trenches, presenting more impassioned or methodologically elegant elaborations of their basic worldviews to their fellow travelers.[1]

I suggest in this chapter that the lack of engagement and progress in the metropolitan governance debate arises, in large part, for two reasons. First, there is an excessive dichotomizing tendency within the debate, an inclination to approach the subject from the point of view of ideal types of consolidated or polycentric government rather than to consider the range of alternative forms that metropolitan governance often takes. Second, there exists an implicit normative disagreement between the advocates of regional integration and polycentric government as to the most desired ends for government in metropolitan areas—the value of efficiency or of equality. By turning to a more expansive typology of urban governmental arrangements, and to a wider set of policy outcomes or authoritative allocations of value against which to examine those arrangements, social scientists may be able to begin a more productive dialogue about the implications of metropolitan political structure.

This altered set of priorities may also be important in wrestling with the new empirical realities of American metropolitan areas, where, to be sure, much has changed since the intellectual debate began nearly half a century ago. While not aiming for a definitive analysis, I link theory to an empirical trend by examining important questions raised by one emerging type of metropolitan political structure, the very large suburban municipality. This governmental form confounds many of the traditional assumptions of consolidationists and polycentrists alike. Neither fish nor fowl, such large suburbs (defined here as suburban municipalities with at least 50,000 residents), on the one hand, represent an example of substantial competition with and separation from the traditional central city; yet on the other hand, being on such a large scale, these jurisdictions hardly embrace the small-scale, "communities of interest" approach to local governance embraced by the Tiebout school. Steadily growing in number, these "supersuburbs" are a reality of metropolitan governance experienced by millions of Americans, and they are worthy of closer attention. I argue that it matters for metropolitan development whether the suburban portion of a metropolitan area takes the form of small jurisdictions or of supersuburbs.

CONCEPTUALIZING METROPOLITAN STRUCTURE: BEYOND LEVIATHAN AND LILLIPUTIA

Much social science theorizing proceeds from a consideration of so-called ideal types. Thus, for example, scholars have deduced regularities of behavior from considerations of full information or total noncommunication in games of strategy, and they have predicted legislative outcomes conditioned on whether there are open or closed rules for amending bills. Studies of metropolitan politics, similarly, have made such simplifying comparisons.

Many propositions arise, overtly or implicitly, from a contrast of one metropolitan jurisdiction to many. For example, a single, consolidated metropolitan jurisdiction, or ("leviathan,") has certain monopolistic qualities that may hurt its motivation to offer public services efficiently, while at the same time it allows for intrametropolitan redistribution and a unified approach to economic development. A large multiplicity of jurisdictions—the closer to infinity, seemingly the better—allows for extensive sorting of the population by "tastes" for public services and tax levels, permitting a more efficient match of preferences to publicly provided goods. To its critics, multiplicity also offers a seemingly endless potential for "secession of the successful" into smaller, more socially advantaged units, and thus more metropolitan stratification (Reich 1991).

The one-versus-many comparison is a useful heuristic that is often employed in studies of metropolitan governance.[2] Scholars acknowledge, however, that the real world falls somewhere in between total consolidation and complete fragmentation. The assumption is generally made, then, that any given metropolitan statistical area (MSA) can be situated along a continuum between governmental unity and polycentric government. In practical measurement terms, ordinarily this is done by examining the density of municipalities (and perhaps counties or special districts) per capita, or occasionally the density of such governments per square mile.[3]

In comparison with the confusing menu of real-world metropolitan governance structures, this assumption of a linear continuum from consolidation to fragmentation may be an oversimplification. Public choice advocates do at least take into account the presence of overlapping jurisdictions for relevant functions such as regional air quality districts or interjurisdictional service agreements. The assumption has tended to be that where needed, such entities will arise to take care of coordination issues (Friesma 1970; Ostrom, Parks, and Whitaker 1978; but see also Lowery 2000; Visser 2002).[4] For their part, the advocates of greater centralization complain that such units are disproportionately involved in so-called system maintenance functions—technical realms like sewage treatment or mass transportation development—but typically ignore lifestyle issues involving redistribution or schooling (Williams 1971).

However, the real world presents varieties of governance beyond the case of overlapping jurisdictions. Even if we only consider the case of general-purpose local governments, there are complex variations. Consider three possible governance structures for a hypothetical, single-county MSA of 500,000 residents, shown in table 5.1. In Scenario A, a numerically dominant central city is surrounded by numerous tiny suburban

Table 5.1.   Three Scenarios for General-Purpose Governance
in a Hypothetical Metropolitan Area

	Governance Scenario		
Characteristic	A	B	C
Central city population	450,000	100,000	200,00
Other municipalities' populations	10 suburbs, each of 5,000	1 suburb of 150,000, 2 of 100,000, 1 of 50,000	2 suburbs of 50,000 each
Unincorporated area population	0	0	200,000
Governments per 10,000 population[a]	0.24	0.12	0.08
Alternative index of fragmentation	0.189	0.78	0.66

[a]The count of governments in each area includes the county.

municipalities. In Scenario B, only four municipalities exist, but each is sizable, with one suburb outnumbering the central city in residents. In Scenario C, there is a relative population balance between the central city and an unincorporated area ruled by the county government.

In which scenario is the MSA most politically fragmented? I suspect that few real-world observers would label Scenario A as highly fragmented, noting that the central city comprises 90 percent of the metropolitan area, with a sprinkling of tiny suburban towns around it. According to the traditional density measure of governments per capita, however, Scenario A clearly goes the furthest toward polycentric government, with a density of governments twice as high as B and three times higher than C.

For many purposes, a better measure of metropolitan fragmentation is a measure of dispersion of the population across units, based on a variation of the Hefindahl index.[5] This fragmentation index is calculated by summing the squared percentages of the total population accounted for by each unit, and then subtracting that total from 1. The resulting index, which ranges between 0 (total consolidation) and 1 (extreme fragmentation), represents the probability that two randomly selected residents of the MSA live in different political jurisdictions. In the example of table 5.1, we see that in keeping with what I believe is a more realistic perspective on metropolitan structure, Scenario A is the least fragmented area, with only about a 19 percent likelihood that two randomly selected residents live in different political communities. Compare this to Scenario B, where although there are only five primary units of general-purpose local government, the equivalent measure is 78 percent.[6]

That Scenario B is most fragmented is a logical conclusion. The central city comprises only a fifth of the metropolitan population, and there are four major and plausible alternative jurisdictional locations for residents and businesses, particularly as communities of such sizable populations seem likely to include a variety of neighborhood types and business locations. By contrast, the tiny suburbs of Scenario A evoke an image of sleepy bedroom enclaves, or perhaps partially rural exurban towns that happen to be located in this metropolitan county. In Scenario C, one might suspect that the degree of "real" fragmentation depends on the extent to which the county government perceives itself as a full-service government and as an active seeker of economic development, as opposed to a residual hinterland. Also in C, there is likely to be competition with the central city from the other two municipalities, which are of significant size and resources. These competitive factors may make central city claims of dominant centrality suspect.

Although hypothetical, this exercise is more than academic. The number of large suburban municipalities is large and growing, and there are reasons to suspect they have different sorts of ambitions than smaller suburbs. And in the South, where county governments have a long tradition as a powerful level of primary local government, the unincorporated county area is often an active competitor for growth and jobs.

POLICY ENDS AND VALUES: BEYOND EQUITY AND EFFICIENCY

The example above puts a different spin on the scholarly debate over metropolitan political structure, because it suggests that the difference between "one" and "many" governments is not as straightforward as is represented in much of the literature. Another fundamental question for metropolitan governance scholars, however, is "To what end?" Why should we care if governance is more unitary or complex in a given MSA? Neither the public choice school nor the integrationists have trouble in answering these questions—but the answers given are generally different. Even considered in combination, I suggest, the answers are likely to be incomplete in comparison with the concerns of policymakers and civic elites (see also Lowery 2000).

The public choice scholarship on metropolitan structure, and in particular Tiebout's model of local "public economies," has derived largely from public finance concerns about local government. In such studies, by and large, the primary normative end goal or value is *allocative efficiency* in public goods and services. In a given metropolitan area, it is the role of local government to supply bundles of public goods and services that come as close as possible to constituents' tastes, given the tax price of providing such services.[7]

Polycentric governance, then, is seen as optimal because it provides a wider degree of choice for residents, who can vote with their feet, and more competition among service providers, which is likely to reduce the bureaucratic flabbiness of local service provision. In my view, the empirical literature, in the main, leans strongly toward the finding that local government costs less in areas where general-purpose government is more polycentric; in fairness, though, the results are somewhat mixed, and low cost does not necessarily imply higher efficiency, because we do not know the service-bundle preferences of local residents (Zax 1989; Forbes and Zampelli 1989; Oates 1989; Schneider 1989). The relatively few behavioral studies of citizen-consumers also tend to indicate that residents—at least those consumers of major public goods such as education who have recently moved or are considering moving—can be knowledgeable observers of service quality and cost (Teske et al. 1993; Bickers and Stein 1998). By contrast, research shows that a multiplicity of special districts in a metropolitan area tends to increase the absolute amounts spent on district-provided services, and the share of total local expenditure going to such services (Foster 1997). Again, however, more spending is not necessarily evidence for less allocative efficiency, because residents may prefer a high level of service from a special district and be willing to pay for it.

The early advocates of metropolitan consolidation, who tended to come from a tradition of civic reform or traditional public administration, initially focused on service quality and efficiency as well. They made the case, now largely discredited, that consolidation promised cost savings through economies of scale, reduced duplication of effort, and greater technical capacity in service provision. The attack on fragmentation of the past three decades or so, however, has focused mainly on questions of *equity*, not efficiency. In short, it is argued, fragmentation enables elite (often white) populations to escape their obligations to the wider metropolitan society by separating themselves fiscally and spatially into separate jurisdictions (Rusk 1993; Dreier, Mollenkopf, and Swanstrom 2001; Reich 1991). A few studies have made the case for this empirically, albeit without much analytical precision (Hill 1974; Rusk 1993).[8] Still, more rigorous analyses of the topic do bear out some of these arguments, though often with results that show more shades of gray (Miller 1981; Neiman 1980; but see also Morgan and Mareschal 1999).

Assume for a moment that both the public choice and the antifragmentation perspectives are correct in their most extreme positions. What would this tell us? *Fragmented metropolitan areas are less equitable but more efficient.* I would suggest that there is no necessary contradiction in this result, and that it implies there are, unsurprisingly, trade-offs between equality and efficiency (Okun 1975). What one proposes to do about this state of affairs would depend on one's value commitments. With the polycentrists being most enthusiastic about efficiency and the consolidationists seeking equity, not surprisingly they talk past one another.

However, there are at least three other important public values—beyond equity and the efficient provision of routine services—that residents and public officials seek from systems of local government. First, a central question about any form of government is its implications for effective *political representation,* accountability, and promotion of civic involvement. Second, in the American context, local governments are typically assumed to have a role in *economic development,* with a responsibility for the healthy economic growth of a given area in such areas as employment rates, wage growth, and economic stability. Third, a major role for local governments is their *regulation of land use* through their so-called police powers of planning, zoning, and building regulation. The second and third areas are surely connected to one another, as, for example, infrastructure provision in an attempt to improve economic development will also tend to affect land use patterns, and ineffective land use planning (as in growth patterns that lead to traffic congestion or aesthetic deterioration) can hinder an area's economic development.

Social scientists have done less investigation of the linkage of these functions to metropolitan institutional arrangements, although the potential is surely there for governmental structure to powerfully affect outcomes in each of these areas. On the first count, local democracy, only in the past few years have serious studies examined the implications of jurisdictional size and suburban separation for civic participation. Here, the findings indicate that although "smaller is better" for participation, the homogeneity of many suburban jurisdictions has its civic costs, as well (Oliver 2001; see also Gainsborough 2001). No empirical study, however, has focused much on the implications of metropolitan political structure for the capacity of residents to participate and hold officials accountable for issues of regionwide scope, such as air pollution or the health of the regional labor market.

There have been few if any definitive findings on the relationship of metropolitan political structure to regional economic development, though there is no shortage of popular and academic arguments that "regions matter" for economic health—with the implication that some metropolitan-level governance structure may be necessary (Peirce, Johnson, and Hall 1993; Dodge 1996; Pastor et al. 2000). The literature on metropolitan governance focuses heavily on the concept of competition—for both good and ill—among local governments, and one might anticipate that a regional economy will grow differently if one or a few public entities strategize regarding their development focus and the recruitment of firms than if a few hundred entities separately pursue developmental gain. Similarly, one might expect that the provision of regionwide public infrastructure—highways, waste treatment facilities, power plants, flood controls, and so on—could proceed differently in a fragmented area than in a more consolidated area. Such infrastructure differences, in turn, could affect the pace or quality of the region's growth. This area remains ripe for study.[9]

Finally, there has been relatively limited empirical testing of the relationship between metropolitan political structure and various land use outcomes. Policymakers and civic leaders have shown increasing interest in recent years in issues of metropolitan "sprawl," as well as concern for the relative balance of jobs and housing units in subregions of metropolitan areas. Here, social science research has raised interesting hypotheses—for example, that suburban sorting and homeowner dominance in fragmented areas might generate more sprawl or job/housing mismatches (Fischel 1999, 2001). But as of yet, we cannot offer policymakers very definitive conclusions on the relationship between political structure and land use—including the potential effects of polycentric government on the segregation of poor people from rich people or of minority groups from whites.[10]

CENTRALIZATION WITHIN DECENTRALIZATION: THE POTENTIAL IMPORTANCE OF SUPERSUBURBS

Thus far, I have suggested that the debate over metropolitan political structure has been limited and unsatisfying both in terms of its conceptualization and measurement of political structure and in the limited metrics (policy outcomes or values) that have been used to evaluate the effects of different governmental arrangements. In the remainder of the chapter, I make an empirical case for a broader consideration of metropolitan political structure and its potential influence on important policy outcomes with a discussion of supersuburbs and their implications for regional economic development and land use. As in Scenario B of table 5.1, the emphasis here is on very large suburbs as an institutional arrangement that complicates efforts at labeling metropolitan areas as fragmented or unitary. Moving beyond the equity/efficiency standoff, I examine the ways in which large suburban municipalities approach growth and development policy, to see if they are different from their small-suburb counterparts.

I define supersuburbs as municipalities in metropolitan areas that are not central cities but have a population of at least 50,000 residents. There is obviously nothing magical about the threshold of 50,000, but scholars (including Gottman 1961, 25; and Welch and Bledsoe 1988) have often used that size in their studies as a minimum cutoff for cities of significant size or importance, and Dahl (1967) suggested that a population of at least 50,000 may be necessary to support certain important features of democratic self-government. Moreover, the federal government has, with certain exceptions, held that municipalities must be of at least 50,000 residents to be granted central city status.[11]

From Newton, Massachusetts, to Bellevue, Washington, supersuburbs are an increasingly common feature of metropolitan political systems, with the 2000 Census showing that 245 suburbs of this size existed nationwide (see figure 5.1). All told, the supersuburbs had 21.4 million residents, or nearly 8 percent of the U.S. population. Some of these communities are larger than many well-known central cities, with several being the home of more than 200,000 residents (see table 5.2).

Nevertheless, supersuburbs fit uneasily into traditional conceptions of urban structure. Typically "suburban" in their relatively moderate densities and absence of a historical business core, these communities are nevertheless "citylike" in their size, complexity, and often diversity and economic functions. As was suggested above in the discussion of Scenario B in table 5.1, the presence of such communities may have fragmenting tendencies within the metropolis, as they serve as major counterweights to the historic central city; yet, by a density-of-governments standard, they are clearly more centralized than if their areas were instead governed by several smaller suburbs.

This issue of the characteristics and development ambitions of supersuburbs is particularly relevant in the Sunbelt and West. Table 5.3 shows that large suburbs are most prevalent in California (home of 40 percent of all such jurisdictions) but that they are also common in Florida and Texas,

Figure 5.1. Supersuburbs in the United States as of 2000

Table 5.2. The Largest Suburbs (populations of 150,000 or more in 2000)

Suburb	Population
Aurora, Colorado	276,393
Hialeah, Florida	226,419
Plano, Texas	222,030
Glendale, Arizona	218,812
Garland, Texas	215,768
Fremont, California	203,413
Chesapeake, Virginia	199,184
Yonkers, New York	196,086
Glendale, California	194,973
Huntington Beach, California	189,594
Chandler, Arizona	176,581
Henderson, Nevada	175,381
Chula Vista, California	173,556
Oxnard, California	170,358
Garden Grove, California	165,196
Oceanside, California	161,029
Ontario, California	158,007
Santa Clarita, California	151,088

with a handful of Midwestern and Northeastern states also hosting numerous supersuburbs. After California, with nearly 3.0 supersuburbs per million population, they are most disproportionately represented in Utah (2.2 per million), Minnesota (1.8), and Nevada (1.5). Over time, such communities have accounted for a rapidly growing share of such states' total population, with one in four California residents now living in a supersuburb—more than the total in all other non-central-city municipalities. In a discussion of what he calls "boomburbs" (using a somewhat different definition than employed here), Lang (2001) attributes the disproportionate rise of such communities in the West to the prevalence of master-planned communities, and to the necessity of having powerful public institutions to secure a water supply in this semiarid region.[12]

DOES SIZE MATTER? SUPERSUBURBS' DEVELOPMENT ORIENTATIONS

An unexplored research question, then, concerns the manner in which supersuburbs approach economic development. In short, *does it matter for*

Table 5.3. Distribution of Supersuburbs in 2000

State	No. of Supersuburbs
California	100
Florida	18
Illinois	15
Texas	14
Michigan	13
Minnesota	9
Massachusetts	8
Washington	6
Ohio	6
New Jersey	6
Colorado	5
Utah	5
Oregon	4
Missouri	4
New York	4
Arizona	3
Nevada	3
Oklahoma	3
Connecticut	3
Georgia	2
Maryland	2
Virginia	2
Idaho	1
New Mexico	1
Alabama	1
Louisiana	1
North Carolina	1
Indiana	1
Iowa	1
Kansas	1
Wisconsin	1
Rhode Island	1

regional economic development patterns whether the suburban portion of a metropolitan area is organized into numerous small municipalities or whether there are one or more very large suburbs? I hypothesize that such political structure should indeed matter. Urban and regional development is often shaped by the areal and functional scope of the governmental entities that regulate land use and build growth-supporting infrastructure (Danielson and Doig 1982; Lewis 1996).

A supersuburb occupies a larger portion of the metropolitan economy and land area than smaller communities, and its residents are more likely to work within its boundaries. Thus, supersuburban voters are probably more inclined to hold their municipal elected officials somewhat responsible for the state of the local economy—for the availability of jobs, for example. Being larger, supersuburban municipal governments are more distant and likely more insulated from their constituents, which means that slow-growth neighborhood protectionist movements may find it less easy to influence local policies.[13]

Fischel (2001) argues that small suburban municipalities tend to be dominated by the interests of what he calls "homevoters"—homeowners who are vigilant in local affairs for the purpose of maintaining the value of their largest sunk investment, their house. The home-value preservation instincts of such voters lead, in Fischel's terms, to a "race to the top" in local amenities and environmental protection. In larger jurisdictions like supersuburbs, by contrast, such a "median voter" model of local policymaking—in which municipal officials reflect the views of the homeowning majority—may not apply. Rather, developers, employers, and other progrowth interest groups may be more likely to muster and sustain the resources (including campaign contributions) necessary to monitor and influence the actions of local officials (Fischel 2001, 53).

In addition, the large size of supersuburbs implies that they have larger planning and development staffs than their smaller neighbors, and the bureaucratic ambitions of these agencies may lead to more attention to and use of various economic development tools. The greater fiscal resources of large local governments also mean that the municipality is probably more likely to have the wherewithal to engage in such complex arrangements as redevelopment, joint development efforts, or major infrastructure projects (e.g., an airport or major arterial improvement).

These fairly straightforward suppositions about supersuburban governments lead to the hypothesis that they will be more attuned to economic development and have greater ambitions for growth than would the smaller suburbs that might otherwise occupy the same space on the metropolitan landscape. Indeed, size itself may breed municipal ambition, as supersuburbs seem more likely to view themselves as challengers to the economic dominance of the central city, particularly in an era of "edge city" urban development (Garreau 1991). As Mayor Paul Tauer of Aurora,

Colorado—the nation's largest supersuburb—said of his metropolitan
area in 1992, "I see an evolving Minneapolis–Saint Paul type arrangement,
with Denver as Saint Paul: the smaller, older, capital city. Aurora is Minneapolis: progressive, growth-oriented" (quoted in Lewis 1996, 136).

AN EXPLORATORY ANALYSIS USING SURVEYS
OF LOCAL OFFICIALS IN CALIFORNIA

It would probably be wrongheaded to use development "outcomes"—
such as the rate of growth of employment, property valuation, or office
square footage—to measure whether supersuburbs have different orientations to growth than smaller suburbs. There may be many reasons
why growth proceeds differently in large suburbs than in small ones.
Instead, I pursue a brief investigation, meant to be suggestive rather
than causally definitive, examining whether key local officials in supersuburbs espouse different views about their municipal policies and ambitions with respect to economic development than their counterparts in
smaller suburbs. For evidence, I draw upon data from three mail surveys
of municipal officials in California conducted during the past several
years. To reiterate, supersuburbs are defined as municipalities that are
located in MSAs, are not central cities, and have a population of at least
50,000.

Attitudes toward Growth

What are the orientations of supersuburban governments to future
growth? Evidence on this question is drawn from a survey of municipal
planning directors (or other official designated by the planning director as
most knowledgeable about residential development) in 1998–99, regarding city growth orientations and residential policies. The questionnaire
was sent to all municipalities in the three major economic regions of
California—metropolitan Southern California, the San Francisco Bay
Area, and the Central Valley, representing thirty-four counties and the
vast majority of the state's population. The response rate was 76 percent,
meaning that 297 planners responded with usable questionnaires. (Lewis
and Neiman 2000 provide more detail on this survey.)

One of the questions asked, "As to the general attitude of the majority
of your city council towards residential growth, which of the following

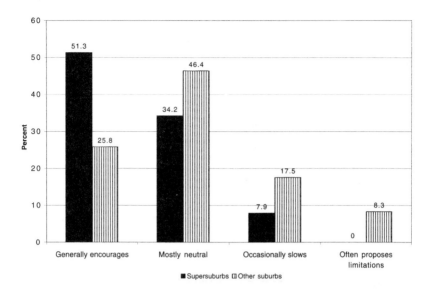

Figure 5.2. Attitude of City Council Majority Toward Residential Growth, According to Planning Director
Note: N = 71 supersuburbs, 95 other suburbs. Differences between supersuburbs and other suburbs (on the 4-point scale) are statistically significant at *p* < .001. Percentages do not sum to 100 due to "don't know" responses.

best describes the situation in your community?" Respondents could indicate that the council encourages growth, is neutral toward it, occasionally slows growth, or often proposes limitations. Figure 5.2 shows the results. A major difference between supersuburbs and suburbs of less than 50,000 population is evident, with planners from the larger communities approximately twice as likely to say that their council encourages residential growth. On a 4-point scale, where 1 is "encouraging" and 4 is "often proposes limitations," the supersuburbs responding to the question averaged a 1.5, compared with a 2.1 for the smaller suburbs, a statistically significant difference. This indicates that city councils in large suburbs are more supportive of sheer growth in housing units than those in small suburbs.

More important for economic development are attitudes toward nonresidential forms of development. Planners were also asked, "Which of the following comes closest to your view of the policies of your city regarding development?" They could respond that their locality "encourages all sorts of residential and commercial growth," "encourages most commercial growth, although it is less receptive to multifamily or 'affordable'

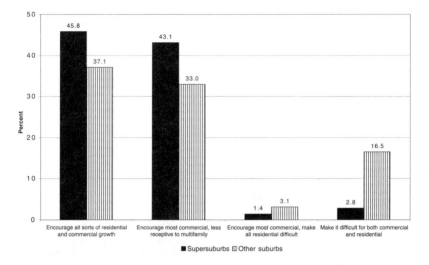

Figure 5.3. Local Policy Toward Growth, According to Planning Director
Note: N = 67 supersuburbs, 87 other suburbs. Differences between supersuburbs and other suburbs (on the 4-point scale) are statistically significant at *p* < .01. Percentages do not sum to 100 due to "don't know" responses.

housing projects," "encourages most commercial growth, but makes all residential development more difficult," or "makes it more difficult for both commercial and residential development." This question was intended to examine development incentives in California's unusual local fiscal system, in which property taxes are a very small share of local revenues in most cities and the property tax rate is not controllable by localities. Instead, sales taxes and business license fees are seen as subject to more local control. This system is often viewed as making retail development much more attractive to localities than residential development.

The results are shown in figure 5.3. Here again, supersuburbs are seen as more amenable to residential development, but at the same time are less restrictive regarding commercial development. Fewer than 3 percent of supersuburb planners choose the most restrictive response, compared with 17 percent of smaller suburb planners. Again, on a 4-point scale from least to most restrictive, the supersuburbs responding had an average score of 1.6 and the smaller suburbs 2.0, a statistically significant difference. In short, supersuburbs in California are more welcoming of both residential and commercial growth.

Using Redevelopment Tools

I hypothesized that supersuburbs would be more likely to make use of complex or innovative policy tools to influence their economic development. Redevelopment policy is one such mechanism, by which municipalities create a redevelopment agency to acquire and assemble land, demolish existing structures, and arrange for new construction, using tax-increment financing. Redevelopment is fairly widespread in California, because it is seen as having notable revenue-raising advantages for municipal governments, which can capture a larger share of local property-tax revenues than is otherwise allowed (Dardia 1998).

In a 1998 survey of city managers or administrators in all California municipalities, regarding city development strategies, respondents were asked to indicate whether their city is engaged in redevelopment very actively, not very actively, or not at all. This survey was completed by respondents from 330 municipalities of the 471 then in existence in California, for a response rate of 70 percent. (See Barbour and Lewis 1998 for more details.) Figure 5.4 shows that about 7 supersuburbs in 10 report a very active redevelopment effort, comparable to the 8 in 10 central cities

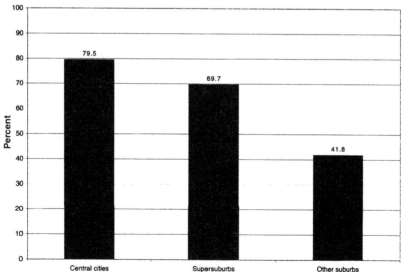

Figure 5.4. Percentage of Municipalities Whose City Manager Reports a "Very Active" Redevelopment Policy Effort

Note: N = 39 central cities, 76 supersuburbs, 110 other suburbs.

reporting the same. By comparison, only about 4 in 10 smaller suburbs report a very active redevelopment policy. This finding provides some confirmation for the notion that supersuburbs have a greater capacity and willingness to make special efforts to achieve their development objectives.

Job Creation as a Motive for Land Use Decisions

As part of the same survey, city managers were asked to rate the importance, to the city administration, of various possible considerations in making development decisions. For example, they were asked to rate in importance motivations such as the service costs associated with a proposed project or its environmental impacts. The city managers were asked separately about development decisions in newly developing (i.e., vacant land) areas of the community and in designated redevelopment areas. They were also asked how important such considerations were in affecting "your plans regarding whether to annex and which properties to annex." To ensure the questions were meaningful to the respondent, only municipalities reporting the presence of vacant land, or the presence of redevelopment activity or annexation plans, were asked to answer the relevant questions.

Here, I focus on responses to a question regarding the importance of the "likelihood of job creation" in evaluating proposed projects in new development or redevelopment areas, and the importance of gaining "land for future development to create jobs" in making annexation decisions. City managers rated the importance of this job-creation consideration on a seven-point importance scale. The results appear in figure 5.5, which indicates that city administrations in supersuburbs attribute significantly more importance to job creation as a motivation to growth decisions than their counterparts in smaller suburbs. Whether because they may be held more responsible by voters for regional economic outcomes, because of concerns of attracting a resource-rich tax base, or because progrowth political actors are powerful in local politics, officials in supersuburbs appear more interested in boosting the fortunes of their communities as job centers than their small-suburb counterparts.

"Visions" for City Development

Taking a more positive view of local officials as relatively autonomous decision agents, it may be that supersuburban governments are more interested in job creation because it fits with an overall vision or plan they have for their community's economic development. Pagano and Bowman (1997) have argued, using evidence from comparative case studies of medium-sized central cities, that the strategic visions city leaders have for their communities are the key factor shaping local development policy and public projects—a process in which officials seek a favorable niche for their city in a competitive, globalizing economy. They write, "Local officials pursue development as a means of reaching an ideal, reflecting an image they hold collectively of what their city ought to be" (1997, 2).

Data from a 2001–2 survey by Max Neiman of local economic development administrators in California municipalities can help cast light on the ambitions, or visions, of supersuburbs. This mail survey included a very relevant question (for which the response rate was 65 percent of municipalities statewide):

> Each city pursues a number of visions. However, it is possible that in a city some visions are more or less important. In thinking about the

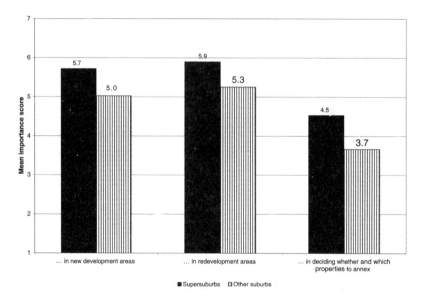

Figure 5.5. Importance of Job Creation to Local Growth Decisions, According to City Manager
Note: N = 47 supersuburbs and 47 other suburbs for new development, 70 supersuburbs and 67 other suburbs for redevelopment, and 38 supersuburbs and 41 other suburbs for annexation. Differences between supersuburbs and other suburbs are statistically significant at *p* < .05 for new development and redevelopment, and at *p* < .10 for annexation.

overall direction of land use and development policy in your city, please indicate how important each of the following is as a feature of your city's policies.

Respondents, who were either the heads of the local economic development agency or were designated as being the most knowledgeable local official regarding this policy area, rated each of eleven visions on a scale from 1 (not very important) to 5 (very important).

The results appear in figure 5.6. The items on the left side of the figure are all visions that reflect an image of economic centrality and increased business presence in the community. Here we see that respondents from supersuburbs are significantly more likely than those from smaller suburbs to envision their community as a source of jobs, as a business-friendly environment, as a retail shopping center, as a source of high-value professional services, and even as a recreation and entertainment

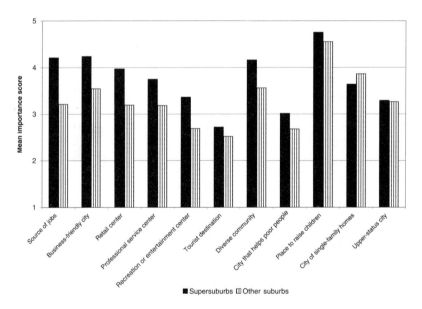

Figure 5.6. Importance to Local Policy of Various Visions for the Community, According to Economic Development Director
Note: N = 68 supersuburbs, 98 other suburbs. Differences between supersuburbs and other suburbs are statistically significant at *p* < .01 for source of jobs, business-friendly city, retail center, professional service center, recreation or entertainment center, and diverse community, and at *p* < .10 for city that helps poor people, and the city as a place to raise children.

center—all functions that point to competition with the traditional roles of central cities.

Interestingly, supersuburban respondents were also more likely than those in smaller suburbs to see their cities as "economically and socially diverse" places (no doubt true), as communities "that help to improve the lives of the poor," and, perhaps contrary to expectations, as "a place to raise families and children" (although differences on this item were not substantively large, for this was a popular and ubiquitous vision across the respondents). There are no significant differences between small suburb and supersuburb respondents in viewing their communities as a tourist destination (which may be largely beyond the control of local policy), as "a community of single-family homeowners," or as "a place of upper-status homes and higher-income residents."

Thus, supersuburbs, although diverse in socioeconomic status and land uses in the eyes of their officials, are no less likely to be envisioned as having strong residential characteristics. Their pronounced, greater degree of aspiration for various types of economic centrality in the metropolis comes *in addition to*, not as a replacement for, their role as bedroom communities, judging by the results of the survey of economic development officials.

Summary of Survey Evidence

The most striking aspect of all the survey results, however, is the portrait they paint of supersuburban governments as being significantly more growth oriented, ambitious, and concerned with jobs and economic development—and of their willingness to use redevelopment tools to achieve such ends. Indeed, it appears, supersuburbs are a different species of municipalities than what is connoted by a more traditional view of the supposedly subordinate suburbs. The case only seems stronger when we consider that some jurisdictions of more than 50,000 residents that many observers would consider to be suburbs—places such as Anaheim or Livermore in California, for instance—are instead labeled central cities by the federal government and were thus excluded from the comparisons above. Indeed, such cases do show the possibility that some supersuburbs may be able to succeed sufficiently in their economic development ambitions that they graduate to a recognized degree of centrality in their MSA: comparable status with the traditional central city.

IMPLICATIONS FOR METROPOLITAN DEVELOPMENT
AND FOR FUTURE RESEARCH

Concerns with the equity and efficiency effects of metropolitan governing arrangements will likely always be with us. But despite the predominant focus of urban scholars on these questions, it is equally likely that policy-makers, civic leaders, and activists considering future changes in metropolitan political structure will be interested in how institutional arrangements may matter for economic development, land use, and democratic accountability. In this chapter, I have suggested that in confronting such research questions, the use of simplifying typologies from the existing literature—consolidation versus fragmentation, the central city versus "the suburbs"—may not provide very useful guidance. In particular, the political organization of the suburban portion of the metropolitan area is a potentially important determinant of policies and outcomes, and it cannot easily be captured in traditional measures of local governments per capita or per square mile.

Assuming that the three surveys reported above capture reasonable approximations of municipal policy intentions, it would indeed appear to matter whether the suburban portion of an MSA is organized into one or more supersuburbs or into numerous small suburban jurisdictions. Supersuburbs, at least in California, have higher ambitions for economic development, are more enthusiastic about growth, and appear to be more willing to use complex policy tools that may help advance the development visions of their municipal leaders.

Of course, having lofty goals or progrowth policies does not ensure that rapid or high-value development will actually occur, because market forces drive most locational decisions of firms and households. Nevertheless, given the expressed preferences of supersuburban leaders, what growth does occur there may take forms that are less likely in smaller jurisdictions—new downtowns, redevelopment areas, mixed-use projects that encompass both housing and jobs, or recreational, cultural, or civic centers. And given that supersuburbs occupy more of an oligopolistic position in the metropolitan land market than do small communities, they have somewhat more leverage over firms or households that want to locate in their portion of the MSA.

What does the presence of supersuburbs mean for the economic development fortunes of the traditional central city? Having larger, more ambitious, and resourceful neighbors implies tougher competition for central city leaders as they seek to maintain their community's preeminence in the metropolitan economy. The supersuburbs—big, diverse, "full-service" local governments—are not easily relegated to the metropolitan back-water, particularly if they contain other locational advantages within their extensive boundaries, such as highway interchanges, airports, or natural amenities. As one observer of metropolitan Portland's development told me, a very large suburb "has the resources to do real damage" to the dominance of the central city (Ethan Seltzer, director, Institute of Portland Metropolitan Studies at Portland State University, and former land use coordinator for Portland's Metropolitan Service District, quoted in Lewis 1996, 198).

A similar story could likely be told about major suburban counties that have large unincorporated areas. This is notably the case in much of the deep South, where zoning decisions are largely made at the county level. When located in fast-growing metropolitan areas such as Atlanta, these counties are often economic powerhouses with the competitive instincts shown by many supersuburbs. Here again, traditional measures of local government fragmentation may be a misleading indicator of economic development policies in such metropolitan areas.

The substantial size of supersuburbs, and their role as a counterweight to the central city, can be seen as having both advantages and disadvantages. On the positive side of the ledger, the pressure that supersuburbs may place upon the central city as the dominant center of the economy may be a source of healthy competition, giving central city policymakers an incentive to compete more effectively. At the same time, supersuburbs tend to be large and diverse enough to carry some of the burdens of the poverty population of a metropolitan area. More broadly, with less effective political pressure from "homevoters," supersuburbs may tolerate more diverse land uses that give rise to a closer match of job and housing opportunities and perhaps greater racial and ethnic integration than in small suburbs. Employing an index of neighborhood ethnic diversity, Sandoval, Johnson, and Tafoya (2002) found that eight of the ten most diverse places in California were large suburbs.

On the negative side of the ledger, a suburban area governed by one supersuburb has less Tiebout choice than the same area governed by several smaller municipalities, implying a less efficient match of residents' tastes to public services. Then, too, feelings of economic independence on the part of some supersuburbs may make them poor neighbors from the standpoint of regional economic development and could portend destructive, perhaps zero-sum, forms of competition with the central city. In addition, the same diversity and poverty burden that I indicated as a potential advantage of supersuburbs could also turn out to be a disadvantage, if the supersuburb's structure and finances—perhaps designed in its simpler days as a smaller community—are not up to the challenges implied.

It is important, finally, to reemphasize that supersuburbs appear most frequently in the American West, which creates an interesting twist for the perceived advantages of the Sunbelt in urban America. Central cities in the Sunbelt have often been viewed as more resilient in the face of suburbanization and economic change than central cities in older parts of the country, largely because of their larger land area, their more auto-mobile-oriented character, the ease of annexation in many Sunbelt states, and the lower density of municipal governments per capita in their MSAs. Ironically, however, some of these same factors make supersuburbs more fearsome competitors for central cities in these states. The large suburbs also have been able to take advantage of annexation powers and the relative lack of small suburban neighbors to add land area; the newness and automobile orientation of these MSAs means there is less inertia in the dominance of core cities; and the transportation system is more likely to have been built to accommodate multidirectional travel, rather than to follow the preautomobile, hub-and-spoke, center-and-periphery model. Supersuburbs seem likely to rise to even greater prominence in the Sunbelt. Urban scholars would be well advised to grant them more attention.

ACKNOWLEDGMENT

I thank Keith Ihlanfeldt and Rick Feiock for helpful comments on this chapter. Ada Chen, an undergraduate summer intern at the Public Policy Institute of California in 2001, helped collect some of the necessary data, prepared the map in figure 5.1, and greatly contributed to my understanding of supersuburbs. Max Neiman graciously provided the data that are discussed in figure 5.6.

NOTES

1. There are some exceptions, of course, to this characterization. E.g., an important attempt to review the overall literature and consider each side's arguments on its own terms is Altshuler et al. (1999); see also Lowery (2000).

2. I have overtly employed this device myself, to analyze likely approaches to suburban development in unitary and fragmented MSAs (Lewis 1996).

3. Chapter 4 in this volume by Stephanie Post illustrates that these two fragmentation density measures are distinct, and the choice of which to use and how to interpret each should be driven by the research question.

4. For new perspectives on cooperation, see chapters 3, 4, and 7 in this volume.

5. In Lewis (2000), I calculated a fragmentation index based on the expenditure level of each local government, not its population size. The hypothetical example presented here is simplified for presentation purposes, but an advantage of such a fragmentation index is its adaptability to different types of research questions. A related measure is developed in Mitchell-Weaver, Miller, and Deal (2000, appendix).

6. In Scenarios A and B, because no residents have the county government as their primary service provider, the county government is irrelevant to this fragmentation index. In Scenario C, where the county serves as the primary municipal service provider for 40 percent of the residents, it is included in the calculation.

7. Note that this approach largely presumes that the costs of public goods and services are internalized in each jurisdiction, with revenue being raised from local property owners through property taxes, assessments, user fees, or in the more theoretical models, a simple head tax. This assumption fits awkwardly in many states, where local sales taxes and hotel occupancy taxes, developer exactions, business license fees, and intergovernmental transfers collectively far outweigh local property-type taxes, meaning that nonresidents bear a large portion of the tax burden.

8. Ihlanfeldt (1999, 239–43) calls for a serious empirical test of Rusk's rudimentary work.

9. Carr and Feiock (1999) have examined the effects of city–county consolidation on growth in manufacturing and retail/service firms, finding no significant linkages.

10. In Lewis (1996), I provide some cross-sectional analysis of the relationship between political fragmentation and several land use outcomes, including the dominance of the central city's business district, the average commute time in the MSA, the number of edge city nodes, and metropolitan density gradients, though I would be the first to argue that more work on the topic is necessary. See also Razin and Rosentraub (2000). There is an intriguing but unsatisfying discussion

of the relationship between central city "inelasticity" and racial segregation in Rusk (1993, 28–31). An analysis showing how political boundaries in a metropolitan area may provide informational cues that reinforce residential and school segregation is Weiher (1991).

11. In this chapter, I use Office of Management and Budget (OMB) definitions of central cities as of 1999. There are other criteria beyond the 50,000 population threshold that OMB and the Bureau of the Census use to designate central cities, most notably their status as employment centers. This brings up the issue that some jurisdictions many people might consider suburban have in fact recently been designated as one of the multiple central cities of their MSAs. (In a few other cases, some former central cities, e.g., Hialeah, Fla., and Burbank, Calif., have been demoted to suburban status.) Here, to have an objective and consistent standard, I hold that only non-central cities (as of 1999) can be labeled supersuburbs. Thus, the count of supersuburbs in this chapter can be thought of as conservative. One can take issue with the government's expansive definition of a central city, but it has been found to be "clear, consistent, and precise," by Hill, Brennan, and Wolman (1998).

12. Lang concentrates more on the demographic character than the governance implications of such communities. He also defines boomburbs, in part, by their growth rate, an approach not taken here.

13. This may depend to some degree on whether the city council is elected by districts or at large.

REFERENCES

Altshuler, Alan, William Morrill, Harold Wolman, and Faith Mitchell, eds. 1999. *Governance and Opportunity in Metropolitan America*. Washington, D.C.: National Academy Press.

Barbour, Elisa, and Paul Lewis. 1998. *Development Priorities in California Cities: Results from a PPIC Survey*. Occasional Paper. San Francisco: Public Policy Institute of California.

Bickers, Kenneth N., and Robert M. Stein. 1998. The Microfoundations of the Tiebout Model. *Urban Affairs Review* 34: 76–93.

Carr, Jered, and Richard Feiock. 1999. Metropolitan Government and Economic Development. *Urban Affairs Review* 34: 476–88.

Dahl, Robert A. 1967. The City in the Future of Democracy. *American Political Science Review* 61: 953–70.

Danielson, Michael N., and Jameson W. Doig. 1982. *New York: The Politics of Urban Regional Development*. Berkeley: University of California Press.

Dardia, Michael. 1998. *Subsidizing Redevelopment in California.* San Francisco: Public Policy Institute of California.

Dodge, William R. 1996. *Regional Excellence: Governing Together to Compete Globally and Flourish Locally.* Washington, D.C.: National League of Cities.

Dreier, Peter, John Mollenkopf, and Todd Swanstrom. 2001. *Place Matters: Metropolitics for the Twenty-First Century.* Lawrence: University Press of Kansas.

Fischel, William. 1999. Does the American Way of Zoning Cause the Suburbs of Metropolitan Areas to Be Too Spread Out? In *Governance and Opportunity in Metropolitan America,* ed. Alan Altshuler, William Morrill, Harold Wolman, and Faith Mitchell. Washington, D.C.: National Academy Press.

———. 2001. *The Homevoter Hypothesis: How Home Values Influence Local Government Taxation, School Finance, and Land-Use Policies.* Cambridge, Mass.: Harvard University Press.

Forbes, Kevin, and Ernest Zampelli. 1989. Is Leviathan a Mythical Beast? *American Economic Review* 79: 568–77.

Foster, Kathryn. 1997. *The Political Economy of Special-Purpose Government.* Washington, D.C.: Georgetown University Press.

Friesma, H. Paul. 1970. Interjurisdictional Agreements in Metropolitan Areas. *Administrative Science Quarterly* 15: 242–52.

Gainsborough, Juliette. 2001. *Fenced Off: The Suburbanization of American Politics.* Washington, D.C.: Georgetown University Press.

Garreau, Joel. 1991. *Edge City: Life on the New Frontier.* New York: Doubleday.

Gottman, Jean. 1961. *Megalopolis.* Cambridge, Mass.: MIT Press.

Hill, Edward, John Brennan, and Harold Wolman. 1998. What Is a Central City in the United States? Applying a Statistical Technique for Developing Taxonomies. *Urban Studies* 34: 1935–69.

Hill, Richard C. 1974. Separate and Unequal: Governmental Inequality in the Metropolis. *American Political Science Review* 68: 1557–68.

Ihlanfeldt, Keith. 1999. The Geography of Economic and Social Opportunity. In *Governance and Opportunity in Metropolitan America,* ed. Alan Altshuler, William Morrill, Harold Wolman, and Faith Mitchell. Washington, D.C.: National Academy Press.

Lang, Robert. 2001. *"Boomburbs": The Emergence of Large, Fast-Growing Suburban Cities in the United States.* Washington, D.C.: Fannie Mae Foundation.

Lewis, Paul. 1996. *Shaping Suburbia: How Political Institutions Organize Urban Development.* Pittsburgh: University of Pittsburgh Press.

———. 2000. The Durability of Local Government Structure: Evidence from California. *State and Local Government Review* 32: 34–48.

Lewis, Paul, and Max Neiman. 2000. *Residential Development and Growth Control Policies: Survey Results from Cities in Three California Regions.* Occasional Paper. San Francisco: Public Policy Institute of California.

Lowery, David. 2000. A Transactions Costs Model of Metropolitan Governance. *Journal of Public Administration Research and Theory* 10: 49–78.

Miller, Gary J. 1981. *Cities by Contract: The Politics of Municipal Incorporation.* Cambridge, Mass.: MIT Press.

Mitchell-Weaver, Clyde, David Miller, and Ronald Deal. 2000. Multilevel Governance and Metropolitan Regionalism in the USA. *Urban Studies* 37: 851–76.

Morgan, David, and Patrice Mareschal. 1999. Central City/Suburban Inequality and Metropolitan Political Fragmentation. *Urban Affairs Review* 34: 578–95.

Neiman, Max. 1980. Zoning Policy, Income Clustering, and Suburban Change. *Social Science Quarterly* 61: 666–75.

Oates, Wallace. 1989. Searching for Leviathan: A Reply and Some Further Reflections. *American Economic Review* 79: 578–83.

Okun, Arthur. 1975. *Equality and Efficiency: The Big Trade-Off.* Washington, D.C.: Brookings Institution Press.

Oliver, J. Eric. 2001. *Democracy in Suburbia.* Princeton, N.J.: Princeton University Press.

Ostrom, Elinor, Roger Parks, and Gordon Whitaker. 1978. *Patterns of Metropolitan Policing.* Cambridge, Mass.: Ballinger.

Ostrom, Vincent, Charles Tiebout, and Robert Warren. 1961. The Organization of Government in Metropolitan Areas: A Theoretical Inquiry. *American Political Science Review* 55: 831–42.

Pagano, Michael, and Ann O'M. Bowman. 1997. *Cityscapes and Capital: The Politics of Urban Development.* Baltimore: Johns Hopkins University Press.

Pastor, Manuel, Jr., Peter Dreier, J. Eugene Grigsby III, and Marta Lopez-Garza. 2000. *Regions That Work: How Cities and Suburbs Can Grow Together.* Minneapolis: University of Minnesota Press.

Peirce, Neal R., Curtis Johnson, and John Stuart Hall. 1993. *Citistates: How Urban America Can Prosper in a Competitive World.* Washington, D.C.: Seven Locks Press.

Razin, Eran, and Mark Rosentraub. 2000. Are Fragmentation and Sprawl Linked? North American Evidence. *Urban Affairs Review* 35: 821–36.

Reich, Robert. 1991. *The Work of Nations.* New York: Alfred A. Knopf.

Rusk, David. 1993. *Cities without Suburbs.* Baltimore: Johns Hopkins University Press.

Sandoval, Juan Onésimo, Hans P. Johnson, and Sonya M. Tafoya. 2002. Who's Your Neighbor? Residential Segregation and Diversity in California. *California Counts* 4: 1–18.

Schneider, Mark. 1989. *The Competitive City: The Political Economy of Suburbia.* Pittsburgh: University of Pittsburgh Press.

Teske, Paul, Mark Schneider, Michael Mintrom, and Samuel Best. 1993. Establishing the Micro Foundations of a Macro Theory: Information, Movers, and the Competitive Local Market for Public Goods. *American Political Science Review* 87: 702–13.

Tiebout, Charles. 1956. A Pure Theory of Local Expenditures. *Journal of Political Economy* 64: 416–24.

Visser, James. 2002. Understanding Local Government Cooperation in Urban Regions. *American Review of Public Administration* 32: 40–65.

Weiher, Gregory R. 1991. *The Fractured Metropolis: Political Fragmentation and Metropolitan Segregation.* Albany: State University of New York Press.

Welch, Susan, and Timothy Bledsoe. 1988. *Urban Reform and Its Consequences.* Chicago: University of Chicago Press.

Williams, Oliver. 1971. *Metropolitan Political Analysis.* New York: Free Press.

Wood, Robert C. 1958. The New Metropolis: Green Belts, Grass Roots, or Gargantua. *American Political Science Review* 52: 108–22.

———. 1961. *1400 Governments: The Political Economy of the New York Region.* Cambridge, Mass.: Harvard University Press.

Zax, Jeffrey. 1989. Is There a Leviathan in Your Neighborhood? *American Economic Review* 79: 560–67.

MARTIN JOHNSON AND MAX NEIMAN

COURTING BUSINESS: COMPETITION FOR ECONOMIC DEVELOPMENT AMONG CITIES

6

Virtually any U.S. metropolitan area is fragmented in the sense that, short of the rare involvement by state government, no entire metropolitan area is governed by a single, general-purpose regime. There are some approximations in the form of city–county consolidations, but even in these instances there are often regional, special-purpose districts that do important things, such as manage water, transportation, or air quality (see chapter 4 of this volume). Concerns about highly decentralized systems continue to produce calls for consolidation and reform—mechanisms intended to promote institutional collective action. As previous chapters have indicated, many policymakers and researchers are concerned that the lack of consolidation and coordination among local governments produces inefficiency, even inequity. Others see decentralization as a vibrant system that allows choice and diversity in local government, efficiently producing a host of benefits and savings overlooked among the advocates of consolidation.

One of the key issues regarding resolving differences between those who advocate consolidation and those who defend polycentrism is recognizing that how one assesses metropolitan governance depends in part on the nature of the problem with which one is concerned. Before advancing the case for either more consolidation or maintaining or extending decentralization, it is important to examine how local governments within metropolitan regions actually function across a range of services and issues. It is likely that findings regarding issues of fairness or efficiency will vary across policies or institutional contexts. Our purpose in this chapter is to focus on one major policy arena—economic development—to investigate how local regimes in one state behave as they seek to attract or retain economic development. After all, decentralization opponents lament competition among communities as causing a host of damaging actions, unnecessary public subsidies to businesses, and ruthless beggar-thy-neighbor actions on the part of localities competing against one another. We ask to what extent this is the case.

When describing how local governments strive to attract and retain economic development, it is not unrealistic to deploy the language of war or extreme sports. The stakes are apparently high, and from time to time expressions of deep concern are raised about whether taxpayers are being gouged, whether on behalf of sports stadiums or to outbid competitors for a putatively job-producing automobile assembly plant (Meder and Leckrone 2002; Isserman 1994). Apart from debates about the efficacy or foolhardiness of state and local incentives, states and cities undertake any number of activities to attract businesses and jobs (Eisinger 1989; Bartik 1991).

Our concern here is "local economic development" policies. These involve the self-consciously directed efforts by communities to shape their local economies. It is conventional to think of cities throughout the United States as being substantially preoccupied with attracting and retaining economic development (Peterson 1981). A number of key studies have explored factors explaining intermunicipal variation in such policies (Bowman 1988; Sharp and Elkins 1991; Fleischman, Green, and Kwong 1992; Wolkoff 1990; Wolman and Spitzley 1996; Clingermayer and Feiock 2001). As is indicated below, localities pursue a wide variety of activities to retain or enhance their economic base. We emphasize the self-conscious aspect of local policy, because communities might also do things or permit things to happen that have unintentional or unanticipated effects on attracting or holding on to commercial activity. For example, local amenities, such as recreational or entertainment resources, can affect the choices made by businesses to locate in one or another place. These amenities might be featured in promotional material, although they are not often directly or methodically incorporated in an economic development strategy.

Schools and educational quality in an area often can affect firms' location choices as well, but rarely do localities and their school districts consolidate their planning or policymaking in ways that maximize the performance of the local economy.

Although there is much debate about the effects of economic development policies enacted by local communities, many local officials claim that such policies are beneficial, in part due to the "folklore" that has emerged from a few successful examples (Feiock 1991). Despite intense disputes regarding the effectiveness or fairness of local economic development efforts (Dardia 1998), as we shall see, there are powerful political incentives for localities competing for jobs and industries. Despite the compulsion to engage in competition with other communities, Lewis and Barbour (1999), for example, find that there is little evidence of general comparative gains or improved relative position among cities in their efforts to boost their local sales tax revenues by attracting local retail businesses.

Of course, regardless of what communities do, the natural course of community development will mean that the fortunes of some communities decline relative to others while the assets of others rapidly increase with economic activity. For whatever reason, communities sometimes do see other localities as "threats" to their economic well-being, and they adopt policies that reflect a sense of competition with other jurisdictions.

We seek to understand the conditions under which communities engage in vigorous economic development activities. In particular, we are interested in competition between communities and want to ascertain whether a community's sense of competition with other communities can account for differences in local economic development policy. The major hypothesis under investigation here is that a greater sense of competition among communities produces higher levels of local economic development effort.

DATA AND SETTING

The units of analysis in this study are cities located in California, with data gathered during 2000 and 2001. Although we did receive responses from a number of the largest cities in the state, the analysis focuses on responding cities with populations of less than 550,000. The fact is that the largest cities (Los Angeles, San Diego, San Jose, San Francisco, and Oakland) are qualitatively different and their scales are of a different order and bias the statistical analysis. As a result, the inquiry here focuses primarily on the remaining independent and suburban small to medium-sized cities in the state.

The questionnaire that provides the core of the data for this chapter was sent in late 2000 to all 475 California cities, and the retrieval of surveys was completed by the spring of 2001. The retrieval effort used the Dillman method to enhance returns (Dillman 1978). Each survey was compiled in booklet format for readability, and a combination of three mailings, reminders, and personal telephone calls and e-mail messages was used to enhance the response rate.

The survey contained detailed items to describe specific local policy actions to promote local economic development. The survey items were designed to tap as many features of local policymaking as theory and prior research suggested were relevant. The instrument queried respondents about local economic conditions, economic development policy actions, the nature of competition between cities for economic development projects, the administrative organization of the city's economic development activities, the politics of economic development policymaking, and the outcomes and effectiveness of economic development activity.

Each survey was mailed to local officials designated as the most appropriate to answer a mailed survey about local economic development policy, such as heads of local housing departments, senior economic development planners, city managers, assistant city managers, and others responsible for economic development. The response rate was slightly higher than 67 percent, resulting in 319 usable surveys. The majority of nonresponding communities were small cities located in the less urbanized regions of the state. The main focus of the survey was to measure local policy efforts in local economic development policy and to identify patterns in policymaking. In addition to the survey data, standard socioeconomic data were gathered on many political traits, including political participation, partisanship, and political structure. Data regarding community characteristics in the 1990s were used, because the policies that were in place by 2001 are conceptualized as being functions of earlier community characteristics.

These data were gathered from official sources and supplemented by research conducted by Dardia (1998), Lewis and Barbour (1999), and Hajnal, Lewis, and Louch (2002). Because about 80 percent of the cities sampled have a council–manager administrative structure, more than 90 percent have at-large elections, and all their local elections are nonpartisan, the basic institutional variables have little variation. Finally, the mean Democratic registration (as of February 1999) for these communities, as a proportion of total Democratic plus Republican registration, is 49 percent, with the maximum Democratic registration among the study communities at approximately 78 percent and the minimum Democratic registration at 17 percent.

Table 6.1. Summary Statistics of Selected Community Characteristics, by Whether City Responded to Policy Questionnaire

Selected Community Characteristics	Responding Communities	Nonresponding Communities
1998 city population	52,913	42,427
Percentage population growth, 1991–98	13.5	13.9
Percentage nonwhite, 1990	38.8	38.2
Percentage Hispanic, 1990	25.3	27.3
Percentage black, 1990	4.6	3.5
Percentage immigrant population	18.8	19.6
Median family income, 1990 (in 1995 dollars)	67,499	68,355
Percentage college graduates, 1990	23.8	22.5
Percentage in poverty, 1990	11.2	12.2
Percentage homeowners, 1990	59.9	60.5
Median home value, 1990 (dollars)	214,844	212,000
Land area, 1990 (square miles)	15.4	10.4

Table 6.1 reports summary statistics for a number of measures comparing cities that responded to the mailed questionnaire with those that did not. The nonresponding communities are quite similar to the responding communities, except in size. The nonresponding communities are, on average, about 20 percent less populous than the responding localities, and they tend to be more than 32 percent smaller in terms of land area.

EXPLANATIONS FOR LOCAL ECONOMIC DEVELOPMENT POLICY

The data permit examination of the following categories of explanation regarding local economic development policies: (1) needs and resources, (2) politics and institutions, and (3) competition with other communities. We pay particular attention to issues associated with perceptions of rivalry, because the presence or absence of interjurisdictional competition plays such a prominent role in accounts of local policies and governance.

Need-based explanations highlight local policies as a feature of communities that are lacking jobs, scrambling for public revenues due to a sparse local tax base, suffering declining or flat property values, or housing disproportionately higher proportions of poor citizens. These cities are compelled to act out of some need to support services and to provide local employment (Bhatta 2001). Even localities whose populations are not especially impoverished can be propelled by a sense of need. For example, rapidly growing communities might face very large increments of housing, with little or no commensurate increases in business or jobs, resulting in long commutes to jobs, commercial, or entertainment destinations.

Efforts to improve the balance of development might be expressed, then, in the form of local policies designed to increase local job sources and provide more in-town services. Thus, need-based factors that incite efforts to retain and attract business development involve those community features that stem from deficiencies in the local socioeconomic profile. Need-based factors create local stress, then, by threatening to undermine the capacity to finance local services or by imposing higher costs on residents by increasing the burden of local taxes and fees or by increasing the costs of everyday life, particularly as it relates to personal security and transportation and commuting costs. Although such deficiencies or disadvantages are most often associated with such social pathologies as poverty, discrimination, unemployment, deteriorating infrastructure, and a declining tax base, they might also include rectifying imbalances in the growth of communities, particularly local concerns over the jobs/houses imbalance.

Many communities are also blessed with abundant resources. It is possible that substantial amounts of land in a locality are devoted to high-revenue-producing uses, whether shopping or automobile centers or very-high-value residential property. Communities with very high levels of household income and median housing values are also likely to have residents for whom the burdens of local services are minor, relative to income. Such places are likely to have residents who do not feel service deprived or stressed and are unlikely to be a source of political pressure for policies to attract or retain economic development.

In resource-rich communities, the link between local economic development policies and community characteristics is likely to be a bit more complex than in the case of need-based linkages. Unlike need-stressed places, localities that are resource blessed, on the one hand, might not feel obliged to seek more development. On the other hand, localities whose initial vision included a sense of being a jobs-rich or highly active retail center might have as part of this vision a panoply of local policies to retain or attract further economic development.

In other words, explanations that emphasize need or resource factors generally think of local governments as accommodating or reflecting external forces, merely reflecting their prevailing social makeup, or being constrained by their endowments and shortcomings. There is little regard for choice or political factors in need- or resource-based accounts of local economic development policy (Hwang and Gray 1991; Hawkins 1971). Such localities are driven by their needs, particularly when they are plagued by social pathology or other disadvantages. Communities with more valuable assets—a lucrative tax base and highly desirable locations suitable for business and commerce, or very expensive homes—tend to have more resources to devote to community development. These more privileged locales are situated, for example, at the intersection of transportation hubs—airports, freeways, railroads, and extensive warehousing districts. They might be more likely to pursue additional business development, often leveraging their locations to produce even more economic expansion. Moreover, for high-status, high-income communities, local economic activity simply is not on the policy radar screen, because there is no perceived need for it.

Political explanations refer to how public policies are affected by formal rules that shape the legal context for making decisions (Dye and Gray 1980; Riposa and Andranovich 1991; Clingermayer and Feiock 2001), such as the form of local government (mayor–council vs. council–manager) or form of local elections (at-large vs. district-level). In our particular setting, a number of key political and institution features have little variance, such as nonpartisan elections, at-large elections, and council–manager forms of local government. However, other political process factors also bear on economic policy issues, including local political affiliations (partisanship) and levels of general local conflict and controversy. For example, locales with a heavy Republican presence might have a more aggressively probusiness economic development agenda focused more on streamlining and easing the permit process and less on traditional redevelopment and subsidy activity.

In addition, a number of political process measures can reasonably be expected to shape or mold local policy. Pagano and Bowman (1995) demonstrated in their case studies the importance, for example, of leadership and city vision. The greater the local level of controversy over development policy, the lower the level of economic activity should be, and perhaps the less emphasis on subsidy and traditional redevelopment approaches. Similarly, the institutional capacity of local government and nongovernmental actors should affect economic development activity. Communities with large numbers of economic development staff and strong economic development agencies housed within local government should be particularly poised to engage in a large number of economic development activities. Communities with powerful nongovernmental economic development officials, (e.g., a strong chamber of commerce) might not need to engage in as much economic development activity, given the presence of such effective efforts outside government.

Finally, we are particularly interested in the effect of competition among communities. When local officials think of themselves as being more or less in competition with other communities to attract and retain local businesses, one can expect the level of policy activity seeking to attract businesses to also increase. Indeed, in some respects, the competition mechanism is critical here. Since the seminal work of Tiebout (1956), scholars have investigated the contests among localities for residents and land uses that enhance their capacity to fund services, while simultaneously minimizing service demands. So on the supply side there are localities doing any number of things to keep taxes low, to project business friendliness, to defend local housing equity, and to ward off threats to the prevailing local lifestyle, particularly if it involves single family homes oriented toward child-rearing. Communities are likely to perceive themselves in competition with one another, when they are located in polycentric metropolitan areas (Ostrom, Tiebout, and Warren 1961; McGinnis 1999).

Our community survey data permit us to investigate each of these explanations: needs and resources, politics and institutions, as well as community competition. The analysis proceeds with an initial presentation of indicators of those characteristics that tap many of these explanations. We then assess the relationship between each indicator and the scope of local economic development policy.

POLICY MEASURES FOR LOCAL ECONOMIC DEVELOPMENT

The dependent variable here is the number of economic development activities each community reported that it undertakes. Survey respondents were asked to indicate whether or not they engaged in thirty-seven different activities. Further, respondents were invited to volunteer any economic development efforts not included on the survey. The highest total activity score a community can have is thirty-seven. If the community does none of these things, it would have a "zero" activity score.[1] The list of activities has been developed over a number of years (Neiman, Andranovich, and Fernandez 2000), and it was reviewed by a number of local economic development officials and other scholars. Table 6.2 summarizes

Table 6.2.   No. of Communities Performing Each Local Economic
Development Activity

Public Policies and Actions	Responses
Assuring consistency in development rules	306
Working with private promotional groups such as chambers of commerce	304
Streamlining review of licenses and permits	298
Working with area's council of governments or area's regional government	288
Emphasizing improvements of local amenities (e.g., school, shopping, recreation)	284
Contacting or networking with businesses	280
Community Development Block Grant programs	279
Property site referrals	274
Rezoning land for commercial use	262
Public improvements to declining areas to stimulate private investment	257
Encouraging industrial parks	249
Promotion of specific industry/activity (e.g., high technology, tourism)	246
Improving the quality of the local public schools	244
Working with local colleges and universities	241
Local government assisted advertising and other public relations	241
Establishing single agency to encourage economic development	222
Relief from payment of fees, licenses, permits, etc.	217
Subsidizing or amortizing on- or off-site infrastructure	214
Increasing space for business by permitting higher densities and building heights	211
Ombudsman service for businesses	210
Issuance of bonds to support development projects	209
Tax increment financing	207
Technical assistance for small businesses	197
Public acquisition of smaller parcels for clearance or resale as larger parcels	189
Government assembly of and writing it down for private-sector purchase	186
Annexation to provide serviced land for new business	182
Low interest loans to business	171
Subsidy or support for employee training	163
Financial grants to businesses	152
Loan packaging for business startups	148
Federal job training programs	145
Sales tax rebates to business	137
Rebates of other non-sales taxes (e.g., property tax)	127
Establishment of local enterprise zones	121
State of California Enterprise Zones	102
Lower operating costs by subsidizing utility rates	90
Other activities	58

how many respondent localities indicated that they undertook each activity included in the thirty-seven economic development activities we explore.

The data indicate that the economic development activities that are most frequently reported are in some ways the "easier" ones. Encouraging industrial parks, streamlining, consistency, "working" with groups, emphasizing amenities, and contacting and networking do not involve large expenditures by the city. Conversely, activities such as tax-increment financing, which involves a serious commitment of resources, ranks lower, at twenty-second out of thirty-seven potential development activities.

The mean number of economic development activities respondent communities undertook in 2001 was 24.2, with a median of 25. Figure 6.1 graphs the distribution of the count of economic development activities in this sample. The modal respondent community undertakes thirty-six of the activities on this list. Two communities had scores of 0, both of which are affluent communities with virtually no commercial development inside their boundaries; they are more than 75 percent white, have virtually no person in poverty, and had 1990 per capita incomes in excess of $70,000. These are built-out, exclusively residential communities, with exceptionally expensive residential housing.

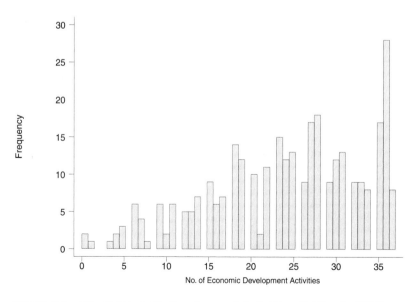

Figure 6.1.   No. of Economic Development Activities, California, 2001

MEASURES OF LOCAL NEEDS AND RESOURCES

Local needs refer to those community features that tend to swell the demand for local services. One such category of variables is often associated with "crisis" communities, in the sense that these are older, poorer, more crime-ridden places, with disadvantaged populations suffering the ravages of low education and higher unemployment levels. Fast-growing communities are also likely to find a need to balance increasing residential development with additional commercial development. Increased commuting might produce a desire to attract more jobs. If growth involves primarily large amounts of housing, the result might be to undermine the jobs/housing balance, and increased efforts to attract economic development can be seen as a way of managing that problem. The "need" measures we employ here are

- unemployment, 1990;
- population change, 1980–98;
- population, 1990;
- city size, by land area, 1990;
- age of the city, in years since incorporation;
- percentage of the population that is nonwhite, 1990; and
- average commute time to work, 1990.

The operational hypothesis is that communities that are larger, with higher rates of growth; older; of lower status, as measured by higher unemployment rates and proportionally more minority residents; and larger in land area are more likely to feel compelled to seek resources through higher forms of economic development activity. In addition, the commute-time measure indicates that communities with poorer jobs/residence ratios will strive to improve this situation by adopting more economic development policies. Communities with residents that have longer commutes are assumed to be under greater pressure to provide more local jobs to minimize congestion and transportation costs. This is a problem of particular concern in California, where traffic congestion and commuting times have become very salient policy issues (Baldassare 2002). The resource measures are

- total per capita sales tax revenue, 1997;
- mean per capita income, 1990;
- per capita assessed property value, 1999;
- fiscal effort relative to property tax base, measured as city revenues divided by the total assessed value of local property;

- fiscal effort relative to income, measured as total city revenue divided by aggregate community income, 1990; and
- per capita total own-source revenue, 1993.

It is not easy to anticipate the direction of the relationship between these fiscal measures and local economic development policy. On the one hand, communities that are better off might not only be so blessed because of previous economic policies, but they are also in a better position to support such policies. On the other hand, they have less of a need to seek more economic development. Having adequate resources, in property, sales-tax revenues, and personal incomes, such communities are perhaps less likely to undertake local economic development activity.

POLITICAL AND INSTITUTIONAL MEASURES

We also employ a number of institutional and political process measures. There is a long tradition of thinking about the ways in which local institutions affect public policies. Much of that work has focused on the differences among localities regarding the presence or absence of "reform institutions," such as nonpartisanship, at-large versus district elections, and council–manager versus mayor–council forms of government. Indeed, an entire range of policies has been studied as functions of local institutions (Dye and Gray 1980; Hawkins 1971; Clingermayer and Feiock 2001).

In addition, a host of political process factors bear on such issues as patterns of local political affiliations (partisanship), levels of general local conflict and controversy (e.g., the prevalence of recall elections or initiative battles), or the perceptions among communities of competition from other communities. Localities with higher Democratic registrations or greater support for "liberal" policies should be more supportive of government intervention in the economy. Hence, such communities might not only have more active local economic development policies, but they might also be marked by greater reliance on more intrusive approaches, such as redevelopment and subsidy approaches. Less "liberal" or "more Republican" locales might have lower scores for overall local economic development activity, and, insofar as these localities have an economic development agenda, it might be more focused on streamlining and easing the permit process and less on traditional redevelopment and subsidy activity.

A number of political process measures also can reasonably be expected to shape or mold local policy. For example, the greater the local level of controversy over development policy, the lower the level of economic activity should be, and perhaps the less emphasis on subsidy and traditional redevelopment approaches. We include a number of measures of political characteristics that previous work suggests are important in explaining public policies:

- local economic development officials' assessment of the general level of controversy usually associated with economic development policies;
- the size of the local economic development staff;
- the perceived importance of local economic development staff in shaping local policy;
- the perceived importance of the local chamber of commerce in shaping local policy; and
- the percentage of local registered voters who are Democrats, 1998.

The hypotheses regarding these measures are that the greater the level of community controversy in general and over economic development in particular, the lower the level of economic development policy. In short, we expect negative relationships between the level of economic development policy and the specific level of controversy associated with economic development policies. We also expect that localities with larger economic development staffs, where economic development staffs and local chambers of commerce are considered salient and important, and where Democratic registration is high, will have higher levels of economic development policies.

MEASURING COMPETITION AMONG COMMUNITIES

This study focuses on three indicators of competition. Two of these are based on the survey used in this study. Each city was asked in the study questionnaire to list up to five communities perceived as its competitors for economic development. On the basis of this item in the questionnaire, we use three measures of competition:

- the total number of times that a city is mentioned by other cities as a competitor, weighted by its rank as a competitor;
- the total number of communities, up to five, that a respondent lists as a competitor; and
- the number of cities within a 5-mile radius of each respective city.

The first measure taps the idea that a city that is mentioned by different communities more often than others is more competitive. However, the measure also includes information about the degree of competition between dyads of cities. Specifically, survey respondents were asked to rank their competitors, naming as many as five competitors. Each time a city is named as another community's top-ranked competitor, it receives five points on this measure; second-ranked communities receive four points; third-ranked communities, three; and so on. Consequently, cities with high competitiveness scores both are mentioned frequently and are primary competitors.

The second competition score taps the idea that communities listing more other communities as competitors feel a deeper rivalry with other cities. The assumption in using the third measure is that the greater the number of communities within an area, the greater the likelihood that they are aware of what other communities are doing and are more sensitive to the actions of these communities. In this sense, we are tapping into a key feature of the decentralized, governmentally fragmented metropolitan region. The greater the numbers of other jurisdictions within a 5-mile radius, the more decentralized and jurisdictionally "rich" a region is likely to be. Moreover, in jurisdiction-rich urban areas, businesses will find more opportunities for eliciting offers and thereby reinforce the perception of competition. In the case of all three measures, the expectation is that they are positively related to our measure of local policy—the number of local economic development activities.

EXPLAINING LOCAL ECONOMIC DEVELOPMENT EFFORTS

To what extent is the effect of competition among neighboring communities independent of the more traditional need, resource, and political explanations for economic development activities? To investigate this question, we turn to a multivariate analysis of our count of local economic development activities. In table 6.3, we model this count of economic development activities[2] using a Poisson regression, which is more appropriate than an ordinary least squares (OLS) regression for these particular data (King 1988, 1989). OLS assumes that a dependent variable is distributed normally and has values that extend, in theory or in practice, to positive or negative infinity. However, given the counting process that underlies the data, we think the Poisson model is more appropriate.[3]

Coefficients estimated using a Poisson regression are not directly interpretable in units of the dependent variable. However, the results are

Table 6.3. Multivariate Analysis of Economic Development Activities

Characteristic or Measure	Coefficient	Standard Error
NEEDS		
Unemployment, 1990	0.0041	0.0057
Population change, 1980–98	0.0002	0.0002
Population, 1990 (thousands)	−0.0005	0.0003
City area in square miles, 1990 (thousands)	0.9557	0.8644
Age of the city since incorporation	−0.0004	0.0005
Percentage of population that is nonwhite, 1990	−0.0018	0.0012
Average commute time to work, 1990	−0.0049	0.0037
RESOURCES		
Per capita sales tax revenue, 1997 (thousands)	−0.0946	0.1017
Mean per capita income, 1990 (thousands)	−0.0192***	0.0029
Per capita assessed property value, 1999 (thousands)	−0.0005	0.0005
Fiscal effort relative to property tax base, 1990	3.8840	7.2860
Fiscal effort relative to income, 1990	−2.7139***	1.0426
Per capita total own-source revenue, 1993 (thousands)	0.1496**	0.0604
POLITICAL AND INSTITUTIONAL FACTORS		
Economic development officials' assessments of controversy, 2001–2	0.0703***	0.0177
Size of economic development staff, 2001–2 (natural log)	0.0404***	0.0138
Importance of local economic development staff, 2001–2	0.0348*	0.0182
Importance of local chambers of commerce, 2001–2	−0.0216**	0.0110
Percentage of local registered voters who are Democrats, 1998	−0.0033*	0.0018
COMPETITION		
Times city mentioned by others as competitor (natural log, weighted for importance as competitor)	0.0596***	0.0147
No. of cities listed as competitors (0–5)	0.0347***	0.0095
No. of cities within 5 miles (natural log)	0.0336*	0.0207
CONSTANT	3.2237***	0.1654
N = 228		
Likelihood ratio χ^2 = 398.79***		
Pseudo R^2 = 0.20		
Log likelihood = −775.08		

*$p < .10$.
**$p < .05$.
***$p < .01$.

intuitively interpretable, in the sense that positive coefficients suggest that increases in a particular independent variable produce additional economic development activities. In the multivariate analysis, none of the need indicators affect the economic development activity score with a conventional level of statistical significance. The resources indicators fare somewhat better, with per capita income, fiscal effort relative to income, and per capita total own-source revenue significantly related to economic development activity.

Among the political and institutional factors we examine, the controversy associated with economic development, the size of the economic development staff, the importance of government economic development personnel, external development actors such as a chamber of commerce, and the partisan balance in a community each has a statistically significant influence on the number of economic development activities undertaken. Contrary to our expectations, controversy is positively associated with economic development activity. We expected a negative relationship because we expected controversy to affect the ability of policymakers to agree on policy adoption.

However, there may be another causal effect we did not anticipate: Each policy adopted may affect additional controversy in a community. In any case, the size of a community's economic development staff also affects its efforts to attract business. External development actors such as chambers of commerce appear to remove the burden of economic development from the public sector. As these grow in importance, city governments reduce the scope of their economic development efforts.

As expected, our measures of competition also affect economic development policies in these California communities independent of need or resource and political or institutional explanations. Cities in competitive environments, as indicated by our weighted competition indicator—which measures the frequency and the fierceness of competition between a city and its competitors—and the number of communities a respondent city perceives to be in competition with it, engage in more economic development activities than cities facing less competition. An objective measure of competition in polycentric metropolitan areas—the number of cities within 5 miles of a respondent community—was also related to the economic development activities of a community.

For a clearer indication of the effects of the significant independent variables, we rely on predicted expected values: the number of economic development activities predicted by the model at important values of each significant independent variable, as is shown in table 6.4. Holding all

Table 6.4. Effect of Significant Predictors on Count of Economic Development Activities

Independent Variable	25th percentile	75th percentile	EV at 25th percentile	EV at 75th percentile
Mean per capita income, 1990 (dollars)	11,443.00	19,676.00	27	23**
Fiscal effort relative to income, 1990	0.02	0.03	27	26**
Per capita total own-source revenue, 1993 (thousands of dollars)	291.06	607.18	20	21**
Economic development controversy, 2001–2	1 (low-key)	2 (occasional)	23	25**
Economic development staff size, 2001–2	1	5	23	25**
Importance of economic development staff, 2001–2	4 (somewhat)	5 (very)	24	25*
Importance of chamber of commerce, 2001–2	2 (not very)	5 (very)	25	24**
Percentage of local voters registered Democrats, 1998	37.2	55.9	25	24**
Times city mentioned as competitor (weighted for importance as competitor)	2	12	23	26**
No. of cities listed as competitors (0–5)	3	5	24	25**
No. of cities within five miles	1	13	23	25*

Note: EV = expected value. Expected values are rounded to whole integers for ease of interpretation; asterisks indicate the significance level of expected-value changes across the interquartile range (* = $p < .10$, ** = $p < .05$).

other variables at their mean values, we computed the number of expected economic development activities across the interquartile range of each independent variable—the predicted activity count at the twenty-fifth and seventy-fifth percentiles—using Clarify for STATA statistical software (Tomz, Wittenberg, and King 2002).

As with the predicted probability scores often used to interpret discrete-choice models such as logit or probit, this table of expected values makes it a bit easier to see the effect of each independent variable on the number of economic development activities a community undertakes. For example, a city at the twenty-fifth percentile of income had residents with an average per capita income of $11,443 in 1990. Holding the other variables in the regression at their mean, the model predicts that this community would engage in twenty-seven economic development activities. Communities with more affluent residents at the seventy-fifth percentile of income, an average per capita annual income of $19,676, are predicted to engage in four fewer economic development activities.

Most of the effects across the interquartile range of each variable are modest, affecting the count of economic development activities by one or two policies or activities. The fiscal effort of communities, own-source revenue, economic development staff, chambers of commerce, resident party identification, and number of cities listed as competitors had these relatively modest affects on the economic development activities that a city pursues. The controversy of economic development programs, economic development staff size, and community density had a stronger effect on the number of economic development activities, with interquartile changes in the values of each associated with two additional or fewer economic development activities. However, the weighted competitiveness measure had a relatively strong effect on economic development activities, with its interquartile change producing a three-activity difference in our count of economic development policies.

Across the full range of these competition indicators, the effects of competition are more interesting than table 6.4 alone suggests. Figure 6.2 shows the effects of the weighted competitiveness measure on a respondent city's economic development activities. Given the natural log specification of the variable, it is not surprising that competition has a diminishing marginal effect on economic development activity. Additional mentions and more strongly perceived competition have larger effects at lower values, with incremental changes in the competitive environment producing little additional economic development activity as the competitive environment grows increasingly fierce.

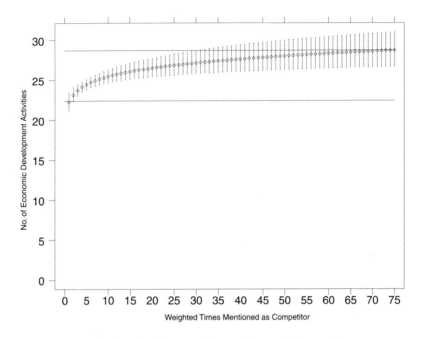

Figure 6.2. Weighted Mentions as Competitor and Economic Development Effort

CONCLUSION

Although competition is not the only thing that affects the economic development activity initiated by a local government, it has a clear influence on a community's efforts to attract business and industry, particularly the competition *perceived* by our survey respondents. In fact, the substantive effect of competition on development activity is stronger even than a community's resources or internal political attributes. Although future work will be required, these results suggest that as the number of local governments within a given metropolitan terrain increases, the perception of competition is likely to increase. With even a relatively few jurisdictions in a given region, increasing numbers of communities are associated with a heightened sense of competition. As the number of communities increases, the number of development activities tends to climb at slower rates. This suggests that a great deal of consolidation could be required to contain competitive economic development pressures. Indeed, virtual wholesale consolidation might be necessary to make a significant dent in the competitive activity of a group of communities that see the others as being in competition with them.

It is also possible that despite the effect of perceived competition on local economic development activity levels, we might be exaggerating the degree to which localities are directly competing with each other. Cities could be exerting themselves along different development tracks. The present investigation groups economic development activities together without regard to the underlying dimensionality of government development programs (Pelissero and Fasenfest 1989; Reese 1993). Other research has demonstrated that in these California communities, economic development offices may proceed along multiple tracks (Neiman, Andranovich, and Fernandez 2000). Some communities might focus on direct subsidy programs to attract business, while others could prefer less revenue-intensive efforts, such as easing bureaucratic requirements and permitting processes. It is possible that different economic and political conditions affect different strategies for economic development. For example, the partisanship or ideology of community residents might give rise to differently oriented development programs. Similarly, competition may affect some types of economic development programs but not others.

The findings here suggest additional avenues for research into the effect of (1) the level of fragmentation on promoting competition among cities and thereby adding to the ongoing concern about efficiencies of polycentricity; (2) the degree to which competition might generate positive spillovers in such factors as increased information and reduced spatial friction as economic development looms in a particular area; (3) the influence of mutual perception among communities in more jurisdiction-rich regions, where the sense of competitiveness can be generated by the mere existence of other communities striving to retain or attract business; (4) the constraints and incentives that state fiscal and institutional frameworks have on local regime behavior; and (5) the manner in which rent-seeking conduct by businesses is likely to act as a propellant and accelerate community efforts to attract business.

One particular area of economic development effort we have not explored here is a community's interest in cooperative endeavors with other municipalities. We removed an indicator that allowed respondents to rate the importance of "joint ventures with other cities" from the count of activities analyzed here because of our interest in competition in the present investigation. However, it is worth noting that cities that do engage in cooperative efforts engage in more overall economic development activities (twenty-seven activities on average for cooperating cities, compared with eighteen for cities that are not inclined to cooperate with other communities; $t = 5.4$, $p <. 001$) and are more frequently mentioned as a competitor (2.9 mentions on average, as compared with 1.8 mentions on average for noncooperators; $t = 3.6$, $p <. 001$).

Such findings are consistent with the idea that communities engage in higher levels of activity not merely as a consequence of some antagonistic perception of competition. Higher levels of exertion also might simply reflect a sense that communities share information about what best practices apply in attracting development. Of course, localities that become aware of other communities' actions might adopt them not only out of some sense that their neighbors are seeking to draw away development but also because their closer interaction and, apparently, higher levels of cooperation jointly produce more policy innovation. In a sense, then, communities that exist in the context of a jurisdiction-rich environment are more likely to be in communication with neighboring jurisdictions and therefore are more likely to become aware of and share best practices and, in some cases, formally cooperate with one another.

The interplay between cooperation and perceived competition is intriguing and suggests a provocative area for future research. This is of no small importance. Competition among municipalities is often regarded as a welfare-optimizing arrangement that introduces a quasi-market for local bundles of taxes and services (Tiebout 1956). However, our results associate competition with a flurry of activity aimed at attracting capital, raising the concern that competition among local governments also drives duplication of services for the businesses and industries targeted by these development policies and ultimately inefficient subsidies. Collective action—cooperative development activities—could mitigate the potential problems with the zealous competition that researchers associate with a race-to-the-bottom model of "smokestack chasing."

NOTES

1. The total number of activities possible is thirty-seven, after the inclusion of open-ended responses to the economic development activities count and the exclusion of self-reported activities aimed at forging interjurisdictional alliances and cooperative efforts with other communities. Given our interest in competition, we felt it was important to weed the dependent variable down to competitive activities.

2. The average inter-item Pearson's r correlation between each of these activity measures is 0.296.

3. The Poisson approach used here is not perfect because it assumes the dependent variable could have infinite positive values and our data are bound on the right at thirty-seven activities. Nonetheless, the results produced using OLS and left- and right-censored tobit specifications produced results similar to those reported in table 6.3.

REFERENCES

Baldassare, Mark. 2002. *A California State of Mind: The Conflicted Voter in a Changing World.* Berkeley: University of California Press.

Bartik, Timothy. 1991. *Who Benefits from State and Local Economic Development Policies?* Kalamazoo, Mich.: Upjohn Institute.

Bhatta, S. D. 2001. Are Inequality and Poverty Harmful for Economic Growth? Evidence from the Metropolitan Areas of the United States. *Journal of Urban Affairs* 23: 335–59.

Bowman, Ann O'M. 1988. Competition for Economic Development among Southeastern Cities. *Urban Affairs Quarterly* 23: 511–27.

Clingermayer, James C., and Richard C. Feiock. 2001. *Institutional Constraints and Policy Choice: An Exploration of Local Governance.* Albany: State University of New York Press.

Dardia, Michael. 1998. *Subsidizing Redevelopment in California.* San Francisco: Public Policy Institute of California.

Dillman, Donald. 1978. *Mail and Telephone Surveys: The Total Design Method.* New York: John Wiley.

Dye, Thomas R., and Virginia Gray, eds. 1980. *The Determinants of Public Policy.* Lexington, Mass.: Lexington Books.

Eisinger, Peter. 1989. *The Rise of the Entrepreneurial State: State and Local Economic Development Policy in the United States.* Madison: University of Wisconsin Press.

Feiock, Richard C. 1991. The Effects of Economic Development Policy on Local Economic Growth. *American Journal of Political Science* 35: 643–55.

Fleischman, Arnold, Gary Green, and T. Kwong. 1992. What's a City to Do? Explaining Differences in Local Economic Development Policies. *Western Political Quarterly* 45: 677–99.

Hajnal, Zoltan L., Paul G. Lewis, and Hugh Louch. 2002. *Municipal Elections in California: Turnout, Timing, and Competition.* San Francisco: Public Policy Institute of California.

Hawkins, Brett W. 1971. *Politics and Urban Policies.* Indianapolis: Bobbs-Merrill.

Hwang, S. D., and Virginia Gray. 1991. External Limits and Internal Determinants of State Public Policy. *Western Political Quarterly* 44: 277–98.

Isserman, Andrew. 1994. State Economic Development Policy and Practice in the United States: A Survey Article. *International Regional Science Review* 16: 49–100.

King, Gary. 1988. Statistical Models for Political Science Event Counts: Bias in Conventional Procedures and Evidence for the Exponential Poisson Regression Model. *American Journal of Political Science* 32: 838–63.

———. 1989. *Unifying Political Methodology: The Likelihood Theory of Statistical Inference.* New York: Cambridge University Press.

Lewis, Paul G., and Elisa Barbour. 1999. *California Cities and the Local Sales Tax.* San Francisco: Public Policy Institute of California.

McGinnis, Michael D., ed. 1999. *Polycentric Governance and Development: Readings from the Workshop in Political Theory and Policy Analysis.* Ann Arbor: University of Michigan Press.

Meder, J., and J. W. Leckrone. 2002. Hardball: Local Government's Foray into Sports Franchise Ownership. *Journal of Urban Affairs* 24: 353–68.

Neiman, Max, Gregory Andranovich, and Kenneth Fernandez. 2000. *Local Economic Development in Southern California's Suburbs: 1990–1997.* San Francisco: Public Policy Institute of California.

Ostrom, Vincent, Charles Tiebout, and Robert Warren. 1961. The Organization of Government in Metropolitan Areas: A Theoretical Inquiry. *American Political Science Review* 55: 831–42.

Pagano, Michael, and Ann O'M. Bowman. 1995. *Cityscapes and Capital: The Politics of Urban Development.* Baltimore: Johns Hopkins University Press.

Pelissero, John, and David Fasenfest. 1989. A Typology of Suburban Economic Development Policy Orientations. *Economic Development Quarterly* 3: 301–11.

Peterson, Paul. 1981. *City Limits.* Chicago: University of Chicago Press.

Reese, Laura. 1993. Categories of Local Economic Development Techniques: An Empirical Analysis. *Policy Studies Journal* 21: 492–506.

Riposa, Gerry, and Greg Andranovich. 1991. Implementing Economic Development in Middle America: An Analysis of Political, Administrative, and Organizational Constraints. *American Review of Public Administration* 21: 17–32.

Sharp, Elaine, and Stephen Elkins. 1991. The Politics of Economic Development Policy. *Economic Development Quarterly* 5: 126–39.

Tiebout, Charles. 1956. A Pure Theory of Local Expenditures. *Journal of Political Economy* 64: 416–24.

Tomz, Michael, Jason Wittenberg, and Gary King. 2002. *CLARIFY: Software for Interpreting and Presenting Statistical Results* (version 2.0); http://gking.harvard.edu/stats.shtml.

Wolkoff, Michael. 1990. New Directions in the Analysis of Economic Development Policy. *Economic Development Quarterly* 4: 334–44.

Wolman, Harold, and David Spitzley. 1996. The Politics of Local Economic Development. *Economic Development Quarterly* 10: 115–50.

RICHARD C. FEIOCK, JILL TAO, AND LINDA JOHNSON

INSTITUTIONAL COLLECTIVE ACTION: SOCIAL CAPITAL AND THE FORMATION OF REGIONAL PARTNERSHIPS

7

The potential for regional cooperation among governments in metropolitan areas has captured tremendous interest. Regionalism entails traditional prescriptions for metropolitan areas, such as the centralization and consolidation of governments and functions, as well as decentralized approaches to governance (Savitch and Vogel 2000). The consolidationist school portrays competition and cooperation as incompatible, but students of decentralized governance describe a regionalism that is based on both cooperation and competition among decentralized governmental units in urban areas (Feiock 2003).

Decentralized regional governance emphasizes self-governance through horizontally and vertically linked organizations. Although primarily among governments, these linkages can also include voluntary, not-for-profit, and private organizations and service producers. Institutional collective action is central to the achievement of metropolitan governance without a unitary metropolitan government. Local governments act collectively to create "a metropolitan civil society to integrate the metropolis across multiple jurisdictions through a web of voluntary agreements and associations and collective choices by citizens to constitute the provision side of a local public economy" (Oakerson 1999, 104). Recent work by Post (2002a, 2002b) demonstrates that fragmented local governments can and do act collectively in service delivery. This cooperation usually takes the form of interlocal service agreements.

Can fragmented local governments cooperate to address larger metropolitan issues, such as income inequality, economic development, and the environment? A recent study by Olberding (2002b) concluded that fragmented areas lack the social capital and cooperative norms necessary for regional partnerships. Olberding acknowledges the importance of cooperative norms for regional partnerships, but she assumes that the presence of more governments (i.e., fragmentation) indicates an absence of cooperative norms. She reports significant negative relationships between the number of various types of local governments in metropolitan areas and the formation of regional economic development organizations.

Although governmental fragmentation might increase coordination problems for collective action, it does not necessarily indicate low social capital. Cooperative norms are not absent from a decentralized system of governance. Social capital in general, and cooperative norms in particular, are products of interaction—not static characteristics of political culture. Rather than assume a lack of cooperation in fragmented areas, we test the relationship between cooperative norms and regionalism. Patterns of actual cooperative interaction among cities within metropolitan areas are defined by interlocal fiscal transfers through service agreements. The results reported here provide evidence that the social capital resulting from experience with interlocal agreements is strongly related to the formation of regional economic development partnerships. Moreover, after controlling for cooperative activity, the negative influence of municipal fragmentation on partnerships disappears. We conclude that social capital fostered by local interactions and agreements encourages the exchange of commitment and reinforces norms of reciprocity by overcoming local service delivery problems.

REGIONAL GOVERNANCE AND REGIONAL PARTNERSHIPS

Interdependence among cities within a metropolitan region has increased during the past few decades as social, economic, and political linkages between cities have strengthened and interjurisdictional issues and problems have grown in number and intensity. Cities may have become more socioeconomically connected in recent years because telecommunication and transportation systems have reduced the competitive advantage to firms being located close to suppliers and consumers. Cities may have a greater need to work together as a region to build competitive advantages that are not related to location (Grell and Gappert 1993; Dodge 1990, 1992).

Empirical work reports important economic linkages between central cities and their suburbs. Voith (1998) found only a weak relationship between city and suburban income in the 1960s but a much stronger one in the 1970s and 1980s. Likewise, Savitch and others (1993) and Ledebur and Barnes (1992) each reported that the correlation between central city income and suburban income in U.S. metropolitan areas increased significantly from the late 1970s to the late 1980s. Gainsborough (2001) reported that as suburbs age, their political affiliations begin to align more closely with those of the central cities they surround, challenging the conventional assumption that suburban cities can be counted on as enclaves for those escaping "big city problems." These findings would also seem to suggest that shifts in political alliances may make regional coordination more palatable than was previously thought possible.

Although the creation of multipurpose governments through the consolidation of existing units has declined in recent years, there has been a tremendous increase in targeted regional action through interlocal agreements (Post 2002a), the creation of special districts (McCabe 2000, 2005) and regional compacts or partnerships among local governments in a metropolitan area (Olberding 2002a). The nature of regional cooperation appears to have shifted during the past three decades. The use of targeted regional strategies has risen at the same time that federally mandated regional planning efforts and city–county consolidation proposals have declined. Top-down solutions have been replaced by voluntary cooperation among governments and sectors through public–private, "intercommunity partnerships" (Dodge 1990, 354).

An increasingly popular regional governance strategy is the formation of a regional partnership. Development partnerships are an "alliance formed by local governments, often with the help of private-sector firms and nonprofit organizations, that has a mission of enhancing the economy of a multijurisdictional area" (Olberding 2002a, 253). Regional partnerships typically begin with the task of studying a regional issue or problem and then developing a strategic plan to address it. Often, though, the partnerships take on additional activities, including program development and provision of services and incentives. Olberding's recent work makes a valuable contribution to the study of local governance by providing the only quantitative investigation of why regional partnerships for economic development are formed. Nevertheless, it is hampered by several conceptual and empirical limitations, which are discussed in the following sections.

REGIONAL PARTNERSHIPS AND COLLECTIVE ACTION PROBLEMS

Efforts to form regional economic development partnerships face collective action problems. Recent work by Lubell and others (2002) found that partnerships to cooperatively manage watersheds emerged when the potential benefits of cooperation outweighed the transaction costs of forming new institutions. Feiock and Carr (2001) observe similar patterns in the creation of a municipal government or special district. Studies of government formation highlight how contextual factors—such as economic conditions, the local political culture, and state-level rules—shape boundary choices. Local jurisdictions seeking to realize gains from cooperation on economic development programs face collective action problems because each government unit would be better off if others took on the burden of forming the organization. Furthermore, an individual government unit can often realize political or economic gains from being a free rider. In the absence of confidence that other actors will abide by agreements and continue to cooperate, the anticipated payoffs from cooperation are low. Both theoretical and empirical work suggests that there are powerful incentives for the parties to defect—to abandon agreements to cooperate and instead pursue individual interests (Feiock 2001).

Certain provisions of state laws affect the possibilities for collective action by providing incentives and disincentives for cooperation. State governments play a central role in specifying the solutions to the local collective action problem by taking on some of the organizational burden of local actors, by setting requirements at the state level, and through laws that define the powers of local units and the processes necessary to form interjurisdictional organizations.

These external factors can be critical to the success of collective action. Voluntary collective action occurs in small groups because the transaction costs of collective action and enforcement of agreements are minimal. Collective action among larger groups of actors typically requires coercion or selective incentives (Olson 1965). Burns (1994) identified three "solutions" to collective action problems in the formation of local governments that are linked to provisions of state laws. First, the need for collective action is determined by the availability of other mechanisms to address regional development. Second, an existing organization or group can be used to pursue the desired policy. Third, state laws influence the incentives for a single jurisdiction or other actors to shoulder a disproportionate share of the financial burden and mobilize diffuse interests in regional development. The entrepreneur provides the start-up resources necessary for organizing the effort and eventually is able to attract other jurisdictions to join the effort.

Where external coercion and incentives are absent or inadequate to overcome social dilemmas, studies of social capital suggest that internal mechanisms could overcome collective action problems (Ostrom 1998). Face-to-face communication raises cooperation and builds social capital through the exchange of commitment, increased trust, the reinforcement of norms, and the development of a collective identity. Innovation and small-scale cooperation build norms of reciprocity that facilitate larger actions (Ostrom 1998).

Previous work has not combined the contextual elements of the boundary or collective action frameworks with the internal explanations for overcoming social dilemmas. Though several studies have laid claim to testing social capital explanations for local governance or policy, social capital has generally been measured contextually by indicators of civic culture rather than by measures of interaction among the institutional actors. The following section elaborates on how social capital reduces barriers to collective action.

THE ROLE OF SOCIAL CAPITAL IN OVERCOMING BARRIERS TO COLLECTIVE ACTION

The idea of social capital was articulated most systematically by Coleman (1987, 1990), in conjunction with the concepts of physical and human capital. Physical capital refers to investment in the tools of production, whereas human capital refers to investment in skills and knowledge. Social capital is the product of changes in the relations among individuals that facilitate action. Coleman (1987) argued that such actions include obligations and expectations, both of which depend on the trustworthiness of the social environment, the information-flow capability of the social structure, and the establishment of norms accompanied by sanctions. Putnam defines social capital as "features of social life—networks, norms, and trust—that enable participants to act together more effectively to pursue shared interests by facilitating coordinated actions" (1993, 664–65).

Much recent work casts social capital as a feature of political culture. In doing so, this work treats social capital, like cultural values generally, as a contextual variable (Jackman and Miller 1998). We argue that trust can be seen as a product or by-product of interactions among actors facing a collective action problem. Social capital can be thought of as a public good that is a by-product of organization and interaction. Individual cities routinely engage in cooperative agreements with neighboring local governments in a region with the expectation of securing services or other benefits to their residents (Post 2002a). As cooperation continues to provide those benefits, the parties to these exchanges build reputations for being trustworthy, providing in the process a feedback mechanism that enhances future cooperation and collective action.

Thus, interlocal agreements provide mechanisms for the exchange of resources, commitments, and trust that can reinforce cooperative norms. Interlocal agreements also build norms of reciprocity by overcoming small second-order dilemmas regarding service delivery. If local governments enter into cooperative agreements that produce social capital as a by-product, it makes formation of metropoliswide cooperative organizations easier.

Recent efforts to apply the concept of social capital to state and local governance have ignored Coleman's original argument, which casts social capital as endogenous, and have instead treated social capital as a characteristic of the environment (Rice and Sumberg 1997). Olberding (2002b) measured the number of voluntary associations in a region and the numbers of cities, counties, school districts, and special districts. These indicators of the number of governments are based on her assumption that the presence of more governments indicates norms of competition rather than cooperation. Her conclusions are shaped by the exogenous treatment of social capital and the assumption that competition is incompatible with cooperation. The next section provides a design to examine the formation of regional economic development partnerships with a model that includes contextual forces, such as civic culture, sociodemographic factors, and external constraints on collective action on the one hand, and endogenous social capital based in interlocal accords on the other.

ANALYSIS

The following analysis is designed to explain whether or not a metropolitan area adopted a regional partnership for economic development. Metropolitan areas are our units of analysis. The population consists of all areas in the United States that the Bureau of the Census defined as consolidated metropolitan statistical areas (CMSAs), metropolitan statistical areas (MSAs), and New England county metropolitan areas (NECMSAs). On the basis of these definitions, there are a total of 242 metropolitan areas.

We measure the formation of regional partnerships for economic development by whether or not a regional partnership for economic development was established in a metropolitan area between 1990 and 2001. This dichotomous variable equals 1 if a metropolitan area adopted at least one regional partnership for economic development, and it equals 0 if a metropolitan area did not adopt such a partnership. Olberding assembled a listing of regional partnerships formed through 1997:

> Regional partnerships were identified using a systematic and extensive search process. First, *Site Selection's* 1998 listing of economic development groups was reviewed to identify those which are regional in scope. Second, the *Worldwide Chamber of Commerce Director's* 1998 listing of economic development organizations was reviewed to identify those which are regional. Third, *Trends in Economic Development Organizations: A Survey of Selected Metropolitan Areas* published by the National Council for Urban Economic Development in 1995, was reviewed to identify regional organizations. Fourth, a search of Internet Web sites was conducted using various combinations of key words such as "regional" and "economic development."
>
> Finally, state economic development departments were called to interview officials who work with local governments and ask them if any organizations in the state fit the definition of regional partnerships for economic development (i.e., organizations or networks of governmental officials—and often business leaders and other individuals—to facilitate cooperation on enhancing the economy of a multijurisdictional area). Some state officials provided information over the telephone while others sent lists of regional partnerships via a facsimile machine or the postal service. This search process identified 194 regional partnerships for economic development in 150 metropolitan areas. (Olberding 2000, 153–54)

We extended the research to a larger set of metropolitan areas and updated the list of partnerships through 2001 on the basis of a search of Web sites and the online resources of *Site Selection* and the International Economic Development Council. In addition, we identified the date on which partnerships were formed to exclude partnerships that existed before 1990. The analysis includes Olberding's (2002b) measure of cooperative norms in the citizenry and the number of civic associations per capita, as reported in *County Business Patterns*. In addition, we included a measure of inter-local agreements involving fiscal transfers to indicate endogenous social capital. We calculated the number of municipal governments receiving intergovernmental revenues from other local governments in the metropolitan area from the 1992 *Census of Government Finance*. The numbers of cities, counties, and special districts in each metropolitan area, which, Olberding contends, indicate a lack of cooperative norms in government, are also in the model (Olberding 2002b). On the basis of the description above and extant research, we added measures of population in 1990, per capita personal income in 1990, land area, and an index of state constraints on local government annexation, incorporation, and borrowing.

The model is estimated using probit maximum likelihood techniques. The parameter estimates are reported in table 7.1. The results provide strong support for a link between endogenous social capital and the formation of regional partnerships. Regional cooperation was more likely in metropolitan areas that had more frequent interaction among local gov-

Table 7.1. Probit Estimates of the Formation of Regional Economic Development Partnerships

Variable	B	Standard Error
Population	.0000259	.0000023
Income	−.0000329	.0000414
Civic association	.2138645	.1513676
Land area	.0000835	.0000615
Total cities	−.0011991	.0042145
Total counties	.1962058**	.0878722
Total special districts	−.0053993*	.0031876
Constraints	−.2382334*	.1243458
Interlocal agreements	.0299446**	.0118298
Constant	.7165653	.8714065
Number of observations	208	
Log likelihood	−128.31	
Likelihood ratio χ^2 (10)	31.26	
Probit > χ^2	0.0005	
Pseudo R^2	0.1686	

*$p < .10$.
**$p < .05$.

ernments. Where more cities entered into interlocal service agreements, there was a significantly higher likelihood that an economic development partnership would be formed.

Civic culture, as evidenced by voluntary organizations, had a positive effect, but the coefficient fell short of statistical significance. Olberding (2002b) found that the number of cities and special districts in a metropolitan area decreased the likelihood of collective action. We also found that special districts decreased the likelihood of regional partnerships, but our specification found no evidence that the number of cities reduces the likelihood of metropoliswide cooperation. Moreover, we found that the number of counties in the metropolitan area had a positive effect on the formation of economic development partnerships. Table 7.1 also reports that metropolitan areas with larger populations have a greater likelihood of forming a regional partnership but that higher incomes and larger land areas did not have a significant influence on the formation of partnerships.

CONCLUSION

Our results strongly repudiate the recent work that argues that governmental fragmentation and competition are destructive of regional cooperation. Olberding (2002b) found that the number of local governments in a metropolitan area had a negative effect on the formation of regional partnerships. However, after controlling for actual cooperative behavior through interlocal agreements, much of this relationship disappears. The number of cities is unrelated to cooperation, and the number of counties has a positive rather than negative effect. We do find that special districts reduce the likelihood of regional partnerships, but this result more likely reflects the fact that these districts can provide an alternative avenue for solving regional problems (McCabe, 2005), not that special districts are destructive of cooperative norms.

The results presented here also highlight the importance of the endogenous role for social capital in theories of institutional cooperation. Empirical studies of cooperative action need to account for the endogenous social capital that results from institutional interactions, not just contextual measures of community civic culture. This assertion is reinforced by the finding that interlocal agreements had a much greater impact on collective action to form economic development partnerships than did civic associations.

The results reported here have implications beyond economic development and may extend to a wide array of regional issues affecting citizens and governments in metropolitan areas. Recent research has directed attention to the institutional reform of local government institutions and to efforts to create new jurisdictions or modify the boundaries of existing local governments through annexation (Carr and Johnson 2002). Each of these contributions to the literature has applied collective action models to institutional choice with some success. The results presented here suggest that these models might be augmented to account for internal resources for overcoming social dilemmas as well as the contextual elements of the collective action framework.

ACKNOWLEDGMENT

The research for this chapter was supported by National Science Foundation Grant SES-0214174 and a grant from the Devoe Moore Center of Florida State University. The authors thank Julie Olberding for making her data available to us; In-Sung Kang, Moon-Gi Jeong, Seung-Bum Yang, and Sang-Seok Bae for assistance in data collection; and Annette Steinacker for helpful comments and suggestions.

REFERENCES

Burns, Nancy. 1994. *The Formation of Local Governments: Private Values and Public Institutions*. New York: Oxford University Press.

Carr, Jered B., and Linda S. Johnson. 2002. A War of Words: The Heuristics of Creating Regional Governance. Paper presented at the annual meeting of the American Political Science Association, Boston, September 3–5.

Coleman, James S. 1987. Norms as Social Capital. In *Economic Imperialism: The Economic Approach Applied Outside the Field of Economics*, ed. Gerald Radnitzky and Peter Bernholz. New York: Paragon House.

———. 1990. *Foundations of Social Theory*. Cambridge, Mass.: Cambridge University Press.

Dodge, W. 1990. Regional Problem Solving in the 1990s: Experimentation with Local Governance for the 21st Century. *National Civic Review*, July–August, 354–66.

———. 1992. Strategic Intercommunity Governance Networks: "SIGNETs" of Economic Competitiveness in the 1990s. *National Civic Review*, fall–winter, 403–17.

Feiock, Richard C. 2001. A Quasi-Market Framework for Local Economic Development Competition. *Journal of Urban Affairs* 24: 123–42.

———. 2003. *Decentralized Governance: The Organization of Local Governments in Metropolitan Areas*. Washington, D.C.: Georgetown University Press.

Feiock, Richard C., and Jered B. Carr. 2001. Incentives, Entrepreneurs, and Boundary Change: A Collective Action Framework. *Urban Affairs Review* 36: 382–405.

Gainsborough, Juliet F. 2001. *Fenced Off: The Suburbanization of American Politics*. Washington, D.C.: Georgetown University Press.

Grell, Jan, and Gary Gappert. 1993. The New Civic Infrastructure: Intersectoral Collaboration and the Decision-Making Process. *National Civic Review* 82, no. 2: 140–48.

Jackman, Robert W., and Ross A. Miller 1998. Social Capital and Politics. *Annual Review of Political Science* 1: 47–73.

Ledebur, Larry C., and William R. Barnes. 1992. *Metropolitan Disparities and Economic Growth*. Washington, D.C.: National League of Cities.

Lubell, Mark, Mark Schneider, John Scholz, and Mihriye Mete. 2002. Watershed Partnerships and the Emergence of Collective Action Institutions. *American Journal of Political Science* 46, no. 1: 148–63.

McCabe, Barbara. 2000. Special-District Formation among the States. *State and Local Government Review* 32, no. 2: 121–31.

———. 2005. Special Districts as an Alternative to Consolidation. In *City–County Consolidation and Its Alternatives: Reshaping the Local Landscape*, ed. Jered Carr and Richard C. Feiock. Armonk, N.Y.: M. E. Sharpe.

Oakerson, Ronald. 1999. *Governing Local Public Economies: Creating the Civic Metropolis*. Oakland: ICS Press.

Olberding, Julie C. 2000. The Formation, Structure, Process and Performance of Regional Partnerships for Economic Development in Metropolitan Areas. Ph.D. dissertation, University of Kentucky, Lexington.

———. 2002a. Diving into the "Third Waves" of Regional Governance Strategies: A Study of Regional Partnerships for Economic Development in U.S. Metropolitan Areas. *Economic Development Quarterly* 16: 251–72.

———. 2002b. Does Regionalism Beget Regionalism? The Relationship between Norms and Regional Partnerships for Economic Development. *Public Administration Review* 62: 480–91.

Olson, Mancur. 1965. *The Logic of Collective Action*. Cambridge, Mass.: Harvard University Press.

Ostrom, Elinor. 1998. A Behavioral Approach to the Rational Choice Theory of Collective Action. *American Political Science Review* 92, no. 1: 1–22.

Post, Stephanie. 2002a. Local Government Cooperation: The Relationship between Metropolitan Area Government Geography and Service Delivery. Paper presented at the annual meeting of the American Political Science Association, Boston, August 29–31.

———. 2002b. Metropolitan Area Governance and Institutional Collective Action. Paper presented at DeVoe Moore Symposium, Florida State University, Tallahassee, October 5–6.

Putnam, Robert. 1993. *Making Democracy Work: Civic Traditions in Modern Italy*. Princeton, N.J.: Princeton University Press.

Rice, Tom W., and Alexander F. Sumberg. 1997. Civic Culture and Government Performance in the American States. *Publius: The Journal of Federalism* 27, no. 1: 99–114.

Savitch, Hank V., David Collins, Daniel Sanders, and John P. Markham. 1993. Ties that Bind: Central Cities, Suburbs and the New Metropolitan Region. *Economic Development Quarterly* 7: 341–57.

Savitch, Hank V., and Ronald Vogel. 2000. Metropolitan Consolidation versus Metropolitan Governance in Louisville. *State and Local Government Review* 32, no. 3: 198–212.

Voith, Richard. 1998. Do Suburbs Need Cities? *Journal of Regional Science* 38, no. 3: 445–64.

ELAINE B. SHARP

METROPOLITAN STRUCTURE AND THE SEX BUSINESS

8

Analysis and argumentation about the consequences of metropolitan structure have focused on a variety of topics, including racial segregation, income inequalities, government spending, satisfaction with basic services, and economic development (Dreier, Mollenkopf, and Swanstrom 2001; Carr and Feiock 1999; Morgan and Mareschal 1999; Boyne 1992; Lowery and Lyons 1989). It has not, however, examined the impact of metropolitan structure on local "morality policy"—that is, local government's handling of those issues that involve conflict over first principles and where at least one side defines the issue "as one of morality or sin and uses moral arguments in its policy advocacy" (Mooney 2001, 3). This chapter undertakes such an analysis of an important subcategory of local morality policy— that involving the "business of sex."

City governments are in fact frequently confronted with issues involving the sex industry. At the local level, the sex industry includes two sets of phenomena that may at first appear quite different: (1) prostitution (either in the form of streetwalkers, conventional brothels, or various businesses, e.g., escort services and massage parlors, that frequently serve as thinly disguised covers for prostitution) and (2) businesses purveying sexually explicit entertainment (such as nude dancing establishments, X-rated theaters, and adult book and videocassette stores). Prostitution is nearly universally illegal in U.S. localities (with the exception of a few counties in Nevada); but First Amendment considerations constrain localities from completely banning sexually explicit businesses, though they may be regulated in various ways.

Despite this seemingly fundamental difference, the two elements of the sex industry at the local level are considered together here, for at least two reasons. First, while the "law on the books" makes prostitution illegal, enforcement of that law is quite episodic (i.e., periodic crackdowns) and typically focuses only on visible prostitutes (i.e., streetwalkers) while over-looking less visible prostitution (escort services and the like) (Miller, Romenesko, and Wondolkowski 1993, 313). Meanwhile, though sexually explicit businesses such as X-rated theaters and adult bookstores have a constitutionally protected right to exist, municipalities have devised a variety of regulations that have withstood court tests and can be used to strongly limit sexually explicit businesses. These include zoning regulations that limit the proximity of such businesses to other land uses, including schools or churches, or that restrict them only to designated zones (Gerard 1996); and prohibitions against the sale of alcohol in adult entertainment establishments and regulations distancing nude dancers from patrons—both of which make the adult business less lucrative (Gilmore 1999). The lax and haphazard enforcement of laws against prostitution on the one hand and the increasingly aggressive regulation of sexually explicit businesses on the other hand give the two elements of the sex business a de facto legal status that is more similar than the "law on the books" would suggest. Second, the two elements of the sex industry frequently can be related in practice, as when nude dancing establishments are alleged to provide a venue for prostitution.

From at least one point of view, the sex industry can be an asset, at least to some central cities. The sex business is, after all, a key element in an economic development strategy of culture and tourism that has become increasingly important for core cities as they "accepted . . . the pointlessness of trying to compete head-to-head with suburbs for certain kinds of wholesaling and retailing" (Judd 1999, 35). In Atlanta, for example, nude dancing clubs are widely acknowledged to contribute to the city's success as a convention center and are a key part of the city's image; the nude dance clubs also account for 10 percent of all the liquor taxes collected in Atlanta, even though they constitute fewer than 5 percent of the businesses paying liquor-by-the drink taxes (Osinski 1995, 4G). A substantial literature on "sex tourism" documents the growing importance of "varieties of leisure travel that have as a part of their purpose the purchase of sexual services" (Wonders and Michalowski 2001).

But the sex industry is also a problem for cities, in a variety of ways. Most obviously, prostitution is a public health threat, especially with respect to the spread of HIV/AIDS. And especially where it impinges on residential neighborhoods, prostitution evokes a host of other problems, including disorderly conduct and the accumulation of condoms and syringes in streets and alleyways, the accosting and propositioning of neighborhood women who are not prostitutes, the cost of lost customers for some businesses, and the potential for all these externalities to lead to overall neighborhood decline (Weitzer 2000, 166–69). Furthermore, while prostitutes, nude dancing establishments, pornographic film theaters, and the like may function as support services for the convention and tourist business in *some* parts of *some* cities at *some* times, the use of urban space for seedy, sex-industry purposes can sometimes conflict with plans for major urban redevelopment efforts.

Indeed, as the Times Square redevelopment project in New York City illustrates, prostitution and pornography are often lumped with crime and drug use in an amalgam that symbolizes urban decline, thus providing a justification for local officials to supplant these land uses (Reichl 1997, 521). Similarly, Judd (1999, 37–39) depicts the "tourist bubble" that core cities construct in an effort to succeed with a culture and tourism strategy that emphasizes the building of standard components, such as a domed stadium, festival mall, and convention center. The tourist bubble needs to have a sanitized character so as to project a safe and idealized image of city life rather than a gritty or dangerous one. From this perspective, the visible aspects of the sex industry must be moved out of the tourist bubble. Finally and perhaps most generally, the sex industry—whether in the form of prostitution or of nude dancing clubs, X-rated theaters, and the like—is frequently problematic for local officials because such activities and establishments lead to the mobilization of individuals and groups that object *on morality grounds* and that demand that the government take action to restore decency (Weitzer 2000, 170–71).

METROPOLITAN STRUCTURE AND THE LOCAL SEX INDUSTRY

This chapter examines the impact of metropolitan structure on official action concerning the sex industry in the core cities of metropolitan areas. More precisely, the chapter investigates whether variation in the extent to which a metropolitan area is governmentally fragmented or is inelastic will have a bearing on the extent to which local officials in the metropolitan core take aggressive action against the sex industry.

Although there has been virtually no research on this precise matter, a series of hypotheses can be derived by extension from research on other relevant policy areas. If we assume that the sex industry is generally viewed as problematic and undesirable on any of the grounds outlined above (an assumption that will be relaxed below) and yet inevitable (either because sex businesses cannot on constitutional grounds be completely regulated out of existence or because of limitations on the resources that can be committed to enforcement of restrictions), we can begin to think about the sex industry as a specific form of a locally unwanted land use (LULU), subject to the same dynamics as other LULUs in decentralized metropolitan areas. Thus, just as Hartford officials tired of serving as the dumping ground for the region's poor people and put a moratorium on homeless shelters and other facilities serving poor people to force the suburbs to do their fair share (Dreier, Mollenkopf, and Swanstrom 2001, 174), so also might we expect core cities in decentralized metropolises to try to "export" the problem of sex-industry LULUs by engaging in law enforcement crackdowns on prostitution, enacting more stringent regulations involving sexually explicit businesses, or more aggressively enforcing the regulations that currently exist.

More generally, officials in one jurisdiction may be motivated to crack down on the sex industry if neighboring jurisdictions do so, out of fear that passivity in the face of neighboring jurisdictions' action would open the city's door to an influx of sex business activities. There is some basis for such fears. Research suggests that police crackdowns in general have displacement effects, and police sweeps of prostitutes in particular have been shown to be a factor in prostitutes' decisions to move to another city (Miller, Romenesko, and Wondolkowski 1993, 314). And case study evidence from several metropolitan areas that are the source of data for this analysis also exemplifies this dynamic.

In one of these metropolitan areas, a flock of municipalities rushed to adopt ordinances prohibiting the sale of alcohol in nude dance clubs the moment that the state's supreme court affirmed such an ordinance as adopted by one of the metropolitan area's suburban municipalities. Such ordinances were seen as a means for local governments to discourage the location of adult entertainment clubs within their community, because most clubs would fail to turn a profit without the revenues generated by liquor sales. A police official in another metropolitan area was even more explicit about the effects that crackdowns on the sex industry by other metropolitan area municipalities have on his core city jurisdiction. In a local newspaper article on the subject, he is quoted as indicating that when a neighboring jurisdiction started putting law enforcement pressure on prostitutes and their johns, "we felt we had to respond or they'd all come here."

Although the ensuing "arms race" of anti-sex-industry action is possible even in metropolitan areas that are minimally decentralized, the multiplicity of jurisdictions in highly fragmented metropolises enhances the potential for such an arms race and makes coordinated, areawide action more difficult. In parallel fashion, because inelastic cities are spatially limited, they would presumably find it more difficult to deal with sexually explicit businesses by using zoning rules to concentrate them in one or a few areas that do not threaten negative spillover effects for either residential areas or other business districts. And lacking this ability to innocuously accommodate the sex industry within their borders, officials of such inelastic cities would be expected to enact more restrictive policies to discourage sexually explicit businesses from operating in their jurisdiction. In short, the initial and simplest hypothesis (H_1) stipulates that the more decentralized the metropolitan setting, the harsher is city officials' action toward the sex industry.

However, the structure of the metropolitan context is only one of several factors that can be expected to shape official action with respect to sex-oriented businesses. A more sophisticated version of H_1 would suggest that, *other things being equal*, the more decentralized the metropolitan setting, the more aggressively will core city officials oppose sex-industry activity in their jurisdiction (H_2). But what other variables constitute the potential significant factors that should be controlled?

A growing body of research on morality policy suggests that key variables representing cultural, economic, and institutional explanations should be included. With respect to cultural explanation, existing research on morality policy more generally suggests that socioculturally defined values are the basis for varied reactions to morality issues and that public officials are highly responsive to such values. Variables such as level of church membership (Button, Rienzo, and Wald 1997; Sharp 2002), fundamentalist religious attachment (Button, Rienzo, and Wald 1997; Pierce and Miller

1999), the extent of Catholicism (Norrander and Wilcox 1999; Smith 1999), and the political empowerment of women (Berkman and O'Connor 1993; Smith 1999) have been found to be important predictors of local or state action on a variety of morality policy issues, including pornography and other "decency" issues.

A more theoretically satisfying line of research suggests that a number of such sociodemographic variables combine to distinguish locations with "new political cultures" (Clark and Inglehart 1998) or "unconventional sub-cultures" (Rosdil 1991; Miranda and Rosdil 1995) from locations with conventional or traditionalistic subcultures. In particular, postindustrial trends have created urban locations where changing women's roles, the increasing prevalence of postsecondary education, increases in nontraditional household arrangements such as unrelated individuals living together and female-headed families, and the growing importance of human services employment (Rosdil 1991, 81) create an unconventional subculture that challenges traditional social values.

Both because of the leftist-progressive values that have been linked to unconventional subcultures (Miranda and Rosdil 1995) and the emphasis on freedom of speech, individual participation, and expressive political activity in such subcultures (Inglehart 1990), cities with more unconventional subcultures may be expected to push official action with respect to the sex industry in a more permissive direction. By contrast, in cities with more conventional subcultures, officials would be expected to take action more averse to the sex industry, to stand up for traditional moral values.

At first blush, it might seem that economic variables have less of a place in models of morality policymaking than they do in other types of policy. After all, if morality policy is about "values, not the economics on which most nonmorality policy centers" (Studlar 2001, 38), then explanatory variables reflecting material stakes, financial pressures, resource capacity, or other economic considerations have little place in the analysis. However, for some morality policies, such as lottery adoption, both logic and empirical evidence support the relevance of economic considerations (Berry and Berry 1990, 1992) and the potential tug-of-war between economic considerations and the cross-cutting pressures of socioculturally based values is of great theoretical interest. Similarly, economic considerations may be expected to drive urban policymaking with respect to the sex industry, which, as was noted above, can occupy an interesting niche in the economic base of cities. In particular, officials in cities with economies that make them more desperate for economic development may be hypothesized to take a more permissive approach to the sex industry.

An assessment of the impact of metropolitan structure on core city officials' response to the sex industry should also control for the institutional arrangements of core city governance. Both logic and a substantial body of empirical research suggest that the institutional differences that distinguish reformed from nonreformed city government have an impact on policy outcomes of many kinds (Morgan and Hirlinger 1991; Feiock and Clingermayer 1992; Clingermayer and Feiock 2001; Schneider and Teske 1993; Elkins 1995). When applied to the case at hand, this line of work suggests that officials in nonreformed settings should be more likely to take aggressive action against the sex industry.

In part, this is because directly elected mayors have more incentives than do city managers for the sort of political entrepreneurship (Schneider and Teske 1992, 1993) and credit claiming that can so readily be generated in crusades against the sex industry—a key lesson of Downs's (1989) case study of the development of antipornography regulations in Minneapolis and Indianapolis.[1] Likewise, the nonreform institution of district elections provides many incentives for officials to be responsive to the neighborhood-level complaints that are inevitable, given the spatially defined, negative externalities of the sex industry (Weitzer 2000, 166–69).

Alternatively, it may be argued that the direct effect of variation in local governing institutions is not the relevant matter. Rather, such institutions are arguably important because they mediate the effects of pressures stemming from the community subculture. From this point of view, we would expect that where governing institutions are the least reformed (and hence the most open to community demands and expectations), the relationship between subculture and official action toward the sex industry should be maximized, and that where governing institutions are the most reformed (and hence insulated from community demands and expectations), the relationship between subculture and official action toward the sex industry should be minimized. In the analysis that follows, both the direct effects and the mediating effects of local governing institutions are examined.

Hypothesis 2 thus stipulates that, controlling for differences in (1) local subculture, (2) economic circumstance, and either (c_1) institutional arrangements or (c_2) institutional arrangements interacted with subculture, officials in decentralized metropolitan areas will take stronger action against the sex industry than officials in more centralized metropolitan areas.

Alternatively, the linkages between local subculture, economic circumstance, and local governing institutions on the one hand and official action toward the sex industry on the other may be mediated by the character of the metropolitan context. In highly fragmented areas, a Tiebout-like hypothesis stipulates that there would be greater opportunity for a match between preferences with regard to toleration of the sex industry and governmental policy with respect to the sex industry. To the extent that preferences are derived from socioculturally derived values, this would suggest that the impact of subculture on governmental action toward the sex industry is much greater in decentralized areas than in centralized ones (H_3). In parallel fashion, Hypothesis 3 would stipulate that metropolitan structure may mediate the impact of economic considerations on the official posture toward the sex industry. The desperation for economic development that makes cities with poor economic circumstances more tolerant of the sex industry may be expected to be especially pressing among the core cities of fragmented or inelastic metropolitan area, because the competitive environment of the metropolitan area leaves them without the luxury of being choosier about allowable enterprises.

Similarly, Hypothesis 3 envisions metropolitan structure as mediating the impact of local institutional arrangements on the official posture toward the sex industry. It posits that the link between nonreformed institutions and crusading against the sex industry should be most pronounced in fragmented or inelastic metropolitan contexts where core city officials can most readily make claims of taking action lest the city become a dumping ground for the metropolitan area's sleazier establishments and practices.

DATA AND MEASUREMENT

This analysis draws upon data from a larger study of morality policy in ten study cities—each of which is a core city in a major metropolitan area (see the appendix for more details on study city selection). A search of local newspaper files and relevant documentary evidence (e.g., city ordinances) combined with personal interviews with government officials (mayors, city managers, council members, police and public health officials, city attorneys, and prosecutors) and community leaders or activists on morality issues (i.e., leaders of gay rights organizations, abortion clinic directors, and antipornography activists) yielded information on a total of 451 "incidents" or cases in which local officials took action on any of a defined core set of morality issues (gay rights, needle-exchange programs, abortion, and "decency," including pornography, prostitution, and the reg-

ulation of adult entertainment enterprises). Official "action" was not limited to formal policy adoption. It also included implementation decisions
and taking a position at the agenda-setting stage.

For this study, all 97 incidents involving the sex industry (i.e., all the
"decency" incidents) were extracted for analysis. Given the broad definition of official action, they include incidents in which city councils adopted
(or refused to adopt) policies instituting more restrictive zoning or licensing regulations targeted at sexually explicit businesses; incidents in which
law enforcement officials engaged in crackdowns on prostitution and incidents of decision making about alternative approaches to the prostitution
problem, such as "john schools" or legalizing prostitution; incidents in
which elected officials took a public stance against pornographic bookstores; and incidents in which officials refused to install filters to block access to pornographic Web sites at the public library. The dependent variable is a five-category ordinal scale of official action in each incident, ranging from action that is greatly restrictive or unfavorable toward the sex
industry to action that is highly permissive or favorable.[2] The variable is
scored such that higher values indicate more permissive action.

The extent to which metropolitan areas are decentralized has been measured in a variety of ways, ranging from counts of political units (Stephens
and Wikstrom 2000), usually adjusted for population (Schneider 1986;
Dolan 1990) to measures of the core city's share of metropolitan population (Savitch et al. 1993) to growth in central city land area (Morgan and
Mareschal 1999). In their study of the effect of metropolitan fragmentation on central city–suburban inequality, Morgan and Mareschal (1999)
use all three types of measures, but they find that only two of the three—
cities per metropolitan statistical area (MSA) and central city population
share—are significant predictors of any aspect of central city–suburban
inequality.

Meanwhile, in a report prepared for the National Research Council,
Altshuler and others (1999) argue that the central city share of metropolitan population and growth in core city land area are measures of elasticity
(and its converse, inelasticity)—not measures of fragmentation. Fragmentation, they argue, "should be measured by the number of relevant local
governments per capita in a metropolitan area" (Altshuler et al. 1999, 65).
Note that, as used here, the term "elasticity" derives from Rusk (1993),
who conceptualizes metropolitan elasticity as the extent to which core
cities can *annex* new growth areas, not necessarily whether core cities are
relatively successful at attracting new population within their original
boundaries.

This chapter takes a middle ground in this controversy, using indicators of both relevant local governments per capita (i.e., fragmentation) and of core city share of metropolitan population (inelasticity). More specifically, the measure of fragmentation is the number of municipalities and counties in the metropolitan area[3] in 1997 per 100,000 population in 1997. Special districts and townships were not included in the measure because neither have jurisdiction over the matters at issue in this analysis. The measure of inelasticity is the core city's share of metropolitan population in 1997.

The community subculture for each city is measured by using an index of cultural unconventionalism that averages six indicators of degree of unconventional culture, all for 1990: same-sex-partner households per 100,000 households; percentage of individuals *not* living in households with married parents and children under age nineteen years present; percentage of women in the labor force; percentage of the workforce in professional, scientific, technical, or educational categories; percentage of the over-age-twenty-five population with a bachelor's degree or higher; and percentage of the county population *not* adhering to a church.

The measurement of local institutional reformism versus nonreform may at one time have been a simple matter of distinguishing cities with city managers from those with mayors and cities with district elections from those with at-large elections. Now, however, there is a considerable blending of institutional arrangements as many mayor–council cities have added city manager–like chief administrative officers, and many cities have adopted electoral systems that combine some council members elected at large and some elected by ward. Recent work suggests that by the late 1990s, only about one-fifth of all cities fit into the pure reformed or pure nonreformed category. The remainder are hybrids (Frederickson, Wood, and Logan 2001; Frederickson and Johnson 2002).

Consistent with this new reality, the measurement approach for local institutional arrangements used here is an additive index of *non*-reformism that combines a score for chief executive arrangement (coded 0 if there is a city manager and no directly elected mayor, 1 if there is a city manager but the mayor is directly elected, 2 if there is a strong mayor and an appointed chief administrative officer, and 3 if there is a strong mayor and no appointed chief administrative officer) with a score for council election arrangement (scored 0 if all are elected at large, 1 if most are elected by district but there are some at-large members, 2 for the special case of a city with all district elections except for two members elected from "superdistricts," and 3 if all are elected by district). To assess the mediating effects of local institutional arrangements, an interaction term (the index of nonreformism multiplied by the index of cultural unconventionalism) is used.

The extent to which a city's economy puts it in a privileged position or a desperate one may be measured, and indeed conceptualized, in a variety of different ways. For simplicity and for consistency with the major, existing study of subnational governmental stance toward the sex industry (Smith 1999), per capita income is used.

RESULTS

When only bivariate relationships are considered, neither fragmentation nor inelasticity is significantly associated with governmental action vis-à-vis the sex industry. The former correlation[4] is 0.135 and the latter is −0.074. Hence, there is no evidence for the metropolitan structure hypothesis in its simplest form (H_1).

However, as Hypothesis 2 stipulates, a more appropriate assessment of the direct effects of metropolitan structure requires multivariate analysis, in which the relevant metropolitan structure measure is investigated while other, theoretically important, variables are controlled. Table 8.1 presents the results of ordered logit analyses,[5] in which each measure of metropolitan structure is modeled along with the key indicators representing cultural, economic, and institutional explanations of variation in city officials' actions vis-à-vis the sex industry.

The results show that, as hypothesized, a community's level of cultural unconventionalism predicts a more permissive official posture toward the sex industry, and that wealthier communities are more restrictive of the sex industry. However, cities with the more politicized and neighborhood-oriented institutions of nonreformed government are *not* predisposed toward aggressive restriction of the sex industry. Finally, the impact of cultural unconventionalism is not mediated by the extent to which local governing institutions are nonreformed.

Most important for the purposes at hand, table 8.1 shows that with these factors controlled, fragmentation has precisely the impact hypothesized—officials in core cities of more fragmented metropolitan areas are harsher in their handling of the sex industry than are officials in less fragmented metropolitan areas. By contrast, the other indicator of metropolitan structure—inelasticity—is not a significant predictor of official action.

Hypothesis 3, however, suggests that metropolitan structure is best understood as mediating the impact of subcultural, economic, and local insti-

Table 8.1. Official Action Toward the Sex Industry: Multivariate Analysis

A. MODELS USING FRAGMENTATION AS THE MEASURE OF DECENTRALIZATION

	Model 1	Model 2
(a) Fragmentation	−0.231 (0.021)	−0.282 (0.007)
(b) Index of unconventional culture	3.087 (0.001)	4.474 (0.001)
(c) Index of nonreformism	−0.013 (.928)	−0.105 (0.486)
(d) Interaction of (b) and (c)	—	−0.555 (0.118)
(e) Income	−0.001 (000)	−0.001 (0.001)
N	97	97
Pseudo R^2	0.10	0.11

B. MODELS USING INELASTICITY AS THE MEASURE OF DECENTRALIZATION

	Model 1	Model 2
(a) Inelasticity	0.012 (0.446)	0.009 (0.600)
(b) Index of unconventional culture	2.980 (0.002)	3.186 (0.006)
(c) Index of nonreformism	0.030 (0.842)	−0.002 (0.992)
(d) Interaction of (b) and (c)	—	−0.112 (0.751)
(e) Income	−0.001 (0.003)	−0.001 (0.015)
N	97	97
Pseudo R^2	0.10	0.07

Note: Figures shown are ordered logit coefficients and (in parentheses) significance levels, except where otherwise indicated.

tutional forces on officials' handling of the sex industry. Table 8.2 presents the results of a pair of ordered logit analyses testing this thesis. Panels A and B show that, whichever indicator of metropolitan decentralization is used, the results are consistent with the hypothesis that metropolitan fragmentation mediates the impact of sociocultural forces on governmental officials' response to the sex industry.

As table 8.2 shows, *when the metropolitan context is fragmented (or inelastic)*, higher levels of unconventional community subculture are associated with local action that is more permissive with respect to the sex industry, while lower levels of unconventionalism are linked with official action that is less permissive and generally consistent with traditionalistic preferences for restrictions or crackdowns. However, *when the metropoli-*

Table 8.2. Official Action Toward the Sex Industry: Multivariate Analysis with Metropolitan Structure Mediating

A.	Highly Fragmented Areas (Score of 3 or More)	Less Fragmented Areas (Score of 2.87 or Less)
Index of unconventional culture	16.386 (0.003)	1.699 (0.096)
Income	−0.004 (0.010)	−0.004 (0.061)
Index of nonreformism	0.883 (0.016)	−0.712 (0.028)
N	39	58
Pseudo R^2	0.26	0.09

B.	Inelastic Areas	Elastic Areas
Index of unconventional culture	10.439 (0.001)	1.788 (0.132)
Income	−0.002 (0.001)	−0.001 (0.138)
Index of nonreformism	0.556 (0.048)	−0.250 (0.316)
N	40	57
Pseudo R^2	0.20	0.10

Note: Figures shown are ordered logit coefficients and (in parentheses) significance levels, except where otherwise indicated.

tan context is not fragmented (or is elastic), the association between cultural unconventionalism and official action toward the sex industry is much smaller in magnitude and statistically insignificant. These results suggest that, apart from any other considerations about the sex industry, core city officials in decentralized metropolitan areas are pressed to respond to the socioculturally defined preferences of their citizens, whereas officials in more centralized contexts are not.

The results with respect to income are also consistent with the mediating effects hypothesis. Among core cities of either fragmented or inelastic metropolitan areas, the wealthier cities are more aggressively restrictive of the sex industry, whereas the officials of poorer core cities are constrained by their circumstances to tolerate an industry that, while unsavory, is at least a going enterprise and potentially one that supports certain elements of the city's convention and tourism aspirations. By contrast, the linkage between core city wealth and tolerance of the sex industry does not hold in less fragmented and elastic cities. Though the coefficients are in the same direction as those for cities in fragmented or inelastic contexts, they are not statistically significant.

As in the examination of direct effects, the results with respect to local governing institutions are contrary to expectations. They suggest that *in more decentralized metropolitan contexts (whether fragmented or inelastic)*, governing arrangements that are politicized and neighborhood focused are linked with a *more permissive* stance toward the sex industry; and though there is no significant association between the index of nonreformism and official action on the sex industry in elastic settings, the negative and significant coefficient for less fragmented areas suggests that it is in this *less* localistic context that the politicization and localism of nonreformed institutions translates into harsh action against the sex industry.

FUNCTIONAL COORDINATION DESPITE DECENTRALIZATION

The findings presented so far highlight the importance of metropolitan decentralization in fostering governmental responses to the sex-industry issue that are based upon competition rather than cooperation with other local governments. But what of the claim that, even in metropolitan areas that are structurally decentralized, a great deal of cooperative, coordinated problem solving can nevertheless occur through joint efforts among local governments? Public choice theorists have long argued that the existence of interlocal service agreements, functional consolidation, and other formal or informal agreements among local governments can yield coordination even in fragmented and inelastic settings. And the policing function that is central to at least one aspect of local response to the sex industry has long been cited as evidencing just such cooperation and coordination. Ostrom, Parks, and Whitaker (1978) document numerous examples of interlocal cooperation and coordination involving the police, and Finney (1997) notes that in the Los Angeles area, more than 45 percent of jurisdictions provide police service through intergovernmental agreements of some kind.

However, the significance of measures of metropolitan decentralization in the quantitative analyses presented above casts a shadow on expectations of "governance without government" consolidation with respect to sex-industry regulation. And when narrative histories of the case study cities' recent experience with the sex industry are examined, they reveal relatively little in the way of interlocal cooperation and coordination with respect to sex-industry regulation, especially in the more fragmented metropolises where such joint efforts are presumed to be especially important compensatory devices.

There are two clear examples of cooperation or coordination with respect to policing prostitution. In 1995, Western City[6] collaborated with two suburban municipalities to conduct simultaneous prostitution stings so that, in the words of one police official, "We don't just push them back and forth across the borders." And in the mid- to late 1990s, Valley City police cooperated with police from several jurisdictions in the metropolitan area to coordinate their efforts in battling a prostitution industry that had begun to use tanning salons as a front and that had begun to involve international prostitution rings locating in the area. Although the information sharing and coordinated arrest actions in these cases epitomize the possibilities for interlocal cooperation, it is notable that the examples are from two jurisdictions with relatively low fragmentation scores. Similar examples were not evident among the study jurisdictions with higher fragmentation scores.

There are also, in principle, other important institutions for achieving a coordinated, even unified response to the sex industry despite metropolitan decentralization. One of the ways of having a more coordinated, regional approach even in a fragmented metropolitan area involves the emergence of the urban county. As Miller (2002, 107) notes, to the extent that county governments become active in areas that effect multiple municipalities within the county, they "serve to further the regionalizing of metropolitan America." And there is some evidence of coordinating institutions involving the core urban county. In some metropolitan areas, land use planning and regulation are functionally centralized through the existence of joint city–county land use commissions or control boards. In South City, such a joint city–county land use control board engaged in efforts in the mid-1990s to change zoning regulations so as to confine adult entertainment businesses to light or heavy industrial zones. Countywide officials with prosecutorial powers can also be instrumental in imposing a uniform stance toward the sex industry that discourages undesirable businesses in both the core city and surrounding areas.

There is evidence that core county district attorneys in both the South City and Border City metropolitan areas played such roles. Though the South County prosecutor's crusade against topless clubs ultimately foundered when legal challenges by the clubs were successful, the Border County prosecutor's crusade against pornography and obscenity led to a string of successful prosecutions that appear to have discouraged sexually explicit businesses from locating throughout the area. Meanwhile, in the River City metropolitan area, two core county officials—a prosecutor and a judge—were instrumental in getting the city to adopt a "john school"—

an innovative approach that focuses on the customers of prostitutes—sentencing them to a program that educates them about the various personal and societal costs that the use of prostitutes' services entail.

As important as these various cooperative arrangements may be in principle, they appear in practice to have very little effect on the overall climate for official action with respect to the sex industry in decentralized metropolitan areas. This is in part because some of the cooperative arrangements are actually being undertaken in the metropolitan areas that are already relatively centralized—that is, those that score relatively low on fragmentation and inelasticity. And though collaborative, integrating institutions involving core county officials may have what Miller (2002) calls a "regionalizing effect," that effect will be minimized in multicounty metropolitan areas where the core county and the core city are similarly "divorced" from a substantial portion of metropolitan suburbia. For all these reasons, functional coordination within the sectors that deal with the sex industry does not appear to go very far to compensate for the competition and lack of coordination that a decentralized metropolitan setting entails.

DISCUSSION

Core city activists often complain that their community is a "dumping ground" for a host of unwanted land uses, objectionable facilities, and unregulated practices that simply would not be tolerated in suburbia; and research on a variety of locally unwanted land uses involving facilities for redistributive services confirms that their complaints are justified. Are core cities similarly the dumping grounds for LULUs involving the sex industry? The research reported here focuses only on core cities and offers no direct assessment of the comparative pervasiveness of sex-industry LULUs in core cities and their respective suburban areas.

However, the results indirectly suggest some limited support for this extension of a key equity-based argument. The results show that, among core cities in decentralized metropolitan settings, there is a significant connection between core city economic disadvantage and more permissive treatment of the sex industry—a finding that can be interpreted as revealing how the desperation for economic development that is to be found in core cities of limited wealth forces them to accept a larger sex-industry presence to establish an economic niche for the city.

By the same token, the "dumping ground" interpretation must be tempered by the finding that in decentralized metropolitan areas, the socioculturally defined preferences of residents are a much more substantial factor than city wealth in determining the sex-industry stance of core city officials. Thus, though economic distress partly determines which core cities are dumping grounds for sex-industry LULUs, the powerful influence of community subculture shows that official actions concerning the sex industry are largely constrained by responsiveness to what can be tolerated within the community's dominant value system.

Public choice theory has always been controversial from the viewpoint of those who argue that the metropolitan "marketplace" of governments is relatively inaccessible to many core city residents, either because of a lack of personal resources for mobility or exclusionary practices by suburban jurisdictions, thus forcing core city residents to endure a package of service quality and tax levels that may be far from what they prefer. Viewed from the standpoint of this equity-based argument, the findings here with respect to subculture are somewhat reassuring. They suggest that, at least with respect to this key morality issue, core city residents do not have to endure a policy position on the sex business that is far from their cultural values.

By the same token, the findings suggest that public officials in the core cities of *some* highly fragmented and inelastic metropolitan areas face an interesting dilemma. On the one hand, it is precisely in such metropolitan areas that subcultural forces are at their strongest, driving officials in unconventional settings to be more tolerant of risqué businesses and officials in conventional settings to be more inclined toward prostitution crackdowns and more restrictive regulations on sexually explicit businesses. But it is also in decentralized metropolitan areas that core city officials are constrained by economic development imperatives toward a more permissive posture toward the sex industry. In unconventional cities, this poses no conflict. Officials can both accommodate culturally derived preferences of the citizenry *and* cater to their presumptions that the sex industry is necessary for the city to build a better future in the convention and tourism sector. But for officials in conventional cities, there will be crosscutting pressures stemming from the socioculturally based values of the community, which demand a relatively restrictive posture toward the sex industry, and economic considerations, which demand a permissive posture. Though cynics might suggest that money always trumps morality, the results here suggest that the subcultural politics of morality have a more substantial impact than economic considerations.

But the cross-cutting pressures facing public officials in economically distressed, conventional cities may lead them to respond to the community's subcultural values through symbolic action that gives the *appearance* of strict regulation of the sex industry while allowing prostitution and sexually explicit businesses to flourish. For example, crackdowns on prostitution (i.e., law enforcement sweeps that generate high volumes of arrests) are, for purposes of this analysis, treated as unfavorable action toward the sex industry, and in some cases they may function as such. However, they can all too easily function as high-profile actions that only give the appearance of "doing something" about a perceived problem, while those arrested are quickly back in action.

In this regard, Miller, Romenesko, and Wondolkowski (1993, 313) characterize city policy with respect to prostitution as a relatively meaningless regulatory strategy involving periodic crackdowns that are followed by periods of relative inattention; even when there are crackdowns, they typically involve only visible prostitution—that is, streetwalkers—while prostitution in other settings (e.g., escort services, massage parlors) is allowed to go on. Similarly, the adoption of what appear to be highly restrictive regulations and licensing standards for nude dancing establishments may in reality mean relatively little if implementation and enforcement are haphazard.

But regardless of whether action is symbolic or substantive, the clearest implication from this research is that metropolitan decentralization does evoke an arms race of anti-sex-industry action. This may be viewed as a good thing by those opposed to the sex industry. But such action, especially if undertaken as a pressured response to what neighboring jurisdictions are doing, can have a variety of negative consequences. To the extent that prostitution crackdowns function as more than symbolic shows, they may do no more than to simply move prostitution around within the metropolitan area—an outcome that does not really solve the public health or other problems of prostitution. And the "arms race" against nude dancing, pornographic movie theaters, and the like may lead cities to enact restrictions that subsequently bury them in expensive litigation and that ultimately cannot withstand constitutional scrutiny.

Furthermore, if the results observed here are at all generalizable to morality issues more broadly, metropolitan decentralization may have an adverse impact on cities' handling of important public health problems. Consider, for example, needle-exchange programs (NEPs), which provide clean needles to intravenous drug users to fight the spread of HIV/AIDS infection among intravenous drug users. Although many NEPs try to use their contact with drug abusers as a vehicle for encouraging them into drug treatment programs (Bertram et al. 1996, 170), NEPs are controversial because many people view them as inappropriately sending the message that an immoral behavior—drug abuse—is tolerated. It is for this reason that they fall into the morality policy category. Although the larger project from which the sex-industry cases for this analysis were drawn does not include enough needle exchange cases for a parallel, quantitative analysis, logical extension of the findings here would lead us to expect that the greater the extent of metropolitan decentralization, the more difficult it will be for core city officials to initiate or sustain NEPs.

APPENDIX: STUDY CITY SELECTION PROCESS

The study design envisioned explanations for variation in city governments' handling of morality issues that center not only on the institutional arrangements that are the focal interest here but also on two other categories of independent variables: the sociocultural character of the community, and the economic status of the community. For purposes of study city selection, a key variable for each category of explanation was defined, and corresponding data were collected for each of the fifty-two cities in the United States with a population of at least 300,000. With respect to the city's economic health, population change (1980–90) served as a rough indicator of where the city falls on the continuum from declining local economies to booming ones. With respect to the sociocultural character of the community, the percentage of the population in nonfamily households served as a rough indicator of where the community falls on Rosdil's (1991) conventional–unconventional sociocultural dimension.

The fifty-two cities were winnowed down to those that are both (1) plus or minus 0.75 standard deviation above the mean on percentage of the population in nonfamily households and (2) plus or minus 0.75 standard deviation above the mean on population change, yielding the set of fourteen cities shown in table 8.3, which also presents information on each city's governing institutions. (*Note:* Pseudonyms replace actual city names because the fieldwork protocol called for the promise of anonymity for interviewees, who occupy key decision-making positions in the study cities.) The selection of study cities from each cell maximized the variance of the values of two of the key explanatory variables and minimized the problem of collinearity between those two explanatory variables. To accomplish the same goals with respect to institutional arrangements, study cities were selected within each cell with an eye toward maximizing variation in both aspects of governmental structure.

Table 8.3. Study Site Matrix

Growing, Unconventional	Declining, Unconventional
High growth	
Hill City (at-large; city manager)[a]	River City (district; mayor)[a]
Western City (mostly district; mayor)[a]	Border City (at-large; city manager)[a]
Modest growth	Capital City (unique)
Port City (at-large; mayor)[a]	
Metro City (district; mayor)[a]	

Growing, Conventional	Declining, Conventional
Valley City (district; mayor)[a]	Lake City (at-large; mayor)[a]
Coastal City (at-large; city manager)[a]	South City (district; mayor)[a]
Southwest City (district; city manager)	Rustbelt City (mixed; mayor)
Sunbelt City (district; city manager)	

[a]Selected as a study city.

ACKNOWLEDGMENT

I wish to acknowledge the National Science Foundation, which provided support for this project through Grant 9904482; and I would like to thank the faculty associates whose work on six of the study cities was critical to the project: Yvette Alex-Assensoh, Susan Clarke, Richard DeLeon, Janet Flammang, Michael Rich, and Marjorie Sarbaugh-Thompson.

NOTES

1. Ironically, this logic yields an interpretation that is quite opposite that of a more historical analysis of the reform movement. The latter might suggest that, as products of the sentiments that drove the reform movement, reform cities might be more apt to prefer crackdowns on morality questions.
2. For the larger project from which the data were drawn, local officials' actions with respect to any of the morality issues studied were initially placed into one of six categories on the basis of the field researcher's assessment of the evidence from both interviews and documentary evidence. The six categories (later condensed to five) range from actions that are most favorable to actions that are least favorable to whichever side of the issue is challenging the status quo (e.g., gay rights activists, needle exchange activists, and, in the case of the sex-industry issue, decency activists who op-

pose prostitution or sexually explicit businesses). *Repression* involves action by authorities to discourage collective action. *Nonresponsiveness* occurs when officials take up the policy demands of activists but ultimately make an authoritative decision that is adverse to activists' claims. *Evasion* involves efforts to avoid confrontations with morality issue activists—through symbolic gestures to defer, delay, or defuse their demands. *Responsiveness* involves action that affirms the claims of activists challenging the legal status quo. *Hyperactive responsiveness* also involves authoritative action in support of status quo challengers. However, following Downs (1989) it involves unusual responsiveness in that decisions are made hastily, normal procedures are supplanted by extraordinary ones, and concerns about constitutionality are ignored.

Because only a handful of cases met all these specifications of hyperactive responsiveness, this category was ultimately collapsed into the general responsiveness category. Finally, *entrepreneurial instigation* occurs when government officials take the initiative to push morality issues onto the agenda even in the absence of overt pressure for it by constituency groups. Because the focus of this analysis is on the sex industry (rather than decency activists opposing it), the language of permissive versus restrictive or favorable versus unfavorable action *toward the sex industry* is used—a reversal of the original categorization but one that logically flows from it. Thus, an action that is nonresponsive to decency activists' demands for a crackdown on adult businesses is treated here as a relatively permissive action vis-à-vis the sex industry, while an action that involves local officials instigating a crackdown on adult businesses even in the absence of public pressure for it is treated here as a very restrictive action vis-à-vis the sex industry.

3. For five of the study cities from which cases were drawn, the metropolitan area is straightforwardly defined as the MSA. However, the other five study cities are in consolidated metropolitan statistical areas (CMSAs), leading to the necessity of choosing between defining the relevant metropolitan area as the primary metropolitan statistical area (PMSA) or the CMSA. For purposes of this analysis, the PMSA was used.

4. Because the dependent variable is measured at the ordinal rather than the interval level, Spearman's rho correlation coefficients rather than Pearson correlation coefficients are reported.

5. Because the dependent variable is measured at the ordinal rather than the interval level, ordered logit rather than the ordinary least squares (OLS) regression analysis is used. It might be argued that because maximum-likelihood-estimation methods such as ordered logit are indeterminate with samples less than about 500 cases and because OLS estimates are quite reliable with ordinal data beyond four values, OLS analysis methods should be used. Unfortunately, although the data for the dependent variable were measured on an ordinal scale that included five values, the decency cases at issue here encompass only four values (i.e., there were no instances of repression of prodecency activists). Nevertheless, table 8.1 was cross-checked against a

parallel analysis run with OLS regression. The results were essentially unchanged (i.e., the sign, relative magnitude, and statistical significance of the various coefficients were the same).

6. Here and throughout the chapter, pseudonyms rather than actual city names are used because the fieldwork protocol called for the promise of anonymity for interviewees, who occupy key decision-making positions in the study cities.

REFERENCES

Altshuler, Alan, William Morrill, Harold Wolman, and Faith Mitchell, eds. 1999. *Governance and Opportunity in Metropolitan America.* Washington, D.C.: National Academy Press.

Berkman, Michael B., and Robert E. O'Connor. 1993. Do Women Legislators Matter? Female Legislators and State Abortion Policy. In *Understanding the New Politics of Abortion,* ed. Malcolm Goggin. Newbury Park, Calif.: Sage.

Berry, Frances S., and William D. Berry. 1990. State Lottery Adoptions as Policy Innovations: An Event History Analysis. *American Political Science Review* 84: 395–416.

———. 1992. Tax Innovation in the States: Capitalizing on Political Opportunity. *American Journal of Political Science* 36: 715–42.

Bertram, Eva, Morris Blachman, Kenneth Sharpe, and Peter Andreas. 1996. *Drug War Politics: The Price of Denial.* Berkeley: University of California Press.

Boyne, George. 1992. Is There a Relationship between Fragmentation and Local Government Cost? *Urban Affairs Quarterly* 28: 317–22.

Button, James W., Barbara A. Rienzo, and Kenneth Wald. 1997. *Private Lives, Public Conflicts: Battles over Gay Rights in American Communities.* Washington, D.C.: CQ Press.

Carr, Jered B., and Richard C. Feiock. 1999. Metropolitan Government and Economic Development. *Urban Affairs Review* 34: 476–88.

Clark, Terry Nichols, and Ronald Inglehart. 1998. The New Political Culture: Changing Dynamics of Support for the Welfare State and Other Policies in Postindustrial Societies. In *The New Political Culture,* ed. T. N. Clark and V. Hoffmann-Martinot. Boulder, Colo.: Westview Press.

Clingermayer, James C., and Richard C. Feiock. 2001. *Institutional Constraints and Policy Choice.* Albany: State University of New York Press.

Dolan, Drew A. 1990. Local Government Fragmentation: Does It Drive Up the Cost of Government? *Urban Affairs Quarterly* 26: 28–46.

Downs, Donald. 1989. *The New Politics of Pornography.* Chicago: University of Chicago Press.

Dreier, Peter, John Mollenkopf, and Todd Swanstrom. 2001. *Place Matters.* Lawrence: University Press of Kansas.

Elkins, David. 1995. Testing Competing Explanations for the Adoption of Type II Policies. *Urban Affairs Review* 30: 809–39.

Feiock, Richard C., and James C. Clingermayer. 1992. Development Policy Choice: Four Explanations for City Implementation of Economic Development Policies. *American Review of Public Administration* 22: 49–64.

Finney, Miles. 1997. Scale Economies and Police Department Consolidation: Evidence from Los Angeles. *Contemporary Economic Policy* 15: 121–28.

Frederickson, H. George, and Gary Alan Johnson. 2002. The Adapted City: A Study of Institutional Dynamics. *Urban Affairs Review* 36: 872–96.

Frederickson, H. George, Curtis Wood, and Brett Logan. 2001. How American City Governments Have Changed: The Evolution of the Model City Charter. *National Civic Review* 90: 3–18.

Gerard, Jules B. 1996. *Local Regulation of Adult Businesses*. Deerfield, Ill.: Clark, Boardman, and Callaghan.

Gilmore, John. 1999. Zoned Out. *Planning* 65: 151–53.

Inglehart, Ronald. 1990. *Culture Shift in Advanced Industrial Society*. Princeton, N.J.: Princeton University Press.

Judd, Dennis. 1999. Constructing the Tourist Bubble. In *The Tourist City*, ed. D. Judd and S. Fainstein. New Haven, Conn.: Yale University Press.

Lowery, David, and William E. Lyons. 1989. The Impact of Jurisdictional Boundaries: An Individual-Level Test of the Tiebout Model. *Journal of Politics* 51: 73–97.

Miller, David Y. 2002. *The Regional Governing of Metropolitan America*. Boulder, Colo.: Westview Press.

Miller, Eleanor M., Kim Romenesko, and Lisa Wondolkowski. 1993. The United States. In *Prostitution: An International Handbook on Trends, Problems, and Policies*, ed. Nanette J. Davis. Westport, Conn.: Greenwood Press.

Miranda, R., and D. Rosdil. 1995. Development Policy Innovation in American Cities. In *Local Economic Development: Incentives and International Trends*, ed. N. Walzer. Boulder, Colo.: Westview Press.

Mooney, Christopher Z. 2001. The Public Clash of Private Values: The Politics of Morality Policy. In *The Public Clash of Private Values*, ed. C. Mooney. New York: Chatham House.

Morgan, David R., and Michael W. Hirlinger. 1991. Intergovernmental Service Contracts: A Multivariate Explanation. *Urban Affairs Quarterly* 27: 128–44.

Morgan, David R., and Patrice Mareschal. 1999. Central-City/Suburban Inequality and Metropolitan Political Fragmentation. *Urban Affairs Review* 34: 578–95.

Norrander, Barbara, and Clyde Wilcox. 1999. Public Opinion and Policymaking in the States: The Case of Post-Roe Abortion Policy. *Policy Studies Journal* 27: 707–22.

Osinski, Bill. 1995. Focus on Atlanta's Nude Dance Clubs Naked City. *Atlanta Journal and Constitution*, December 10, 4G.

Ostrom, Elinor, Roger B. Parks, and Gordon P. Whitaker. 1978. *Patterns of Metropolitan Policing*. Cambridge, Mass.: Ballinger.

Pierce, Patrick A., and Donald E. Miller. 1999. Variations in the Diffusion of State Lottery Adoptions: How Revenue Dedication Changes Morality Politics. *Policy Studies Journal* 27: 696–706.

Reichl, Alexander J. 1997. Historic Preservation and Pro-Growth Politics in U.S. Cities. *Urban Affairs Review* 32: 513–35.

Rosdil, Donald L. 1991. The Context of Radical Populism in U.S. cities: A Comparative Analysis. *Journal of Urban Affairs* 13, no. 1: 77–96.

Rusk, David. 1993. *Cities without Suburbs.* Washington, D.C.: Woodrow Wilson Center Press.

Savitch, Henry V., Collins, D. Sanders, and J. Markham. 1993. Ties That Bind: Central Cities, Suburbs, and the New Metropolitan Region. *Economic Development Quarterly* 7: 341–57.

Schneider, Mark. 1986. Fragmentation and the Growth of Local Government. *Public Choice* 48: 255–64.

Schneider, Mark, and Paul Teske. 1992. Toward a Theory of the Political Entrepreneur: Evidence from Local Government. *American Political Science Review* 86: 737–47.

———. 1993. The Progrowth Entrepreneur in Local Government. *Urban Affairs Quarterly* 29: 316–27.

Sharp, Elaine B. 2002. Culture, Institutions, and Urban Officials' Responses to Morality Issues. *Political Research Quarterly* 55: 861–83.

Smith, Kevin B. 1999. Clean Thoughts and Dirty Minds: The Politics of Porn. *Policy Studies Journal* 27: 723.

Stephens, G. Ross, and Nelson Wikstrom. 2000. *Metropolitan Government and Governance.* New York: Oxford University Press.

Studlar, Donley T. 2001. What Constitutes Morality Policy? A Cross-National Analysis. In *The Public Clash of Private Values*, ed. Christopher Z. Mooney. New York: Seven Bridges Press.

Weitzer, Ronald. 2000. The Politics of Prostitution in America. In *Sex for Sale*, ed. R. Weitzer. New York: Routledge.

Wonders, Nancy A., and Raymond Michalowski. 2001. Bodies, Borders, and Sex Tourism in a Globalized World: A Tale of Two Cities—Amsterdam and Havana. *Social Problems* 48: 545–72.

MARK SCHNEIDER AND JACK BUCKLEY

CHARTER SCHOOLS AS A TOOL TO REFORM LOCAL SCHOOLS BY TRANSFORMING GOVERNANCE

In his introduction to this volume, Richard Feiock argues that "the config-uration of local governments is central to governance issues in metro-politan areas" (chapter 1). In chapter 2, Ronald Oakerson elaborates fur-ther on the importance of government organization for a wide range of democratic activities. One of the most important arguments in Oakerson's chapter is that "polycentricity creates civic space—opportunities for con-structive engagement among citizens and officials." Oakerson further sug-gests that we should expect government organizations that embrace poly-centricity "to be more participatory, to feature stronger representation, to engage in more effective problem solving related to the care of common goods (the maintenance of the public realm), to allow for more vigorous public entrepreneurship, and to strengthen the accountability of officials to the citizens they serve."

These are all very strong claims, and the logic behind them is well pre-sented by Oakerson. However, and perhaps reflecting Oakerson's status as a veteran of the long debates over how best to govern metropolitan regions, we find that his argument supporting polycentricity is framed too heavily in terms of a very old struggle over the structure of metropolitan government. Although the controversy over polycentric organization versus metropolitan consolidation produced an important intellectual investigation into the relationship among government, governance, and the local market for public goods, we believe that the focal point of the argument has run its course and that the political movement to create megametropolitan governments has, at least for now, been consigned to the dustbin of history.

In addition, as the debate about polycentricity versus consolidation has played out during the course of the past few decades, it has become highly stylized and stagnant and increasingly removed from the fundament in which the most productive studies of urban politics have always been embedded. Indeed, for us, one of the bedrocks in the study of urban politics has been its focus on what really matters to real people—a concern for where the "rubber meets the road" (or hits the potholes, when a city is not doing its job). In turn, we believe that the intellectual contributions of Oakerson's exploration in chapter 2 can and should be applied to the broader analyses of specific urban services—in so doing, the claims he makes for the benefits of polycentricity can in fact be tested empirically, and the intellectual vigor of the monocentric/polycentric debate enlivened. This challenge motivates the work of this chapter.

In the following pages, we look at how the governance of education—the most expensive and arguably the most important local government service—is being transformed by changing the way in which school systems are organized. In particular, we look at changes in "parent/consumer" satisfaction and participation as a result of expanding school choice.

We can think of the current attempts to promote school choice in terms parallel to the monocentric/polycentric debate. Historically, education has in effect been a monopoly service in which schools are provided by a single district and the enrollment choices of parents and students have been limited by residential location and geographical catchment areas defined by central administrators. With a growing recognition of the failure of many American schools, a wide variety of reforms became common—prominent among them the expansion of school choice. Indeed, during the past decade, school choice has become one of the most highly visible tools aimed at changing the very governance of education. (See Chubb and Moe 1990; Schneider, Teske, and Marshall 2000. For an analysis of the historical roots of choice and estimates of the number of students affected, see Henig 1998.)

Not surprisingly, given the narrow focus on metropolitan governance that has marked so much of the debate about polycentric versus monocentric government, the vibrant and extensive school reform movement has developed without any recognition of the overlap of the concerns of the movement supporting school choice and the movement supporting polycentric metropolitan governance. But clearly the concerns and the goals of these two movements overlap. Moreover, the outcomes we document in this chapter are congruent with the outcomes predicted by the polycentric reform movement; we present evidence below that the decentralization of schooling and the corresponding replacement of a monocentric organization of school districts with a more polycentric one are indeed "opening up civic space" and creating the conditions under which parents are learning civic skills and increasing the responsiveness of government officials.

In the pages that follow, we describe the evolution of the theory linking school choice to citizen behavior, we look at some evidence regarding the satisfaction of parents with their new schools, we show how the decentralization of schools has in fact created civic space that parents are filling, and we present some evidence of increased responsiveness of school officials to parents. All of these outcomes are congruent with the expectations laid out in chapters 1 and 2 by Feiock and Oakerson.

AN EVOLVING THEORY OF THE EFFECTS OF CHOICE

All forms of choice—such as alternative schools, magnet schools, open enrollment programs, vouchers, and charters—expand the range of options available to parents. But the earliest choice reforms did so within the structure of the existing educational establishment; they did not have a view of systemic change. Open enrollment plans, especially interdistrict ones, were among the first choice reforms to present a broader challenge to the existing structure of school systems, but they often did so without an articulated vision of how schools should be organized to operate more effectively.

More recently, reformers have explicitly coupled school choice with a broad challenge to the institutional arrangements that define the U.S. system of education. Current reforms share a vision of good schools and school systems that emphasize small, autonomous schools, unburdened by a large administrative structure, and they share a desire to create a stronger school community bringing parents, students, teachers, and administrators into cooperative, supportive relationships. In this vision, parents are not only given the power to choose but are also viewed as essential to school governance and the creation of effective schools. The emphasis on parents and community intimately links to the concern for high student performance—improved performance becomes an outcome built on a strong school community (Ravitch and Viteritti 1996; Brandl 1998; Hill, Pierce, and Guthrie 1997). In short, in remarkable (and largely unrecognized) symmetry to the claims of polycentricity, choice is viewed as a means of transforming school governance, parent participation, and community *and* as a means of achieving higher performance.

Many of the foundations for the argument linking choice to both performance and community can be traced back to the work of John Chubb and Terry Moe, who, in their 1990 book, *Politics, Markets, and America's Schools,* forged a clear link between choice, markets, and the relationships between stakeholders in schools. Chubb and Moe argued that while school reform has often been considered an "insider's game," played by bureaucrats, administrators, teachers, and other school professionals and fought over what may seem like technical problems (e.g., curriculum, testing procedures, or tenure), the bedrock issue in school reform is the issue of governance: Who has the right to participate in the decision-making process, and at what levels? Chubb and Moe considered this to be a "constitutional" issue, because the outcome of this debate structures subsequent decisions made by school-level officials, parents, and students.

Clearly, then, in any discussion of school choice, we must be concerned with the interaction between the way schools are organized and parental behavior. The work reported in this chapter presents some findings from a survey of parents in Washington, D.C., a city with a large and growing charter school population.[1] Our goal is to show how changes in parental behavior flowing from the expansion of charter schools and the concurrent change in the form of school governance is congruent with the predictions regarding citizen outcomes flowing from theories of polycentric governance.

A FOCUS ON CHARTER SCHOOLS

Across the United States, charter schools have become one of the most frequently used means of increasing choice among educational alternatives. Having first appeared in the early 1990s and then gathered momentum throughout the past decade, charter schools now play an increasingly large role in the public education system. As of the fall of 2002, 2,700 charter schools were operating in thirty-six states and the District of Columbia, serving more than 575,000 students—representing a double-digit rate of increase from previous years (Center for Education Reform 2002).

One apparent reason for the growth in enrollments is that parents and students think charter schools are better than the traditional public schools in which the students were previously enrolled. Finn and others (1997) found that a large majority of parents felt that charter schools in which their children were presently enrolled were better than the traditional public schools they left, with respect to class size, school size, teacher attentiveness, and the quality of instruction and curriculum. In contrast, fewer than 5 percent of parents found their new charter schools inferior. Finn and others also found high levels of student satisfaction, ranging across the whole gamut of school conditions, including teachers, technology, class size, and curriculum. Teachers also seem to like charter schools, with high levels of teacher satisfaction having been found among charter teachers (Koppich 1998).

There are several foundations for this greater satisfaction with charter schools. Perhaps the strongest is that of the increased "allocative efficiency" flowing from the choice process, in which parents get to choose the schools that deliver the kind of education they want for their children. This particular link between choice, allocative efficiency, and higher parent satisfaction dates at least as far back as Friedman's original argument in favor of vouchers in the 1950s (Friedman 1955)[2] and constitutes a core argument upon which choice is built (Schneider, Teske, and Marschall 2000). The argument is quite simple: Education is a multidimensional good, and parents legitimately want different things from the schools. According to popular theories of school reform, as choice expands, new schools will emerge offering distinct curricula and strong programs, and existing schools will innovate and improve in response to this competition. *Allocative efficiency* increases as children can attend a school that is higher on the dimensions of education that the parent (and the student) hold important, and *productive efficiency* increases as the forces of competition lead schools to improve.

This idea clearly parallels many of the core ideas upon which the model of polycentric governance is built; rather than a "one-size-fits-all" set of services delivered by a single metropolitan government, in a polycentric system, the diversity of preferences held by citizens is matched by a diversity of products offered in the local market for public goods. Choice becomes central, as the means that allows the "citizen/consumer" to buy the product mix he or she desires. In the polycentric system, this match increases the welfare of individuals and increases satisfaction with the services they receive. In turn, it is not surprising that a core intellectual theme supporting the polycentric approach is the Tiebout model, with its emphasis on shopping around in a local market for public goods and "voting with one's feet" as a mechanism for increasing efficiency in the production and consumption of local public goods (Tiebout 1956; also see Schneider 1989).

To a considerable degree, these same ideas are built into the argument for school choice, but the theories supporting the argument are rather different than in the polycentric debate. Most notably, rather than building on Tiebout, as noted above, prochoice school reformers often turn to the economist Milton Friedman and his emphasis on the importance of consumer sovereignty in the choice of schools (on this idea of "sovereignty" in school choice, see especially Coons and Sugarman 1978; Raywid 1989; and Goldring and Shapira 1993).

In addition to increasing this match between preferences and schools, choice has the potential to change schools themselves—making schools better "products" available for parents to choose among. Indeed, fundamental to the push for choice is the idea that choice unleashes competitive pressure on the schools that makes them improve—and charter schools are often seen as a central tool to leverage such change (see, e.g., Teske et al. 2000).

While the debates still rage about the effect of choice on academic outcomes, other outcomes from choice are less contested, which can increase parental evaluations of schools they choose and which may produce other valuable outcomes as well. For example, many charter schools are designed to improve the relationship between administrators, teachers, parents, and students, in turn creating what Coleman (1988) refers to as "functioning communities." In these communities, the tighter links from the school to parents, families, and students is associated with better educational experiences—and all parties, including teachers, in turn should be more satisfied (Driscoll 1993). This link underlies the basic finding developed in the research on "effective schools," which has shown that good interpersonal relations between members of the school community and shared beliefs and values combine to promote good teaching and a positive learning environment. This may be particularly true for charter schools, which often have a culture (and sometimes a written contract) that provides parents with opportunities to influence school management and to become more involved with the processes of school governance and functioning (e.g., see Peterson and Campbell 2001; Finn et al. 1997).

To the extent that a stronger community grows out of choice, two positive outcomes may flow. First, parental satisfaction with their children's schools should increase. Second, as parents become more involved in school governance, they may learn the skills of citizenship. As we will discuss below, strong school communities can thus be part of building a stronger civil society.

Finally, choice may put pressure on administrators, teachers, and staff to be more "consumer friendly." As Hassel writes with regard to charter schools as schools of choice: "Charter schools cannot take their 'customers' for granted. Their very survival depends on the degree to which families believe the schools are responding to family preferences and working hard to provide the education they demand" (Hassel 1999, 6; also see Teske et al. 2000). Thus, rather than being isolated from the demands of parents, the competitive pressures on charter schools should increase their responsiveness to parent demands.

Clearly, all these ideas—increased citizen participation, competition between service providers, increased responsiveness and citizen satisfaction with services—are themes that resonate with outcomes directly predicted by advocates of the polycentric form of government and inherent in the institutional collective action framework developed by Feiock. In the rest of the chapter, we present empirical evidence about the extent to which these expectations are met. We begin with the issue of satisfaction.

ARE PARENTS WHO CHOOSE SCHOOLS MORE SATISFIED?

In the previous section, we presented strong reasons to believe that choice should lead to higher evaluation of schools by parents. Indeed, almost every study of schools of choice, regardless of type of choice and regardless of evidence of improved performance (or lack thereof), has found higher levels of parent satisfaction (e.g., on vouchers, see Bridge and Blackman 1978; Moe 2001; Peterson 1998; and Witte, Bailey, and Thorn 1992; on charter schools, see Bierlin 1997; and on public school choice, see Schneider, Teske, and Marschall 2000). Moe also finds that parents who changed residences to "buy" good schools were more satisfied, and he argues, "residential choice—the choice of specific neighborhoods or specific schools—promotes greater satisfaction" (Moe 2001, 84).

In this and the following sections, we explore the extent to which the charter school experience in Washington, D.C., leads to greater satisfaction.

To do this, we asked parents to assign an overall grade (on the familiar grade scale of A to F) to their child's school and then to three specific dimensions of the school (teachers, the principal, and the school facility). We compare the grades assigned by charter school parents to those of parents whose children remain in the traditional D.C. public schools.

A Caveat about Using Grades as Indicators

Before proceeding with the analysis, we note that there is a well-known pattern when using grades as measures of parent evaluations of schools—parents almost inevitably give high grades to their children's schools. For example, the *Phi Delta Kappan*, a well-known education journal, regularly asks a sample of parents to grade their children's schools. In 2001, 51 percent of parents gave their own children's schools either an A or a B—11 percent gave the grade of A, while 40 percent gave a B. Note that the grades parents give to their own children's school are higher than the grades they assign to the nation's schools as a whole (to which only 23 percent gave grades of A or B). And also note that parents are more likely to give high grades than nonparents—fully 62 percent of parents gave grades of A or B to schools. However, we believe that this bias is not important for our analysis, because we are interested in comparing parents in the charter schools and the traditional public schools in the same city.[3]

How Do Parents Grade Their Schools?

In figure 9.1, we present the results of a simple comparison between charter parents and traditional public school parents of the reported grades for teachers, facilities, principal, and school overall. Rather than presenting the differences in means, we instead show the relative frequencies of assigned grades for parents in each group.

The results are unambiguous—charter school parents grade their child's school on every dimension of the school that we measure higher than do D.C. public school parents. In particular, there is a marked increase in the frequency of As assigned by charter parents as compared with their traditional counterparts.[4] In short, increasing choice and moving from a monocentric to polycentric form of school provision has increased citizen satisfaction. We move next to the extent to which charter schools build civic capacity.

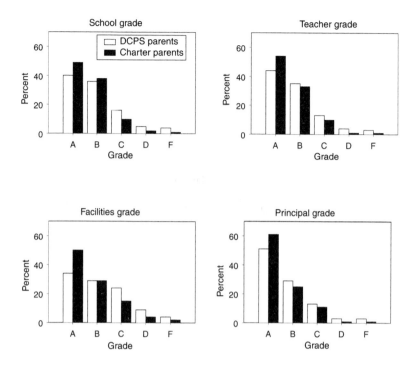

Figure 9.1. Charter School Parents Rate Their Schools Higher
Note: No. of observations = 853. DCPS = D.C. public schools.

ENHANCING CIVIC PRACTICES: POLYCENTRICITY AND SOCIAL CAPITAL

Recall that one of Oakerson's boldest assertions is that government organizations that embrace polycentricity will be more participatory and that citizens in polycentric systems will engage in more effective problem solving in the maintenance of the public sphere. Although the original polycentric arguments developed before the concept of social capital rose to a position of prominence in political science and in contemporary discussions of public policy, clearly the recent debate about the relationship between government and social capital parallels the concerns of the polycentric/monocentric debate.

Although this is not the place to engage in a lengthy discussion of the concept of social capital (the reader is referred to Putnam 2000 or Adler and Kwon 2002, among the many, many pieces that exist), we touch briefly on some highlights in the evolution of the term as it pertains to our concerns.

Though the term "social capital" had been in use in sociology for some time, Coleman (1988) brought it into wider circulation, providing a model in which he attempted to import the economists' principle of rational action into the analysis of social systems. In this work, Coleman's goal was to analyze these systems with a specific focus on the centrality of social organization in the generation of social capital (Coleman 1988, 98). The components of social systems that Coleman identified as generating social capital (obligations, expectations and trustworthiness, more developed informational channels and networks, and effective sanctions on behavior that violates norms) are central to almost every analysis of social capital that has followed.

Whereas Coleman laid an exceptionally strong foundation for the emerging study of social capital, it was Putnam's work, and especially his use of the metaphor of "bowling alone," that propelled the idea of social capital to center stage, certainly in political science and in policy debates. Though many debates swirl around the term, there is wide agreement that social capital is important because it engenders norms of trust, reduces transaction costs, and mitigates the intensity of conflicts, thereby facilitating the emergence of cooperative behavior. Note that these are all central themes in Feiock's theory of intergovernmental cooperation (also see Lubell et al. 2002).

Feiock and Oakerson emphasize the importance of government structure in creating social capital, but that position is controversial. In fact, many analysts of social capital dismiss the idea that government and governance matter. Most notably, though Fukuyama (1995) emphasizes the importance of social capital in creating strong communities, he does not assign a significant role to government in maintaining this link. Specifically, he argues that "social capital is like a ratchet that is more easily turned in one direction than another; it can be dissipated by the actions of governments much more readily than those governments can build it up again" (Fukuyama 1995, 62).

Similarly, for Putnam, social capital is generated mostly through the quality of secondary associations and not through government action. Putnam suggests that "civic virtue" comes from experience in associational life; that experience teaches "skills of cooperation as well as a sense of shared responsibility for collective endeavors" (Putnam 1993, 90). In this regard, Putnam's reference to the "amateur soccer clubs, choral societies, hiking clubs, bird-watching groups, literary circles, hunters' associations, Lions Clubs, and the like in each community"(1993, 91) is often cited, and his image of "bowling alone" (Putnam 1995) summarizes the notion of the decline of such nonpolitical associations in the United States as an indicator of its decline in social capital. The essence of Putnam's social capital framework is the claim that civil societies that are characterized by a richly variegated associational life will also tend to exhibit norms of political equality, trust, and tolerance, and active participation in public affairs.

In contrast to this society-centered approach, from the polycentrist perspective, how governance is structured clearly matters. The polycentric perspective is also linked to the debate about the relative importance of "bottom-up" versus "top-down" processes in nurturing social capital. In this debate, it is agreed that associational life is important in the creation of social capital, but the importance of the broader context within which this associational life either flourishes or starves is at issue—and the role of governance structures is at the center of this debate.

Here again, the tone of the debate has been set by Putnam's work. As Levi (1996, 52) notes, Putnam has a "romanticized image of community," and his concept of social capital is "resolutely society-centered." According to Levi, these views lead Putnam to emphasize a "bottom-up" approach to the generation of social capital in which social capital is generated by grassroots activity and a vibrant associational life. Though this view is broadened in his most recent book (Putnam 2000), the role he assigns to government is still limited.

Yet there is a clear institutional and social context that defines the boundaries of civic engagement and the extent of citizen involvement in social and political events. That is, there are top-down processes that directly affect the quality of grass-roots activity and associational life. In turn, the opportunities for associational groups to generate social capital are affected by the structure and policies of government. From this perspective, the structure of governance cannot be neglected in the creation of social capital and strong communities.

Several analysts have reached the same conclusion and have emphasized the importance of institutions in creating social capital. Levi (1996, 50) argues for the central role of government in the analysis of social capital. Specifically, she argues that more emphasis should be directed toward citizens' trust in government and the central role of governmental performance on that trust. Other analysts have been more directly concerned with participation, which should be viewed as a contributor to the creation of social capital, than with social capital itself. Skocpol (1995), for example, argues that civic associations and citizen participation in the United States developed less from the purely local decisions of collections of individuals and more as a consequence of the institutional patterns of federalism, electoral politics, and political parties.

Similarly, Rosenstone and Hansen (1993) provide empirical evidence to support the argument that participation is indeed firmly rooted in the institutions and organizations that mobilize individuals and structure their involvement. And Verba, Schlozman, and Brady (1995) have also found that networks of recruitment, embedded in institutions and organizations, are critically important for explaining civic volunteerism. They find that institutions "incubate the social networks through which solicitations for activity are mediated. In addition, institutions themselves generate requests for participation" (1995, 369).

Another body of work, focusing on what is often called "policy feedback," reinforces the importance of the relationship between government policies and citizenship, specifically linking the treatment clients of government programs receive to their broader orientations toward government and political action. Schneider and Ingram argue that the way in which government policies are implemented "affect people's experiences with the policy and the lessons and messages they take from it. These, in turn, influence people's values and attitudes, . . . their orientations toward government, and their political participation patterns" (Ingram and Schneider 1995, 442; also see Schneider and Ingram 1997; Mettler 2002).

Although this debate has focused on the general role of government, not surprisingly, scholars of education have also been concerned with the specific role that schools play in the creation of social capital. Indeed, Coleman's classic article specifically addressed the question of how effective school communities can create social capital (Coleman 1988). Other work has followed this lead. For example, Schneider and Coleman (1993), Bryk, Lee, and Holland (1993), and Astone and McLanahan (1991) have examined social capital as a function of the interactions between administrators, teachers, parents, and children. Schneider, Teske, and Marschall (2000) show how choice creates social capital as measured by parent–teacher association membership, volunteering at a school, and sociability—all central dimensions of social capital. Bryk and Schneider argue that "a broad base of trust across a school community lubricates much of a school's day-to-day functioning . . . and is especially important as we focus on disadvantaged schools" (2002, 5–6). Moreover, Bryk and Schneider link high levels of trust not only to the smooth operation of the school but ultimately also to academic performance.

From this perspective, the structure of governance and the practices of government matter. In the next section, we show that the institutional arrangements that increase parental control over the schools their children attend may be able to open up civic space and create the foundations for an increase in social capital.

CHARTER SCHOOLS, SOCIAL CAPITAL, AND BUILDING COMMUNITY

One of the guiding principles of today's educational reform is that effective schools require stronger ties between the various "stakeholders" in the process of education—and, in particular, researchers and reformers have emphasized the importance of parental involvement with the schools in creating strong schools and improving education. Indeed, in a good system of education, the relationships between parents, students, and teachers are more cooperative and interdependent. Studies have shown that many charter schools seek to encourage greater parental involvement. According to Corwin and Flaherty (1995), charter schools have higher rates of parent involvement than other schools. These higher rates stem from a culture as well as policies that nurture (if not quite force) higher involvement (see Peterson and Campbell 2001; Finn et al. 1997; Schwartz 1996; Miron and Nelson 2000).

In one of the most comprehensive studies of charter schools to date, Hill and others (2001) argue that charter schools, while freed from many of the bureaucratic rules and regulations governing traditional public schools, have other key "accountability" relationships, especially with the teachers they hire and on whose performance the schools depend, and with families whom the schools must attract and satisfy (2001, 6). They further argue that "what both schools and parents are learning about charter schools is that choice creates reciprocal accountability. Parents must meet the school's expectations as well as vice versa. This relationship is new and it is one of the charter school movement's greatest contributions to public education" (p. 32).

Relating directly to our study population, Henig and others (1999) also find evidence that public charter schools in Washington do reach out to parents—but they also report that charter schools are finding that enticing parents to become more involved is an exceedingly difficult task.

Our survey of Washington parents contained a battery of questions that allow us to assess the extent to which the attitude of parents toward other members of the school community differ across charter and traditional public schools. We believe that the attitudes we assess in this battery tap into the foundations for more intense parental involvement in the schools and for a more effective school community. We begin with these school-based questions and then investigate broader questions of political efficacy to assess the extent to which more participatory attitudes developed in the schools may spill over to the broader political environment.

Attitudes Show Stronger Trust among School-Based Stakeholders

In creating our set of questions, we built directly on the work of Burns and Kinder (2000), who were seeking to assess the stock of social capital in the nation as reflected in the level of trust that individuals have in others. Burns and Kinder argue that trust is one of the enduring foundations for cooperation and for democratic politics. But more important, they argue that trust is rooted in specific practices and dispositions toward neighbors, coworkers, and others in general; people earn trust by "keeping promises, by being honest and respectful, and by being courteous" (Burns and Kinder 2000, 7).

Clearly, these behaviors can provide the foundation for reciprocity, which in turn is one of the foundations for effective school communities. We adopted the Burns and Kinder approach and asked parents with children in the D.C. public schools and the D.C. public charter schools the following questions:

I'm going to ask you a few questions about the parents of the students who attend your child's[5] school:

- Thinking about those parents, would you say they *treat others with respect* all of the time, most of the time, some of the time, hardly ever, or never?
- What about *irresponsible*? Would you say that *irresponsible* describes these parents extremely well, quite well, not too well, or not well at all?
- Would you say that the word *honest* describes these parents extremely well, quite well, not too well, or not well at all?

The questions were then repeated, substituting teachers for parents.

In figure 9.2, we compare the level of responses for parents in the charter schools and traditional public schools. Across the six measures, we find that charter parents have more favorable attitudes toward their children's teachers and toward other parents. In every case, there is a statistically

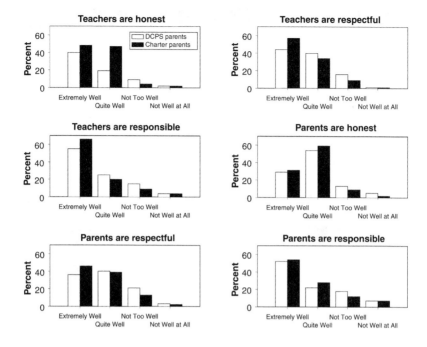

Figure 9.2. Charter School Parents Have More Favorable Attitudes Toward Teachers and Other Parents

Note: No. of observations = 663. DCPS = D.C. public schools.

and substantively significant increase in frequency of response to either of the two most favorable options (or both) for the charter parents.

Attitudes versus Behavior

Clearly, there is strong evidence that parents in D.C. charter schools have developed attitudes supportive of strong and participatory communities. What about behavior? We look first at school-based behavior and then move on to parental behavior in a larger sphere of "traditional" political actions.

In the top two panels of figure 9.3, we present our findings that parents in charter schools are much more likely to interact with both teachers and administrators on a frequent basis than are parents with children in the traditional D.C. public schools. Couple these frequent interactions with the

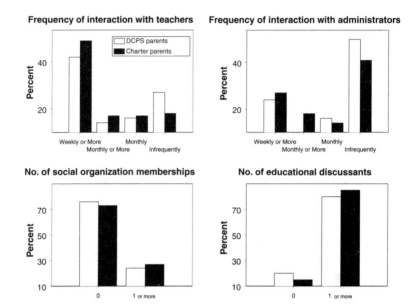

Figure 9.3. Charter School Enrollment Leads to More Participatory Behavior

Note: No. of observations = 996. DCPS = D.C. public schools.

positive feelings that charter parents express toward their child's teachers (demonstrated in figure 9.2), and we have the conditions for the positive policy feedback loop identified by Schneider and Ingram, and by Mettler, as essential for building good citizenship. In short, we believe that the form of governance built into charter schools has begun to open up new and vibrant civic space. But does participation in that school-based community spill over into other political activities?

Unfortunately, according to our study, the benefits that have flowed from the form of governance built into the charter schools have not been completely generalized to broader political attitudes and behavior. Membership in civic organizations and "sociability" (the face-to-face exchange of information) are both critical to most conceptions of social capital. As the bottom two panels of figure 9.3 show, we find modest effects of charter schools on both measures.

When we move to traditional measures of political efficacy, however, we find little or no evidence that being in a charter school community has any effect. This is evident in figure 9.4, in which we compare the groups

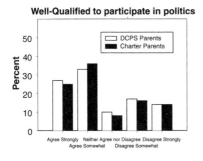

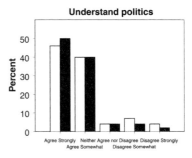

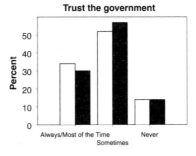

Figure 9.4. Charter School Enrollment Appears to Have Little Effect on Broader Attitudes

Note: No. of observations = 889. DCPS = D.C. public schools.

on three such measures—trust in government, belief in qualification to participate, and belief in understanding politics.

This lack of spillover may be the result of many processes, two of which immediately come to mind. First, Schneider, Teske, and Marschall did find much broader effects of school choice in District 4 in New York City—but the choice program there has been in effect for many more years than in D.C. charter schools. One possibility for the lack of spillover effects in Washington thus may be time related; it may take time for social capital built in a specific domain, in our case, schools, to spread to other forms of behavior. A second possibility is that though school governance has been transformed and leads to enhanced trust and participation within the school community, the political system in Washington (and nationally) remains unchanged. Thus the skills and attitudes developed in a reformed environment cannot be generalized to an unreformed monocentric political and policy environment.

ARE CHARTER SCHOOLS MORE PARENT FRIENDLY?

If charter schools, as schools of choice, are seeking to redefine the relationship between parents and teachers, what about the relationship between parents and staff? One characteristic of monopolies is often their lack of responsiveness toward their customers. In contrast, in more competitive systems, suppliers, lacking the "luxury" of a captive market, have greater incentives to be responsive to consumers. In the world of educational reform, we have seen that creating a welcoming environment for parents is essential for the success of schools. In the next section, we compare the extent to which parents are welcomed by schools in the charter and the traditional public school sectors.

To assess the level of "parent friendliness" of charter schools and traditional public schools, we sent a set of parents to visit a sample of Washington, D.C., schools (both public charter and traditional public schools). We asked them to report on how well they were treated, and how responsive the school staff was to their requests for information about programs and performance. In appendix B, we describe our procedures in more detail.

Parents entered the schools and asked staff about the school's programs and performance. We asked these parents to evaluate how well they were treated by the staff. As is evident in figure 9.5, charter school staff were evaluated as being both more responsive and more courteous than the staff of the D.C. public schools.

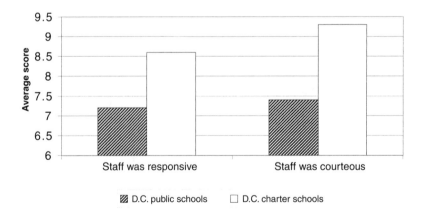

Figure 9.5. How Well Did Staff Treat Parents?

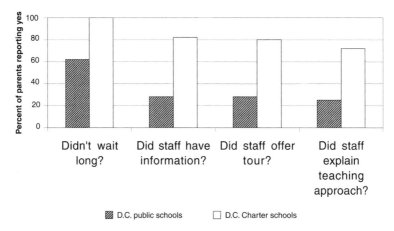

Figure 9.6. Additional Indicators of How Parents Were Treated

In addition, we also asked parents to evaluate how responsive the staff was to a series of requests for information about school programs—this is important because information is a foundation for choice. As is evident in figure 9.6, on each measure that we report, the charter schools were by far more responsive to the legitimate requests of parents for information essential to judging the appropriateness of a school for a prospective student.

We recognize that our findings are based on small numbers (although our parents did visit almost half the charter schools that were open at the time of this research, and they did visit 15 percent of the traditional public schools), and it may be that their relatively smaller size enables their staff to be more parent friendly; nonetheless, the patterns here are strikingly consistent. The staffs of charter schools are more welcoming and open to parents.

We did not study directly how this behavior might affect the behavior of schools accustomed to their traditional monopolistic position; however, the introduction of competition in the institutional collective action and polycentric frameworks posits pressure on all governments to be more responsive to the needs of their citizens. On the basis of their study of forty-nine school districts in five states facing increased competition from charter schools, Ericson and others (2001) found exactly that kind of behavior. More specifically, Ericson and others found that the leadership in nearly two-thirds of the districts changed their public relations policies and parent involvement activities in response to the challenge of charter schools.

Among the most important changes these researchers report in districts facing increased competition from charter schools are the following:

- Almost half of the districts increased their emphasis on customer service, becoming more responsive to parents, and surveying parents to determine their level of satisfaction.
- Over one-third of the districts increased their focus on communication with parents or changed their methods of communication with current and prospective parents and community members.
- About 20 percent reported an increased focus on parent involvement and had expanded their district-wide or school-based parent involvement programs. (Ericson et al. 2001, 14–15)

CONCLUSION

The results we report in this chapter are consistent with the expectations of the advocates of polycentric government and Feiock's institutional collective action framework. Perhaps most important, we have demonstrated that charter schools "open up" space for citizens to develop attitudes supportive of trust and ultimately, we believe, for broader democratic participation. In short, there is a link between the vitality of civil society and the structure of local governance—a highly decentralized structure of local education built around charter schools is providing opportunities for citizens to build social capital and learn democratic practices.

Oliver found that the frequency of contacting local officials and attending different types of civic meetings steadily declines as cities get larger. He also found that people in the smallest metropolitan places (under 5,000 in population) were more likely to work informally with neighbors to solve local problems (Oliver 2001, 42). We believe that the logic of Oliver's argument extends even further downward. Small, decentralized schools of choice, with a philosophy of inclusion, apparently can recreate the results that he found across metropolitan communities. And this can happen in low-income communities in the central city, where the problems of governance may be most severe.

In short, it is not only the configuration of the governance across *metropolitan communities* that matters—the configuration of governance structures *within central cities* can also affect the nature of civil society, the way in which citizens look at their governments, and the way in which these agencies treat citizens. We believe that these findings can breathe new life into the polycentric/monocentric debate and help build a strong micro-level foundation for the concerns that Feiock addresses in his institutional collective action framework.

APPENDIX A: SAMPLE DESIGN AND RESPONSE INFORMATION AND PROBIT RESULTS

Telephone interviews were conducted among parents with at least one child in a Washington, D.C., charter or public school. Interviews were conducted from September 12 through December 11, 2001. All interviews were conducted by the Center for Survey Research of the State University of New York at Stony Brook. As a quality-control measure, up to fifteen callbacks were made per telephone number, and an attempt was made to convert all initial refusals. Almost 52 percent of all interviews were validated on a subsequent call after the interview had been completed.

Sample Design

Parents were drawn from two distinct samples—a random-digit-dialing (RDD) sample of parents with children in charter and public schools, and a sample of parents from a list of charter school parents provided by D.C. charter schools.

RDD sample. A list-assisted method of RDD was used to obtain phone numbers in the main state sample. Numbers were purchased from Genesys. Under the list-assisted sampling method, random samples of telephone numbers are selected from blocks of 100 telephone numbers that are known to contain at least one *listed* residential telephone number. These blocks with at least one residential telephone number are referred to as "1-plus" working blocks. According to Survey Sampling, Inc., roughly 40 percent of telephone numbers in 1-plus working blocks are residences, although proportions are as high as 54 percent when the blocks are screened for nonworking and business numbers.

Charter school sample. A sample of charter school parents was drawn from a list of parents in thirty D.C. charter schools. Not all numbers provided by the schools were valid, and numbers that lacked the appropriate number of digits were eliminated before sampling. This left 7,389 valid phone numbers for charter school parents.

Response Rates

RDD sample. A total of 24,000 numbers were drawn from 1-plus blocks for the main state sample. Of those, Genesys screened out 5,214, or 21.73 percent, as numbers that it detected as nonworking or listed in directories of known business numbers. This left 18,786 numbers that were actually dialed by the Center for Survey Research. Just over 46 percent of all these numbers ($N = 8,734$) were coded as nonhouseholds. This included all numbers coded as disconnected, a business, government office, fax, changed number, or mobile phone. It also included 1,550 numbers estimated as non-households. These 1,550 numbers were drawn from all numbers that were called 15 times and at which there was ever only a busy signal or no answer (but no answering machine). On the basis of research by Westat, we estimated that 75 percent of these numbers are nonhouseholds. This number was based on national estimates. There were 2,067 numbers in this category, and 1,550 were estimated to be nonworking numbers.

This left 9,956 possible households in the sample of phone numbers. Of the remaining households, 6,523 (941 parents plus 5,582 nonparents or non-D.C. parents) were successfully screened for the presence or absence of children in D.C. public or charter schools. This resulted in a screening rate of 62.81 percent for parenting status, which was obtained by dividing the number of D.C. parent plus nonparent households by the total number of households in the sample. The total number of parenting households in D.C. is estimated at 922, or 14.13 percent of all screened households. This number omits 264 (245 nonparents and 19 not in D.C.) households that were coded in at least one contact attempt as parents in Washington but were later recoded as nonparents. The status of these numbers is ambiguous and could reflect the actions of respondents to avoid an interview. If all these numbers are included (probably an overestimate), the incidence of parents in the sample increases to 18.18 percent.

Of those households identified as containing a parent of a child in a D.C. school ($N = 922$), interviews were completed in 504, resulting in a cooperation rate of 54.66 percent. This results in an overall response rate in the sample of 34.33 percent. This response rate is calculated by combining the screening rate for parenting households (62.81 percent) with the cooperation rate among households identified as parents of children in D.C. schools (54.66 percent).

Charter school sample. Charter school parents were drawn from a list of names provided by thirty charter schools in Washington. The sample was self-weighting, which means that unequal numbers of parents were drawn from each school. The number of parents selected from a school was directly proportional to the size of the school in relation to all charter school parents in Washington. Thus, more parents were chosen from large schools and fewer from small schools. This ensured that the final sample represented parents in charter schools across the D.C. area. The sampling fraction was 29.63 percent, or just under a third; parents were drawn in successive random waves from the lists. There were 7,389 parents listed (after bad numbers were culled from the lists), and 2,189 numbers were included in the sample.

Of the total 2,189 numbers, just over 23 percent of all numbers ($N = 522$) were coded as nonhouseholds. This includes all numbers coded as disconnected, a business, government office, fax, changed number, or mobile phone. It also includes 6 numbers estimated as nonhouseholds. These 6 numbers are drawn from all numbers that were called 15 times and at which there was ever only a busy signal or no answer (but no answering machine). There were 24 numbers in this category, and 18 (75 percent) were estimated to be nonworking numbers.

This leaves 1,667 possible households in the sample of phone numbers. Of the remaining households, 1,321 (811 parents plus 441 nonparents and 69 non-D.C. parents) were successfully screened for the presence or absence of children in D.C. public or charter schools. Given the messy status of the sample, we assumed that numbers were not associated with parents of students in charter schools until this had been verified by an interviewer. This resulted in a screening rate of 79.24 percent for parenting status, obtained by dividing the number of D.C. parent plus nonparent households by the total number of households in the sample.

Of those households identified as containing a parent of a child in a D.C. school ($N = 811$), interviews were completed in 510, resulting in a cooperation rate of 62.89 percent. This results in an overall response rate in the main sample of 49.83 percent. This response rate is calculated by combining the screening rate for parenting households (79.24 percent) with the cooperation rate among households identified as parents of children in D.C. schools (49.83 percent).

APPENDIX B: WASHINGTON, D.C., SCHOOL VISITS

Procedures

We contracted D.C. Parents for School Choice, a Washington-based non-profit organization, to train parents to visit both public charter and D.C. public schools. These parents were trained to pose as parents thinking about enrolling their child in the particular school and were trained to ask for information pertinent to that enrollment decision. Because all the parents selected had recently enrolled their own children in new schools, they were already familiar with enrollment procedures and what to look for in schools.

We prepared a checklist for each parent to fill out reporting on the observed conditions in the schools they visited and reporting on what they experienced during their visit. As is evident from the checklist, parents were asked to report on two different aspects of their visit. First, they were asked to evaluate the physical condition of the school and its neighborhood, and, more subjectively, to evaluate the "feel" of the school. Second, parents were instructed to ask school personnel for information about the programs the schools offer and to ask for materials about programs and performance. This second type of data was gathered to assess differences between schools in the degree to which the school staff was responsive to requests for information that is important in allowing parents to evaluate the appropriateness of the schools for their children. (*Note:* In the following list, K = kindergarten, ES = elementary school, JHS = junior high school, MS = middle school, and SHS = senior high school.)

D.C. Public Charter Schools Visited

Chamberlain (K–5)
Children's Studio School (ungraded, age 3–8 years)
Community Academy (K–3)
Edison-Friendship (K–5)
Options (grades 5–8)
The SEED School (grades 7–8)
Village Learning Center (K–8)
Cesar Chavez Public Charter High School (grades 9–10)
IDEA academy (grades 9–12)
Richard Milburn (grades 9–12)
The Washington MST (grades 9–12)

Traditional D.C. Public Schools Visited

Amidon Elementary School
Anne Beers Elementary School
Brightwood Elementary School
Brookland Elementary School
Cook Elementary School
Davis Elementary School
Lafayette Elementary School
Langdon Elementary School
Mildred Green Elementary School
Miner Elementary School
Randle Highlands Elementary School
Backus Middle School
Brown Middle School
Browne Junior High School
Jefferson Junior High School
Lincoln Middle School
Ballou Senior High School
Coolidge Senior High School
Eastern Senior High School
School Without Walls Senior High School

ACKNOWLEDGMENT

The work reported in this chapter was supported by grants from the Smith Richardson Foundation and the National Science Foundation.

NOTES

1. See appendix A for a description of the sample, response rates, and other technical details.
2. Allocational efficiency was also central to J. S. Mill's arguments in "On Liberty," but most discussions of this aspect of the benefits of school choice tend not to go further back than Friedman.
3. For more on these grades, see www.pdkintl.org/kappan/k0109gal.htm#1a. This pattern is also evident among our respondents; e.g., overall, more than 40 percent of the parents in our sample gave their own child's school a grade of A, but only 9 percent gave the D.C. schools as a whole an A grade.

4. The results presented in figure 9.1 (and in the other sections below) are simple comparisons—the only statistical procedure used is the weighting of the frequencies to account for probability of selection to the sample and to adjust for our intentional oversampling of charter parents. In other research using these data, we consider the possibility of bias due to self-selection to charter schools on the part of the parents (Schneider, Buckley, and Kucsova 2003; Buckley and Schneider 2003). All the results presented in this chapter are robust to this effect—indeed, correcting for self-selection actually increases the differences between the groups on average.

5. Earlier in the survey, if the parent respondent had multiple children in the D.C. schools, she was asked to answer all the questions in the survey about the child whose birthday was next (to randomize the survey). In the actual survey, where we use the term "your child," the computer-assisted telephone interview system actually inserted the name of the child upon whom the survey was focused.

REFERENCES

Adler, Paul S., and Seok-Woo Kwon. 2002. Social Capital: Prospects for a New Concept. *Academy of Management Review* 27, no. 1: 17–40.

Astone, N. M., and S. S. McLanahan. 1991. Family Structure, Parental Practices and High-School Completion. *American Sociological Review* 56, no. 3: 309–20.

Bierlin, Louann. 1997. The Charter School Movement. In *New Schools for a New Century*, ed. D. Ravitch and J. Viteritti. New Haven, Conn.: Yale University Press.

Brandl, John E. 1998. Civic Values in Public and Private Schools. In *Learning from School Choice*, ed. Paul E. Peterson and Bryan C. Hassell. Washington, D.C.: Brookings Institution Press.

Bridge, Gary R., and Julie Blackman. 1978. *A Study of Alternatives in American Education*. Family Choice in Schooling Series, vol. 4. Santa Monica, Calif.: RAND Corporation.

Bryk, Anthony S., Valerie E. Lee, and Peter B. Holland. 1993. *Catholic Schools and the Common Good*. Cambridge, Mass.: Harvard University Press.

Bryk, Anthony S., and Barbara Schneider. 2002. *Trust in Schools*. New York: Russell Sage Foundation.

Buckley, Jack, and Mark Schneider. 2003. *Government Institutions and Civic Participation: Can Charter Schools Build a Foundation for Cooperative Behavior?* Occasional Paper 75. New York: National Center for the Study of Privatization in Education, Columbia University, Teachers College. Available at www.ncspe.org/publications_files/OP75.pdf.

Burns, Nancy, and Donald Kinder. 2000. *Social Trust and Democratic Politics*. Available at ftp://ftp.nes.isr.umich.edu/ftp/resourcs/psreport/2000pilot/burns2000.pdf.

Center for Education Reform. 2002. Charter School Highlights. Available at http://edreform.com.

Chubb, John E., and Terry M. Moe. 1990. *Politics, Markets, and America's Schools*. Washington, D.C.: Brookings Institution Press.

Coleman, James S. 1988. Social Capital in the Creation of Human Capital. *American Journal of Sociology* 94 (supplement): S95–S120.

Coons, John E., and Stephen D. Sugarman. 1978. *Education by Choice: The Case for Family Control*. Berkeley: University of California Press.

Corwin, Ronald, and John Flaherty. 1995. *Freedom and Innovation in California's Charter Schools*. San Francisco: WestEd.

Driscoll, Mary. 1993. Choice, Achievement, and School Community. In *School Choice: Examining the Evidence*, ed. E. Rassell and R. Rothstein. Washington, D.C.: Economic Policy Institute.

Ericson, John, and Debra Silverman, with Paul Berman, Beryl Nelson, and Debra Solomon. 2001. *Challenge and Opportunity: The Impact of Charter Schools on School Districts; A Report of the National Study of Charter Schools*. Washington D.C.: Office of Educational Research and Improvement, U.S. Department of Education. Available at www.ed.gov/pubs/chartimpact/district_impact.pdf.

Finn, Chester, Jr., Bruno V. Manno, Louann A. Bierlein, and Gregg Vanourek. 1997. *Charter Schools in Action: Final Report*. Washington, D.C.: Hudson Institute.

Friedman, Milton. 1955. The Role of Government in Education. In *Economics and the Public Interest*, ed. R. A. Solo. New Brunswick, N.J.: Rutgers University Press.

Fukuyama, Francis. 1995. *Trust: The Social Virtues and the Creation of Prosperity*. New York : Free Press.

Goldring, Ellen B., and Rina Shapira. 1993. Choice, Empowerment, and Involvement: What Satisfies Parents? *Educational Evaluation and Policy Analysis* 15: 396–409.

Hassel, Bryan C. 1999. *The Charter School Challenge*. Washington, D.C.: Brookings Institution Press.

Henig, Jeffrey R. 1998. School Choice Outcomes: A Review of What We Know. Paper presented at the School Choice, Law, and Public Policy conference, School of Law, University of California, Berkeley, April 17–18.

Henig, Jeffrey R., Michele Moser, Thomas T. Holyoke, and Natalie Lacireno-Paquet. 1999. *Making a Choice, Making a Difference? An Evaluation of Charter Schools in the District of Columbia*. Washington, D.C.: Center for Washington Area Studies, George Washington University.

Hill, Paul, Robin Lake, Mary Beth Celio, Christine Campbell, Paul Herdman, and Katrina Bulkley. 2001. A Study of Charter School Accountability: National Charter School Accountability Study. Washington, D.C.: Office of Educational Research and Improvement, U.S. Department of Education.

Hill, Paul, Lawrence C. Pierce, and James W. Guthrie. 1997. *Reinventing Public Education*. Chicago: University of Chicago Press.

Ingram, H., and A. L. Schneider. 1995. Social Construction (Continued)—Response. *American Political Science Review* 89, no. 2: 441–46.

Koppich, Julia. 1998. *New Rules, New Roles? The Professional Work and Lives of Charter School Teachers.* Washington, D.C.: National Education Association.

Levi, Margaret. 1996. Social Capital and Unsocial Capital: A Review Essay of Robert Putnam's Making Democracy Work. *Politics and Society* 24, no. 1: 45–55.

Lubell, M., M. Schneider, J. T. Scholz, and M. Mete. 2002. Watershed Partnerships and the Emergence of Collective Action Institutions. *American Journal of Political Science* 46, no. 1: 148–63.

Mettler, S. 2002. Bringing the State Back in to Civic Engagement: Policy Feedback Effects of the GI Bill for World War II Veterans. *American Political Science Review* 96, no. 2: 351–65.

Miron, Gary, and Christopher Nelson. 2000. *Autonomy in Exchange for Accountability: An Initial Study of Pennsylvania Charter Schools.* Kalamazoo, Mich.: Evaluation Center, Western Michigan University.

Moe, Terry M. 2001. *Schools, Vouchers, and the American Public.* Washington, D.C.: Brookings Institution Press.

Oliver, J. Eric. 2001. *Democracy in Suburbia.* Princeton, N.J.: Princeton University Press.

Peterson, Paul E. 1998. School Choice: A Report Card. In *Learning from School Choice,* ed. P. E. Peterson and B. Hassel. Washington, D.C.: Brookings Institution Press.

Peterson, Paul E., and David E. Campbell. 2001. Introduction. In *Charters, Vouchers, and Public Education,* ed. Paul E. Peterson and David E. Campbell. Washington, D.C.: Brookings Institution Press.

Putnam, Robert D. 1993. *Making Democracy Work: Civic Traditions in Modern Italy.* Princeton, N.J.: Princeton University Press.

———. 1995. Bowling Alone: America's Declining Social Capital. *Journal of Democracy* 6, no. 1: 65–78.

———. 2000. *Bowling Alone: The Collapse and Revival of American Community.* New York: Simon & Schuster.

Ravitch, Diane, and Joseph Viteritti. 1996. A New Vision for City Schools. *Public Interest* 122: 3–16.

Raywid, Mary Anne. 1989. The Mounting Case for Schools of Choice. In *Public Schools of Choice,* ed. J. Nathan. Saint Paul: Institute for Learning and Teaching.

Rosenstone, Steven J., and John Mark Hansen. 1993. *Mobilization, Participation, and Democracy in America.* New York: Macmillan.

Schneider, Anne L., and Helen M. Ingram. 1997. *Policy Design for Democracy.* Lawrence: University Press of Kansas.

Schneider Barbara, and James S. Coleman, eds. 1993. *Parents, Children, and Schools.* New York: Westview Press.

Schneider, Mark. 1989. *The Competitive City.* Pittsburgh: University of Pittsburgh Press.

Schneider, Mark, Jack Buckley, and Simona Kucsova. 2003. *Making the Grade: Comparing D.C. Charter Schools to D.C. Public Schools*. Occasional Paper 71. New York: National Center for the Study of Privatization in Education, Columbia University, Teachers College. Available at www.ncspe.org /publications_files/OP71.pdf.

Schneider, Mark, Paul Teske, and Melissa Marschall. 2000. *Choosing Schools: Consumer Choice and the Quality of American Schools*. Princeton, N.J.: Princeton University Press.

Schwartz, Wendy. 1996. *How Well Are Charter Schools Serving Urban and Minority Students?* ERIC/CUE Digest, no. 119. New York: ERIC Clearinghouse on Urban Education.

Skocpol, Theda. 1995. *Social Policies in the United States: Future Possibilities in Historical Perspective*. Princeton, N.J.: Princeton University Press.

Teske, Paul, Mark Schneider, Jack Buckley, and Sara Clark. 2000. Does Competition from Charter Schools Improve Traditional Public Schools? In *Civic Report*. New York: Manhattan Institute.

Tiebout, C. 1956. A Pure Theory of Local Expenditures. *Journal of Political Economy* 64: 416–24.

Verba, Sidney, Kay Lehman Schlozman, and Henry E. Brady. 1995. *Voice and Equality: Voluntarism in American Politics*. Cambridge, Mass.: Harvard University Press.

Witte, John F., Andrea B. Bailey, and Christopher A. Thorn. 1992. *Second Year Report: Milwaukee Parental Choice Program*. Madison: Robert M. LaFollette Institute of Public Affairs, University of Wisconsin.

JERED B. CARR

WHOSE GAME DO WE PLAY? LOCAL GOVERNMENT BOUNDARY CHANGE AND METROPOLITAN GOVERNANCE

10

The process of how human beings create governance structures based on willing consent was discussed at length by Ronald Oakerson in chapter 2 of this volume. He emphasized that governance structures do not come from governments, but instead result from the efforts of human beings doing the work of civil society. Changes in the governance of a metropolitan area reflect local efforts at problem solving, as the people living in these communities alter existing arrangements of government and governance in ways that best serve their needs and solve their own particular set of problems. Oakerson further suggests that "governance structures provide regularized means for identifying and diagnosing problems, elucidating information, arraying and assessing alternatives, and crafting rule-based solutions, as well as monitoring those arrangements for both implementation and possible alteration." This process appears to reflect self-governance in its purest form.

This chapter builds directly on Oakerson's work in two ways. First, it examines local government boundary change, an activity central to the process of governance in communities. With the possible exception of interlocal agreements, changes to jurisdictional boundaries through municipal annexation (and detachment), municipal incorporation (and disincorporation), the formation (and dissolution) of special district governments, and the merger and/or consolidation of two or more general-purpose governments are the most frequent, most permanent—and perhaps most visible—expressions of governance in metropolitan areas. This chapter examines local government boundary change through the development of a framework that reveals how the state laws governing local government powers, formation, and expansion shape the organization of local governments in the context of strategic and adaptive behavior by local actors. This approach is based on the "local public economies" framework developed in a series of papers by Oakerson and his colleague Roger Parks. Understanding how and why local government boundaries are changed sheds light on an important mechanism of local governance.

A second objective of this chapter is to extend Oakerson's work by examining the actors likely to pursue local government boundary change. Oakerson explains that the process of governance permits local actors to modify the institutional base of government in the community in ways that better meet the needs of the community. The fact that these changes are the product of actions by freely consenting local actors and not imposed through coercion by governments is central to the value of this process. However, as Burns's (1994) study of the formation of local governments showed, many local actors lack the resources to successfully utilize the procedures governing the formation of governments. Indeed, she argued that government formation is a means by which these favored actors lock their private values into ostensibly public institutions. This suggests that governance occurring through local government boundary change may be an expression of only a segment of society and, at best, civic society with a very small "c."

I see this as a potentially serious limitation to the conception of metropolitan governance outlined by Oakerson. If we are to view the problem-solving activities of local actors to be the embodiment of civil society and the resulting governmental arrangements as the expression of the will of the community, then it is important that we understand what, if any, restrictions are placed on participation in this civic space. It seems likely that the primary source of these restrictions is found in the state laws that establish the procedures that must be followed to form or expand governments. The framework presented here illustrates how state laws create the collective action problems that actors face and their likely solutions. In doing so, these laws create the incentives within which local actors act strategically to form and expand governments.

Several of the chapters in this volume examine the obstacles to institutional collective action. The logic of institutional collective action builds on Olson's (1965) logic of collective action to explain the obstacles to collective action on the part of governments. In this chapter, I return to Olson's work to examine the collective action problems faced by local actors in pursuing boundary change. When local government officials, business interests, citizens' groups, and individual citizens seek to form or expand governments, they most often have a variety of options. They may be able to choose among multiple procedures to form or expand the new government, or they may be able to choose among multiple types of governments to achieve their goals. In most instances, citizens have each form of boundary change available as they seek to redraw jurisdictional lines of authority, meaning that the use of annexation instead of consolidation, or incorporation in place of annexation, represents a deliberate choice by local actors.

Particular choices might reflect the efficacy of specific instruments, winning strategies for overcoming collective action problems, or simply the constraints on instrument choice imposed by existing patterns of metropolitan organization. The latter part of the chapter is devoted to exploring why a particular form of boundary is chosen over another. Strategy has been the missing element in previous work. By omitting the strategic behavior of local actors from our models of intergovernmental politics, we have overemphasized the importance of collective action difficulties in explaining the effects of state laws in limiting the powers of local governments. In addition, this omission has led urban scholars to overlook the variety of institutions of local governance available to local actors and to not ask *why* this plethora of options exists. When analyzing these questions, it is useful to ask "Whose game do we play?"

WHOSE GAME DO WE PLAY?

The role of boundaries in defining the choices available to people raises Schattschneider's (1960) question, "Whose game do we play?" Metropolitan areas are not simply fragmented. Instead, as Parks and Oakerson (1989) have observed, these areas are complexly organized. Their local public economies approach to understanding metropolitan organization posits that the complex arrangements characterizing most metropolitan areas are the result of local efforts at problem solving (ACIR 1987; Oakerson and Parks 1989; Parks and Oakerson 1989). Central to this approach is the recognition that while local governments may be "creatures of the state," their formation, expansion, and dissolution result from local action (Oakerson and Parks 1989). Therefore, the complexity we observe in these arrangements is the result of efforts over time by local residents to solve problems using the means provided them by state legislatures.

Oakerson and Parks have given us an important lens with which to examine the question of whose game we play. Metropolitan organization is purposely constructed complexity. It is a monument to past and ongoing efforts at problem solving. The unanswered question is "Whose problems?" Does the organization of governments in metropolitan areas reflect problem solving by the entire community or by more narrow segments from within the community? If we are to view local government boundary changes as they do, as an unqualified constructive activity reflecting local efforts to solve problems, then it is important to understand whether metropolitan organization has a bias. And if so, whose game do we play in local government boundary change?

In his classic work *The Semisovereign People*, Schattschneider proposed that whose game we play is a critical choice in politics because the rules of the game determine the requirements for success. "Resources sufficient for success in one game may be wholly inadequate in another" (Schattschneider 1960, 47–48). He concluded that players seek out games they are able to win, and, when possible, games their opponents are most likely to lose. Bridges's research on efforts to "reform" local governments early in the twentieth century provides an illustration of these tactics. She showed that progressive reformers were successful in changing municipal charters (e.g., council-manager government, nonpartisan elections, at-large elections) in those cities where advocates were able to write the rules to win the game (Bridges 1997; Bridges and Kronick 1999). In other words, it was their game that the local population played, and it became their game, Bridges and Kronick argued, because advocates of these reforms systemically disenfranchised those segments of the community likely to oppose them. "Reform succeeded in the Progressive era less from the support of most voters than from the weakness of their opponents in the West, border states, and South. Crucial to opponents' weakness was suffrage restriction, which changed the composition of local electorates, not incidentally disenfranchising the strongest opponents of municipal reform" (Bridges and Kronick 1999, 703–4).

LOCAL GOVERNMENT BOUNDARY CHANGE DEFINED

For the purposes of this chapter, local government boundary change refers to those changes in the legal boundaries of local governments. The county, and in some states, township boundaries established by state legislatures provide the starting point for local government boundary change. These changes may occur in the following ways: municipal annexation or detachment, special district formation or dissolution, municipal incorporation or disincorporation, and the combining of two or more governments, through either mergers or consolidations. In many instances, these boundary changes leave the underlying framework of county and township boundaries unaltered.

Municipal Annexation or Detachment

By far the most common form of boundary change occurs through the expansion of municipal borders to include adjacent, unincorporated territories. Literally thousands of municipal annexations occur each year in the United States; more than 75,000 annexations occurred during the 1980s alone (Miller 1993). Annexation expands the physical size of the municipality and typically increases the city's population as well. In essence, the municipal government assumes the responsibility for providing infrastructure and services to added populations in exchange for the tax base provided by additional territories.

Detachments are the reverse of annexations, amounting to the reduction of area contained within the jurisdiction of the municipal government. Detachments occur less often than annexations and involve relatively few people. Miller (1993) reported that 1,635 detachments occurred in the 1980s, as compared with more than 75,000 annexations during the same period. Additionally, the population detached from cities during the period 1980–86 amounted to less than 1 percent of the population annexed by municipalities during the same years (Miller 1988). However, individual detachments can be significant actions, especially when the action involves a small town. For example, Miller (1988) reported that the population of McLoud, Oklahoma, was reduced by two-thirds through the detachment of a 20-square-mile section of the city. In reality, detachments may not reflect the desire of citizens to escape the jurisdiction of a municipal government. Many detachments are the reversal of annexation actions that have been invalidated by court orders (Miller 1988).

Special District Formation or Dissolution

The second most frequent avenue to boundary change occurs through the creation of special district governments. Citizens have created thousands of these governments in recent decades, totaling 35,356 units in 2002 (U.S. Census Bureau 2002). Special district governments are created to provide services not currently offered by an existing general-purpose government, or to replace service provision by an existing jurisdiction. Of the 35,536 units in operation in 2002, nearly 91 percent perform a single function and about 20 percent perform natural resource functions, such as drainage, flood control management, and soil and water conservation (U.S. Census Bureau 2002). After natural resources, the most frequent function performed by special district governments is fire protection, followed by water supply, and housing and community development districts (U.S. Census Bureau 2002). Generally, special districts exist independent of county or city governments, and they exercise substantial administrative and fiscal independence from these governments.

Within special district governments, there is substantial variation in geographic scope and acceptable means of financing district activities (Foster 1997). District boundaries may encompass several counties, a neighborhood, or a single property. Depending on the specific enabling law, district revenues may be derived from property taxes, user fees, tolls, or other sources. Although not all district governments are directly formed by local citizens—some are formed by state legislatures or by city and county governments—virtually all are formed through local initiative. As governments go, special districts are relatively easy to establish. Many states have enabling laws that provide for the creation of these governments simply through the petition of a majority of property owners within the proposed borders of the district (Bollens 1986). The petitions are usually submitted to a local city or county government, which has the responsibilities of holding a public hearing and either approving or rejecting the petitioned district (Porter et al. 1992).

Occasionally, special district governments are dissolved by citizen action or by special acts of the legislature. Methods of dissolution vary by state and by the process through which the district was formed. For example, Florida law requires special acts of the legislature to dissolve any district created by the legislature; districts created by county or municipal ordinance must be dissolved in the same way (FDCA 1998). The dissolution of special districts is comparatively rare, and nationwide totals are not currently tracked by any central source, as are the other instruments of boundary change.

General-Purpose Government Incorporation or Disincorporation

A third means of local boundary change occurs through the formation of new subcounty general-purpose governments, which typically are carved out of areas served by county or township governments. As of 2002, the 35,937 subcounty general-purpose governments in the United States governed 154 million people (U.S. Census Bureau 2002). Of these 35,937 units in operation, 19,431 were municipalities and 16,506 were townships (U.S. Census Bureau 2002). Only twenty states, mostly in the Northeast and Midwest, use township governments. States utilizing township governments often also provide for the formation of village governments, general-purpose units with powers greater than township governments but less than those provided to municipalities.

This form of boundary change almost always involves the creation of new municipal governments. The formation of new county and village governments does occur, but both actions are fairly rare; the creation of new township governments does not take place at all. In fact, the trend during the past fifty years has been a slow but steady decline in the number of township governments in most states that have them (U.S. Census of Bureau 2002). Citizens form new municipal units to provide general-purpose local government for a specified population living within a particular geographic area. The structure of the new government and the range of permitted functions and financing are spelled out in the municipal charter. Depending on the state, service provision in these areas before incorporation would have been the responsibility of a township or village government, the county, or, in some instances, no general-purpose government. Similar to the case of special district governments, most states have laws setting out petition requirements for the initiation of incorporation proceedings. However, laws governing the formation of new municipalities usually also require that a majority of residents in the area approve the formation of the new city in a local referendum (ACIR 1992).

In the Northeast, municipal and township governments have essentially similar powers and functions. However, in the Midwest, townships are viewed as minimal governments, and when citizens desire expanded services and more home rule, municipal governments can be formed out of part or all of the area served by the preexisting township government.

In states such as Kansas, Minnesota, and South Dakota, the number of township governments has declined substantially during the past half-century as citizens have formed new municipal units with greater powers (U.S. Census Bureau 2002). In contrast, in states such as Michigan, the number of township governments has not declined significantly even as the state has become more suburban in character. Instead of forming new municipal governments, citizens have more often opted to strengthen the powers of the preexisting township units by adopting charter governments (Carr and Feiock 2004).

Boundary change also occurs through the disincorporation of existing municipal governments. Disincorporations are infrequent and generally involve municipalities with very small populations. For example, Miller (1988) reported that Wittenberg, Missouri, had a total population of four when it disincorporated in 1980. Occasionally, substantially larger communities opt for disincorporation. Two Connecticut cities, Willimantic (14,652) and Putnam (6,855), disincorporated with considerable populations during the 1980s (Miller 1988). It is likely that the infrequency of boundary change through disincorporation is due, at least in part, to the fact that many of these communities choose to join (through merger or consolidation) with other municipalities rather than to disincorporate.

Merger or Consolidation of Governments

Least frequently, boundary change occurs through the unification of existing governments. A merger refers to the joining of two or more incorporated governmental units of the same level. Consolidations involve the unification of two or more governments of different levels, often combining cities and a county government. In theory, governmental consolidations leave only a single organization, although in practice this is rarely achieved (Marando 1974). City mergers are substantially more common than city–county consolidations. Forty-eight city mergers occurred from 1970 to 1988 (Halter 1993), as compared with the 23 city–county consolidations approved out of the 134 proposals put before the public from 1921 to 1996 (Blodgett 1996).

Another important difference between the unification of cities and actions concerning a city and county is the population involved. Most city mergers are between very small cities, and often the population of the merged cities is less than 20,000 (Halter 1993). Although several communities of fewer than 20,000 people have attempted city–county consolidation in recent years (Carr and Feiock 2004), many areas with city–county governments have populations in excess of several hundred thousand people (Campbell and Durning 2000).

The other side of this action, the separation of consolidated or merged governments, is rarely, if ever, done. One reason is that there are not many merged or consolidated governments to split. As has been noted, the vast majority of proposals to consolidate city and county governments have been defeated. A second explanation why these actions are rare is due to reasons of terminology. An action to separate a previously unified government would be reported as a detachment of territory or the dissolution of a municipal government, rather than as a "demerger" or "deconsolidation."

STATE LAWS AND LOCAL GOVERNMENT BOUNDARY CHANGE

Oakerson and Parks (1989) have identified two levels of choice at which decisions have an impact on the configuration of local boundaries. Not surprisingly, the two levels are the state legislature and the local community. The power of citizens to create and alter the boundaries of local government derives from a body of rules provided by enabling legislation found in state law or the state constitution.

Thus, local boundary change involves: (1) an "enabling level" prescribing a set of rules local citizens may use to create and modify local governments, and (2) a "chartering level," at which citizens create, expand, reduce, merge, and dissolve local governments within the rules created at the enabling level (Oakerson and Parks 1989). Of particular importance, the distribution of authority between these two levels of constitutional choice is a key factor in the scale and frequency of local boundary changes. The relative balance of this authority has come to be known as "home rule," whereby larger grants of home rule indicate that more of the key decisions regarding the powers of local government are made by citizens at the chartering level (Oakerson and Parks 1989). This section examines two types of enabling rules: state laws governing association, and boundary extension. Chartering-level activities are examined in detail in later sections.

As a group, enabling rules create what Burns (1994) termed the "institutions" of government. She argued that "the stable *institutions* of local government are the laws created by state legislatures and sometimes modified by the federal government that define the powers of local government. Local *governments*, then, are bundles of particular *institutions*—for example, the power to zone, the power to tax, and the power to provide services" (1994, 8). She asserted that people seek to form new governments because they seek access to these institutions. The powers set out in the enabling rules are what she has termed the "prize" of local government formation (Burns 1994, 19).

Rules of Association

Rules of association are made up of (1) "classificatory" decision rules, which provide for the creation of different types of governmental units for different purposes—counties, municipalities, and various special-purpose districts; (2) "constitutive" decision rules, by which local citizens can act to create a new local unit; and (3) "reconstitutive" decision rules for modifying the charter of an existing local unit.

Classificatory rules authorize the creation of different types of local government. For example, these rules create and differentiate municipal governments from special district governments, and they define a number of types within each form, such as cities and towns, and independent and dependent districts. Oakerson and Parks's (1989) framework of constitutional choice outlined an important role for classificatory rules in shaping citizen choice. They contended that the variation in the range and scale of local governmental authority created by these rules enables citizen choice among forms, because different purposes often require different sets of powers. For example, citizens wanting to form a local government for a single purpose may decide to create an independent special-purpose district. This form would be particularly attractive if these citizens did not want to invest in high levels of future decision making to constrain the activities of the new unit to this single purpose. However, if these same citizens were interested in forming a more open-ended unit of local government, one with multiple powers that could be expanded at local discretion, they might instead choose to create a municipality of one type or another.

These same rules also facilitate citizen choice among the subtypes of a particular form of government. Classificatory rules generally authorize a number of permissible forms of municipal governments and variety of special districts, each with different powers, structure, and function. Oakerson and Parks maintained that these choices reflect expected level of municipal activity. For example, decisions to form council–manager or strong-mayor governments may be associated with an expectation of higher levels of service provision, whereas weak-mayor and commission forms may be associated with lower levels of provision. Foster (1997) outlined a similar set of choices for citizens choosing among specific district governments, arguing that citizens decide among these subtypes based on the anticipated fiscal and service delivery implications of each form.

Constitutive decision rules enable the formation of new local units. These rules generally consist of petition and election requirements. Petition requirements will often stipulate the number and type of citizens who must request the consideration of the creation of a new unit. Election requirements consist of procedural hurdles that must be met before a referendum can be held and the voting rules that stipulate which local actors can participate in the referendum and the minimum level of support required for approval of the new government. Constitutive rules vary from state to state and, within states, by the type of local government. For example, dependent special districts (without separate taxing authority), and sometimes independent special districts, may often be created by county or municipal governments without a requirement of a citizen referendum. In contrast, the formation of a new municipal government generally requires the approval of a majority of the affected residents in a local referendum (ACIR 1992). In addition, where states require a referendum on incorporation, voting rules may vary from a simple majority to some extraordinary majority such as two-thirds.

Local governments are created to continue in perpetuity. Reconstitutive rules enable local citizens to reconstitute a unit (e.g., changing the class or the form of the government), to merge with other units, or to abolish the unit. Reconstitutive rules are usually similar to the constitutive decision rules in the state, often stipulating the changes to a local government charter follow the same approval process as do proposals to form new governments. In general, the procedures governing city–county consolidation are an exception to the similarity between constitutive and reconstitutive rules. Whereas the vast majority of states permit municipal incorporation through general law, city–county consolidation can be accomplished through general law in only fourteen states (ACIR 1992). In the other states, a constitutional amendment is required to consolidate these governments (ACIR 1992).

Oakerson and Parks outlined a key role for both constitutive and reconstitutive rules in metropolitan governance. They considered these rules central to ensuring that the provision of public goods reflects local preferences, suggesting that local government boundaries are mechanisms for organizing various communities of interest. They argued that local actors will seek to use these constitutive and reconstitutive rules to reshape the local public economy in ways that serve their own interests. They also saw these rules as playing an important part in the use of citizen voice in the community:

> A local government constitution . . . further amplifies the power of citizen voice in local governance. Local citizens can, on their own initiative, create, modify, or abolish local governments; hold the purse strings of local government by exercising a veto over tax increases in local referenda; approve or disapprove expansions in the boundaries of local units; and through their elected officials, enter into mutually productive relationships with citizens in neighboring and overlapping jurisdictions. (Oakerson and Parks 1988, 111–12)

They maintained that these rules provide a mechanism whereby citizens are able to obtain governmental arrangements that increase the accountability of public officials to citizens, such as low ratios of citizens to elected officials and part-time mayors. These features reduce the obstacles that citizens confront in accessing local government decision makers, thereby enhancing the power of citizen voice.

Boundary Extension Rules

Boundary extension rules establish the processes by which existing governments can be expanded. Similar to the rules providing for the formation of new local governments, boundary extension rules often require petition and local elections. Most states require petitions to initiate municipal annexation, and half the states empower both the landowners in the area or an adjacent municipal government to initiate the procedure (ACIR 1992).

As with government formation, the central issue in boundary expansion surrounds the balance of power between the proponents and opponents of an action. How this power is distributed is largely determined by whether the boundary extension rules require that citizens in outlying areas must give their consent for municipal annexation of their property. Oakerson and Parks (1988) observed that where annexation is viewed as a technical problem associated with service production and delivery, state laws typically empower municipalities to annex fringe areas, almost at will. However, where annexation is viewed as an act of association, then state law gives the preferences of citizens residing in the area to be annexed an equal or greater weight than the service delivery needs of the city government. Nineteen states require a referendum in the area to be annexed; fourteen require a referendum in the city; and ten states require a "dual" referendum, whereby both groups have to approve the proposed annexation in separate elections (ACIR 1992).

BOUNDARY CHANGE AS A COLLECTIVE ACTION PROBLEM

Citizens pursuing local government boundary change face a collective action problem. If a group of people is interested in creating or redrawing government boundaries for collective gains, such as provision of new services or achievement of administrative or production efficiencies, each individual in the group would be better off if someone else took on the burden of forming the new governmental system. These individuals would still receive the benefits of the new institutional arrangements, even if they themselves did not act to promote reform. Thus, among citizens supporting boundary change, the incentives to free ride on the actions of others are high (Carr and Feiock 2001).

State governments play a central role in specifying the solutions to collective action problems because state legislatures both define the extent of these problems confronting local actors and ordain the likely solutions for them through the laws they enact to govern boundary change. These requirements have implications for which actors will be most able to overcome the collective action problem imposed by the law itself. In short, some actors are advantaged and others disadvantaged by the requirements for boundary change set out in state law. In addition, certain organizing and motivating strategies are encouraged and others are discouraged by the requirements included in these laws.

Institutional constraints defining the collective action problem also vary within states. Where state laws provide for multiple procedures for a particular type of boundary change or where these laws provide for multiple stages for the boundary change process, the collective action problem for various groups will be different depending on the procedure in question or the stage in the boundary change process. Boundary change laws in Florida provide an illustration. There are three separate procedures that interested actors may use to annex unincorporated territory. First, annexation can be achieved through a petition of property owners and the enactment of an ordinance for annexation by the city council. Second, in the absence of support from affected property owners, an ordinance for annexation by the city council can be submitted to a referendum of the residents of the area to be annexed (and also city residents, if annual annexation exceeds 5 percent of the land or population of the municipality).

Third, the Legislature is authorized to annex unincorporated property into a municipality by special act. State law also defines a number of different types of special districts, each with its own procedures for creation. The involvement of community groups in boundary change efforts has been shown to vary significantly across annexation procedures and special district types (Carr 2000).

Where state laws define separate procedures for getting boundary change issues on the agenda and for approving the proposed change, the nature of incentives and collective action problems may differ at each stage. For example, state laws generally define a three-stage process for consolidating cities and county governments. The first stage can include petition requirements, special studies, and the appointment of a commission to draft a new charter. The second stage is the creation of the proposed city–county charter. The third stage is a referendum on the proposed charter in all affected areas. In their survey of communities holding a referendum on city–county consolidation, Carr and Feiock (2004) found that the breadth of actor involvement in the issue declined from the agenda-setting stage to the referendum. Significantly, the decline in involvement by supporters far outstripped the decline by opponents of the proposal.

Building on the work of Olson (1965), Burns (1994) identified three collective action "solutions" that typically result from the boundary change laws adopted by states. The first solution to the collective action problem is to reduce the need for collective action. States do this when they enact laws that do not require technical studies, petition signatures, referendum votes, or threshold requirements (e.g., population, tax base, land area) to alter the boundaries of existing units. In this instance, group action is not necessary, and collective action difficulties are avoided. This solution is prevalent in special district formation laws, which often allow these governments to be formed by small groups and even by individuals. This solution also underlies municipal annexation laws that permit unilateral annexation by municipalities, or the voluntary annexation of individual landowners.

The second solution to the collective action problem involves the existence of an organization or group that can be used to pursue the desired jurisdictional change. In this instance, the organizational problem has already been solved, and this group becomes the organizational base for the new collective action. States encourage this solution by adopting provisions that can be met only through organized action, such as requirements for petition and public referenda. Organizations such as business groups, neighborhood associations, and service districts can be critical in organizing the collective efforts that are required for change.

This solution is made more likely if there are few residents or land-owners and if the factors motivating group membership are directly affected by boundary change. Municipal annexations involving a few large property owners, or municipal formations proposed along the boundaries of homeowners' associations or service districts, are examples of preexisting organizations that are vital to successful efforts. Burns contended that this solution is more prevalent in efforts to create new cities than in ones to form special districts, although examples of both can be found. Her own analysis of local government formations identified homeowners' associations as playing this role in the formation of new municipal governments. Similarly, Miller (1981) detailed the role played by the county firefighters' union in securing sufficient petition signatures for municipal incorporations in Los Angeles County. The local's interest in forming new cities was to create customers for their services, and these new cities invariably contracted with the county for fire protection.

The third solution involves the emergence of an elite group to shoulder a disproportionate share of the financial burden and mobilize diffuse interests in seeking the boundary change. In this solution, the entrepreneur provides the startup resources necessary for organizing the effort and eventually is able to attract others to support the effort. States encourage this solution by adopting boundary laws that require substantial financial resources to meet all requirements. For example, states may often require technical studies be made of the feasibility of forming new local governments or demand other information that requires specialized, technical staff or consultants to prepare. Also, where signed petitions are required of large numbers of landowners or residents, volunteer efforts are more likely to fail.

In either case, boundary change efforts may require sizable up-front expenditures, which may not be recovered, regardless of the outcome. A substantial interest in boundary change is necessary to offset the high individual cost of the effort along with an ability to persuade sufficient portions of landowners or residents in the community to support collective action in the referendum or by signing the petition required for the change to go forward. Burns's (1994) analysis indicated that manufacturers often play the role of an interested entrepreneur in forming new municipal governments, and developers often play a similar role in the formation of special district governments. Rosenbaum and Kammerer (1973) also pointed to the role these entrepreneurs play in generating support for consolidation efforts.

INSTITUTIONAL ENTREPRENEURS AND BOUNDARY CHANGE

The next section of this chapter considers the emergence of institutional entrepreneurs in greater detail. Schneider, Teske, and Mintrom (1995) proposed that the appearance of innovative policies on the agenda of local governments is the product of the variation in the supply of potential public entrepreneurs and the presence of certain community conditions and institutions that stimulate entrepreneurial activity. Local government boundary change occurs within a system of state-level rules and constraints. Every state has created laws establishing the procedures that shall be followed to form new local governments or to expand the boundaries of existing ones. In most instances, the burden is on actors within the community to decide whether a change is needed. Some states require that formal initiation may have to be made by the state legislature, or by some other body, but even in these cases the process begins with actors within the community. Thus, whereas state governments may be the architects of local government structure, the structure of local governments is the province of local actors (Oakerson and Parks 1989).

Political entrepreneurs discover ways to maximize individual welfare through institutional change to guarantee for themselves the benefits that these institutions allow them to receive, regardless of whether or not these institutions benefit society as a whole (Knight and Sened 1995, 11). Potential entrepreneurs not only have an interest in reform; many of their skills may translate well into public entrepreneurship. Expertise not only in administrative reform but also in the political process, finance, and real estate is likely to prove valuable. In addition, the use of rhetoric and heresthetics is a valuable resource for entrepreneurship. Heresthetics is a strategy whereby entrepreneurs seek to change people's choices through a strategic reframing of an issue. Rhetoric is intended to persuade, whereas the objective of heresthetics is to structure the decision-making situation to the claimant's advantage (Riker 1986). "Political entrepreneurs can challenge the status quo by rhetoric and heresthetics to make people think differently about political institutions and practices and to lead people to challenge what might otherwise seem like the fixed parameters of the political world" (Schneider, Teske, and Mintrom 1995, 110).

Explanations of boundary change must consider the implications of collective action problems and selective incentives. More than desiring to change local boundaries, actors must be able to assemble and coordinate the teams or networks of individuals and organizations that have the talents and/or resources necessary to undertake change. In other words, it is important to understand which actors—and what situations—are capable of creating boundary change in line with their preferences. Table 10.1 outlines some of the collective and selective incentives that may motivate public officials, business organizations, and resident interests to seek boundary change.

DISCUSSION: WHOSE GAME DO WE PLAY?

In most instances, people have all the instruments of boundary change described above available as they seek to redraw jurisdictional lines of authority—meaning that the use of special district formation instead of annexation, or annexation in place of incorporation, represents a deliberate choice by local actors. How actors choose among these instruments depends on several factors. To some extent, these questions are answered by the particular goals of the actors seeking the boundary change. It is likely that certain instruments are well suited to affect the delivery of particular services and the alteration of specific policies. However, it is also likely that other answers can be found in the instruments themselves. A general explanation of boundary change, then, must also explain how features of the instruments themselves shape citizen choice.

The question of whose game is played is important for at least two reasons. First, proponents of a particular boundary change have a strong incentive to play a game they can win. The insights of Schattschneider and Bridges suggest that people seeking to win the game will choose a game with rules that work to their advantage. If a winnable game does not exist, Bridges's work suggests that actors will seek to change the existing game by rewriting the rules to their advantage. An understanding of the statutory framework governing boundary change, then, provides insight into the likely success different actors will have in drawing local government boundaries in ways that meet their needs.

Second, the organization of local governments in communities reflects winning efforts over time. Existing jurisdictional lines reflect the preferences of the winners of past battles. As was shown above through the discussion of collective action problems, community residents are not equal in their endowment of the kinds of resources necessary to solve problems through local government boundary change. Different procedures favor different resources, and those actors with the resources favored by the procedure will win most often. The preferences of actors for specific forms

Table 10.1. Collective and Selective Incentives for Selected Participants in Boundary Change

Actor	Definition	Collective Goals	Selective Goals
Public officials	Elected officials from local governments (county, municipal, township, and village)	Community leadership	Political power and reelection
	Senior administrators from local governments	Community leadership	Status, prestige, higher salaries
Business associations	Chamber of Commerce, and merchants, media	Community image and status	Financial gain
	Manufacturers	Economic development	Financial gain
	Developers and contractors	Economic development	Financial gain
Resident and citizen organizations	Civic groups, good government organizations	Accountability and "good government"	Status, prestige, and membership
	African American community, racial and ethnic minorities	Representation	Greater influence, access to government
	Homeowners' associations; tax control groups	Lower taxes, greater access, and efficiency	Lower individual taxes, exclusion

of boundary change was discussed at length in an earlier section. This concluding section instead focuses on the dynamics of choice across the four forms.

Choosing the Game

For the past decade, the dominant explanation of local government formation has been Burns's (1994) model of citizen choice based on variations in powers and obstacles to collective action. She argued that citizens seek the formation of new governments because they wish to utilize the powers of these institutions to further certain goals, and differences in the powers attached to these units provide an important basis for choice. Yet boundary-change efforts also involve conflicts among competing interests (Fleischmann 1986; Marando 1974), meaning that in addition to the problem of organizing and motivating supporters to work for the change, the proponents of a particular set of boundaries must compete with others seeking to redraw existing boundaries along different lines, and with those citizens preferring the status quo. Thus, the size and character of the population affected by a potential boundary change must also be an important consideration to the proponents of the change.

Figure 10.1 plots the four forms of local government boundary change discussed in this chapter according to two dimensions: (1) the extent of

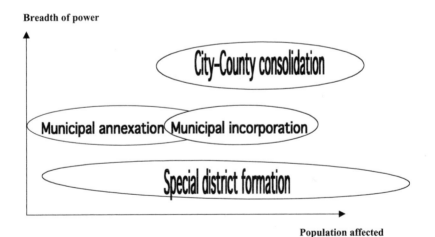

Figure 10.1. Two Dimensions of Local Government Boundary Change

the change in governmental powers associated with each form of boundary change, and (2) the amount of population affected by each form. Plot-
ting these four instruments on these two dimensions provides a simple illustration of the relative frequency of their use. For reasons that will be
explained in the next several paragraphs, higher levels of either dimension
makes boundary change more difficult, and higher levels of both is the
most difficult environment proponents will encounter. The location of municipal annexation and special district formation in the left and lower-left
areas of the figure suggests that these two instruments will be easier to
use. The location of municipal incorporation, and especially city–county consolidation, in the right and upper-right areas suggests that these two instruments will be relatively more difficult to use. Data on boundary change
reported by the Census Bureau supports the conclusions suggested by figure 10.1. Historically, special districts and municipal annexations have
been the two most common forms of boundary change, whereas municipal incorporation, and especially city–county consolidation, is less frequent (Miller 1993; U.S. Census Bureau 2002).

Burns's arguments about the role played by local government powers
in formation decisions relates directly to the breadth-of-power dimension. The breadth of the change in local government powers refers to the
extent to which the boundary change alters the set of preexisting local
government powers available for use in the area in question. Part of the
change stems from differences in powers attached to particular types of
governments (e.g., special districts, municipalities, and county governments), and part is based on whether the change displaces or overlaps
preexisting powers. Figure 10.1 displays the variation of these forms in
terms of the changes in local government power created by their use.
The formation of special districts usually overlaps existing governments, whereas the creation of general-purpose governments typically
displaces much of the existing governmental arrangements. In general,
special districts are the least comprehensive form of boundary change,
usually overlapping existing governments and often adding only a single
function.

Thus, special districts represent an addition to the number of local governments in the community, but only a small change in the distribution
of local government power in the area. At the other extreme, city–county
consolidation displaces many of the existing arrangements, creating an entirely new government. In some instances, one or more subcounty governments are not involved in the unification, but this must be negotiated
as part of the consolidation. Municipal annexations and municipal incor-

poration represent the middle ground for this dimension. These forms displace preexisting powers to provide municipal-level services to the area, but they often leave most of the functions provided by county or special district governments undisturbed.

The second dimension in figure 10.1 is the amount of population directly affected by the use of each form of boundary change. This relatively simple dimension relates directly to Foster's (1997) notion of geographic scope in special district governments. Foster contended that choices made when deciding the geographic scope of special district governments reflect the agenda of those forming the governments. She concluded that the motivation for—and effect of—district governments formed to encompass large populations, and often spanning substantial land area, was to provide services to some constituency at a cost to a much wider population.

In figure 10.1, however, the purpose of this second dimension is far less ambitious; it deals with the potential conflict faced in boundary change, rather than with the agenda of the proponents. It is simply used to illustrate the variation of these instruments in the number of people in the community who *perceive* the boundary change as directly affecting them. The term "perceive" is used deliberately, because boundary changes typically affect many people beyond the parties directly involved, across both space and time. It is clear from the literature on this topic that boundary changes have an important impact on the entire community, including determining patterns of economic development, the prospects for regional planning and growth management, opportunities for racial and economic segregation, and the allocation and costs of public services (Carr 2000; Lowery 2000). It seems likely that much of the affected population is unaware of many of the potential effects of a proposed boundary change.

Broadly speaking, each instrument depicted in figure 10.1 can affect large numbers of people. The ellipses surrounding the words in figure 10.1 illustrate the range of population that may be affected by each form of boundary change. Instruments such as municipal annexation and special district formation are often used in ways such that only a few people seem to be directly affected by a proposed boundary change. Indeed, both instruments can be used to alter the governmental arrangements for a single property. An advantage unique to special district governments is that their narrow breadth of power means that the conflict over their formation will often be low, even when the district spans several counties and encompasses thousands of people. In contrast, city–county consolidation most often affects an entire county's population in a very visible way.

Municipal incorporation will usually involve fewer people than city–county consolidation, but it cannot be targeted at a single property like annexation or the formation of a district government.

The population dimension also illustrates the flexibility of these instruments. The term "flexibility" refers to how easily the boundaries can be drawn in ways that capture homogeneous populations, thereby increasing the likelihood that affected populations have similar preferences and reducing the likelihood of conflict over the proposed boundary change. The degree of flexibility provided by any one form may be key to achieving the objectives that its proponents are seeking. Special districts are the least restricted in how the boundaries of these governments can be drawn. They can be drawn very widely or very narrowly, encompassing several counties or a single neighborhood.

The other three instruments are more limited in the way that boundaries can be drawn. Like special districts, municipal annexation is a very flexible form of boundary change and can be used with great precision. However, unlike special district governments, this instrument is restricted to unincorporated areas, and many states do not permit annexations to cross county lines (Carr and Feiock 2003). The same is true for municipal incorporation; the boundaries of a new municipality cannot overlap existing municipal governments. The formation of a new municipal government will almost always involve more people than the largest annexations, making it a less precise instrument than municipal annexation. However, municipal incorporation does offer the possibility that the boundaries can be drawn so as to have a direct impact on a relatively homogeneous population. City–county consolidation is geographically limited by the size of the county. In practice, this instrument will visibly affect virtually every person in an entire county. Thus, from this perspective, city–county consolidation is a very blunt instrument indeed.

What does the empirical literature show about how actors choose among these forms of boundary change? Studies by Burns (1994), Foster (1997), and Rigos and Spindler (1991) have confirmed a connection between municipal annexation and the formation of new municipal and special district governments. Rigos and Spindler (1991) showed that residents in outlying areas will sometimes preempt an impending annexation by incorporating all or part of the area as a municipal government, an action they termed "defensive incorporation." Burns's analyses showed that the choice between municipal and special-purpose government hinges at least in part on whether the actors seeking the change seek the power to zone.

Similarly, Foster's analysis of the same choice confirmed this factor, and it added several more (i.e., political visibility, and financial, administrative, and geographic flexibility) that directly affect these decisions. Foster (1997) and McCabe (1997) both examined how the use of minimum provisions (e.g., land area, population, tax base) for municipal incorporation affected the formation of new special district governments, with Foster concluding the presence of these provisions reduced reliance on special district governments, and McCabe concluding that the provisions made district formations more likely.

The connection between city–county consolidation and these other forms has received less attention by analysts, although this is changing. (See Carr and Feiock, eds., *Reshaping the Local Government Landscape: City–County Consolidation and Its Alternatives*, 2004.) As the most comprehensive form, there is little that can be achieved through the others that cannot also be gained through city–county consolidation. However, the reverse is not true; typically, none of the other forms achieves everything that a city–county consolidation does. Yet, especially when they are used in combination, these other instruments can achieve virtually all the objectives used to justify city–county consolidation. In addition, the four forms of boundary change considered in this chapter are not the only means to these ends. Other ways to meet some of these objectives include, for instance, selected functional consolidations between city and county governments, contracting between local governments for the production of public services, and the use of regional jurisdictions such as councils of governments and metropolitan planning organizations to facilitate planning and coordination among local governments.

Changing the Rules?

The power differentials among local governments may become less of a basis for choice in the future. As table 10.2 shows, more and more state legislatures are creating an environment in which local governments act as service delivery competitors. The table presents information on functional responsibility compiled by the U.S. Census Bureau for twenty-four different service areas. It shows that, as of 2002, a majority of states empowered two or more types of local governments to engage in the same service areas. In some service areas, such as fire protection, utilities, solid waste management, and parks and recreation, provision is often available through all three types of governments.

Table 10.2. Local Government Competition in Service Provision

| Core Government Function[a] | County | Municipality | | Special District |
		City	Township	
Air Transportation	42	45		28
Cemeteries	33	19		13
Community development	31	49	2	22
Education	10	11		5
Elections	46	49	3	2
Electric power				31
Fire Protection	39	48	1	33
Gas supply				14
Health and welfare	31	27	1	31
Highways	42	45	4	28
Hospitals	31	27		31
Housing	33	19	1	42
Libraries	31	48		26
Natural resources	35	49		39
Parking facilities				7
Parks and recreation	31	48	1	35
Public Safety	39	48	1	26
Sewerage			1	40
Solid waste management	42	45	2	39
Taxation	46	49	4	2
Transit	42	45		21
Utility	42	45		42
Water supply			1	45
Water transport and terminals	42	45		37

[a]Functions are permitted by state law, not required.
Sources: Compiled by author on the basis of data in U.S. Census Bureau (2002) and Krane, Rigos, and Hill (2000).

It is worth noting that this table shows permissible service areas and that in many instances local governments may choose not to participate in a particular service area. In addition, these service area categories are fairly broad and, at times, multiple governments may be providing services that are complementary instead of competitive. Still, the information in table 10.2 shows that actors seeking boundary change for the purpose of service delivery have options, whereas in previous years there may have been only one means to obtain desired public services. Situations that were once candidates for municipal annexation are now open to multiple forms of boundary change. Some actors may find it easier to obtain service delivery through special district formation, rather than through municipal incorporation. Or equally important, some actors may prefer service delivery by the county to annexation by a neighboring municipality. The trend by states to empower different types of local governments to provide similar kinds of services gives local actors more options or, in other words, more games to play.

Recently, state legislatures have also adopted multiple procedures that may be used for a single boundary change. Many states have enacted several different procedures for municipal annexation (Carr and Feiock 2001), and most states have created dozens of different special district enabling laws (Carr 2000). Once a particular form of boundary change has been settled upon, these different sets of procedures create opportunities for actors to select the procedure that best meets their strengths. For example, provisions imposing filing fees, petition collection, lobbying public officials, and managing a public campaign for or against a proposed boundary change require substantial organizational and financial resources to be successfully met, effectively limiting the set of actors that can win this game.

In contrast, other provisions do not affect the organizational and financial resource threshold, but instead alter the scope of conflict by adding or subtracting actors from the formal approval process. Referenda requirements and provisions authorizing county governments to approve boundary changes are just two examples of provisions that affect the scope of conflict in addition to whatever impact they might have on collective action difficulties. It is important to remember that in Schattschneider's (1960) conception of the scope of conflict, which actor prevails in the battle is thought to depend upon the arena in which the decision is made. He argued that the losing side (or the side that anticipated losing in this arena) would seek to expand the scope of conflict. The scope of conflict, then, also involves keeping likely opponents out of the decision-making process. Actors may have sufficient resources to successfully engage in collective action, but they may be reluctant to invite others into the fight except when it cannot be avoided.

Theories of intergovernmental politics, particularly in areas such as local government boundary change—for which state legislatures have devised a great variety of government forms and differing procedures to create these forms—must incorporate strategic and adaptive behavior by local actors in explaining how state constraints affect outcomes at the local level. Local government boundary change is driven by the logic of "selective action." This logic suggests that the procedural rules set out in a particular state law do have consequences for collective action, but any single law is only part of the network of rules that creates the incentives faced by these actors. Viewed as a set, these laws create obstacles and opportunities for action, and both outcomes must be addressed when examining local government boundary change.

REFERENCES

ACIR (Advisory Council on Intergovernmental Relations). 1987. *The Organization of Local Public Economies.* Washington, D.C.: ACIR.

———. 1992. *State Laws Governing Local Government Structure and Administration.* Washington, D.C.: ACIR.

Blodgett, Terry. 1996. *Current City–County Consolidation Attempts.* Washington, D.C.: National Association of Counties.

Bollens, Scott A. 1986. Examining the Link between State Policy and the Creation of Local Special Districts. *State and Local Government Review* 18: 117–24.

Bridges, Amy. 1997. Textbook Municipal Reform. *Urban Affairs Review* 33: 97–119.

Bridges, Amy, and Richard Kronick. 1999. Writing the Rules to Win the Game: The Middle-Class Regimes of Municipal Reformers. *Urban Affairs Review* 34: 691–706.

Burns, Nancy. 1994. *The Formation of American Local Governments: Private Values in Public Institutions.* New York: Oxford University Press.

Campbell, Richard W., and Dan Durning. 2000. Is City–County Consolidation Good Policy? A Symposium. *Public Administration Quarterly* 24: 133–39.

Carr, Jered B. 2000. The Political Economy of Local Government Boundary Change: State Laws, Local Actors, and Collective Action. Ph.D. dissertation, Florida State University, Tallahassee.

Carr, Jered B., and Richard C. Feiock. 2001. State Annexation "Constraints" and the Frequency of Municipal Annexation. *Political Research Quarterly* 54: 459–70.

———. 2003. Annexation. In *Encyclopedia of Public Administration and Policy,* ed. Jack Rabin. New York: Marcel Dekker.

Carr, Jered B., and Richard C. Feiock, eds. 2004. The Politics of City–County Consolidation: Findings from a National Survey. In *Reshaping the Local Government Landscape: City–County Consolidation and Its Alternatives,* ed. Jered B. Carr and Richard C. Feiock. Armonk, N.Y.: M. E. Sharpe.

FDCA (Florida Department of Community Affairs). 1998. *The 1998–1999 Official List of Special Districts.* Tallahassee: FDCA.

Fleischmann, Arnold. 1986. The Goals and Strategies of Local Boundary Changes: Government Organization or Private Gain? *Journal of Urban Affairs* 4: 63–75.

Foster, Kathryn A. 1997. *The Political Economy of Special-Purpose Government.* Washington, D.C.: Georgetown University Press.

Halter, Gary. 1993. City–City Consolidations in the United States. *National Civic Review* 82, no. 3: 282–89.

Knight, Jack, and Itai Sened. 1995. *Explaining Social Institutions.* Ann Arbor: University of Michigan Press.

Krane, Dale, Platon Rigos, and Melvin Hill. 2000. *Home Rule in America: A Fifty-State Handbook.* Washington, D.C.: CQ Press.

Lowery, David. 2000. A Transaction Costs Model of Metropolitan Governance: Allocation versus Redistribution in Urban America. *Journal of Public Administration Research and Theory* 10: 48–78.

McCabe, Barbara C. 1997. Revenue, Structure and the Grassroots: The Causes and Consequences of State Tax and Expenditure Limits on Local Governments. Ph.D. dissertation, Florida State University, Tallahassee.

Marando, Vincent L. 1974. The Politics of Metropolitan Reform. *Administration & Society* 6: 229–62.

Miller, Gary. 1981. *Cities by Contract: The Politics of Municipal Incorporation.* Cambridge, Mass.: MIT Press.

Miller, Joel. 1988. Municipal Annexation and Boundary Change. In *Municipal Year Book.* Washington, D.C.: International City Management Association.

———. 1993. Annexations and Boundary Changes in the 1980s and 1990–91. In *The Municipal Year Book.* Washington, D.C.: International City Management Association.

Oakerson, Ronald J., and Roger B. Parks. 1988. Citizen Voice and Public Entrepreneurship: The Organizational Dynamic of a Complex Metropolitan County. *Publius* 18: 91–112.

———. 1989. Local Government Constitutions: A Different View of Metropolitan Governance. *American Review of Public Administration* 19: 279–94.

Olson, Mancur. 1965. *The Logic of Collective Action: Public Goods and the Theory of Groups.* Cambridge, Mass.: Harvard University Press.

Parks, Roger B., and Ronald J. Oakerson. 1989. Metropolitan Organization and Governance: A Local Public Economy Approach. *Urban Affairs Quarterly* 25: 18–29.

Porter, Douglas, Ben C. Lin, Susan Jakubiak, and Richard B. Peiser. 1992. *Special Districts: A Useful Technique for Financing Infrastructure,* 2d ed. Washington, D.C.: Urban Land Institute.

Rigos, Platon N., and Charles J. Spindler. 1991. Municipal Incorporation and State Statutes: A State-Level Analysis. *State and Local Government Review* 23: 76–81.

Riker, William H. 1986. *The Art of Political Manipulation.* New Haven, Conn.: Yale University Press.

Rosenbaum, Walter A., and Gladys M. Kammerer. 1973. *Against Long Odds: The Theory and Practice of Successful Governmental Consolidation.* Beverly Hills, Calif.: Sage Publications.

Schattschneider, E. E. 1960. *The Semisovereign People: A Realist's View of Democracy in America* (reissued 1983). New York: Holt, Rinehart, and Winston.

Schneider, Mark, Paul Teske, and Michael Mintrom. 1995. *Public Entrepreneurs: Agents for Change in American Government.* Princeton, N.J.: Princeton University Press.

U.S. Census Bureau. 2002. *Government Units in 2002.* 2002 Census of Governments GC02-1(P), Washington, D.C.: U.S. Government Printing Office.

CONCLUDING THOUGHTS: REGIONALISM, URBAN POLITICS, AND GOVERNANCE

The theoretical frameworks introduced in part one of this book provide the conceptual handle to better grasp the dynamics of decentralized systems of governance and to identify the various ways governments cooperate and compete. Institutional collective action in metropolitan areas has proven difficult both to understand and to achieve because it confronts strategic interactions among numerous organizations and jurisdictions, multiple potential solutions, and a high degree of uncertainty. Strategic interaction among governments underlies many of the regional governance problems discussed in this volume. In economic development, land use management, service coordination, and other decisions, each jurisdiction chooses its own policies, but the outcomes are directly affected by the decisions of other local actors. Where benefit spillovers exist, each jurisdiction will choose its best response to the choices of other jurisdictions (Brueckner 1998).

Local government actors must anticipate how those with whom they interact will respond to a set of institutional incentives. Will they choose to cooperate if I cooperate, or will a cooperative overture be exploited?

Even if their cooperation is reciprocated and regional institutions are in place, local government leaders may be unsure whether or not cooperation will generate the benefits ascribed to it by academics or higher-level governments promoting regional reform.

A related problem is that of coordinating behavior around one of several competing, plausible alternatives. The problem of coordination arises when there are what game theorists refer to as "multiple equilibria": situations in which there are several jointly preferred possible outcomes around which actors can coordinate their behavior. Governance alternatives can range from the informal coordination of services among local organizations and governments to the creation of metropolitan governments. Such situations often result in inaction, even if action would have benefited the participants. Multiple equilibria result in coordination and distribution problems that are exacerbated by uncertainty (Heckathorn and Maser 1987). Decentralized governance arrangements combine both a strategic element and uncertainty about the nature of the new payoffs to cooperation.

Because decision makers are boundedly rational when it comes to evaluating gains from cooperation, there is inevitably a high degree of uncertainty regarding what will happen if they cooperate and their partner cooperates (i.e., what is the new payoff?). Such uncertainty can easily impede efforts at regional cooperation. In this situation, the circulation of information on the benefits of joint action may not be sufficient to overcome barriers to cooperation unless it is accompanied by interorganizational learning gained through experience interacting with other local actors. The theories and evidence in this volume suggest that a decentralized system of governance can provide the civic, political, and administrative interactions that can facilitate future cooperation.

COMPETITION AND COOPERATION IN LOCAL GOVERNANCE

The focus of the theoretical frameworks advanced in part one extend beyond the traditional debate between fragmented and consolidated government. The empirical chapters that follow build on this foundation. For example, Paul Lewis argues in chapter 5 for a broader consideration of metropolitan political structure and its potential influence on important policy outcomes by examining how land use and development are different in supersuburbs (non–central cities in metropolitan areas with populations that exceed 50,000 residents) than other suburban areas. In chapter 9,

Mark Schneider and Jack Buckley also contend that arguments supporting decentralization and polycentricity have been framed too heavily in terms of a struggle over the structure of metropolitan government. They argue for broader analyses of specific urban services to extend Ronald Oakerson's exploration of decentralized governance in chapter 2.

To understand the dynamics of governance in metropolitan areas, it is necessary to examine specific policy issues and how local governments and other local actors interact in managing these issues. This directs attention to decentralized governance where, in the words of Schneider and Buckley, "the rubber meets the road."

Competition and cooperation are often portrayed as alternative and even incompatible mechanisms for governance. The empirical studies reported here demonstrate that elements of both competition and cooperation are present in virtually all systems of local governance, and that they are quite often complementary.

Competition and cooperation in metropolitan areas are evidenced through many mechanisms. Although the urban policy literature gives much attention to intergovernmental competition over taxes and service provision, less attention has been directed to how competitive forces shape the services communities choose to provide, the qualities of these services, and what organizations or actors are responsible for production. In particular, the role of nonprofits as competitors and complements to local governments needs to be more fully explored.

Competition is central to Buckley and Schneider's application of Oakerson's framework to education policy. They identify changes in how school systems are organized. In particular, they identify changes in "parent/consumer" satisfaction and participation as a result of expanding school choice. The account of development policy by Martin Johnson and Max Neiman in chapter 6 documents how intergovernmental competition influences developmental decisions regarding land use and economic subsidies. They find that perceptions of rivalry with other local governments lead cities to provide more development programs.

Intergovernmental and intersectoral competition in a local political economy shapes not only developmental policy but also allocation and redistribution. In chapter 8, Elaine Sharp examines how variation in the extent to which a metropolitan area is governmentally fragmented influences the extent to which local officials in the metropolitan core take aggressive action against the sex industry. She finds that metropolitan decentralization evokes an arms race of anti-sex-industry action not unlike the economic development rivalry reported by Johnson and Neiman. In addition, as Jered Carr demonstrates in chapter 10, competition often underlies efforts to modify local boundaries or create regional governments.

Cooperation also takes on many forms. It is evidenced by interlocal agreements between two or more government units (Post 2002), by coalitions of local governments seeking federal grants that are often brokered by a member of Congress (Bickers and Stein 2002), by public–private regional partnerships, by the creation of regional authorities or districts, and by consolidated metropolitan governments (Feiock and Carr 2001; Carr and Feiock 2003). Though the scale and scope of these cooperative institutions vary tremendously, each of them represents successful efforts by local government units to overcome free-rider problems and other barriers to cooperation through institutional collective action.

In chapter 7, Richard Feiock, Jill Tao, and Linda Johnson report that even in the traditionally competitive economic development arena, local governments can engage in cooperative action and that cooperation is positively influenced by service-delivery interactions among local actors. Though Johnson and Neiman focus primarily on competitive forces shaping development, they note that some cities do engage in cooperative development efforts and that these cities had more, not fewer, overall economic development activities.

In education policy, Schneider and Buckley argue that the decentralization of schools has created a civic space that parents are filling, and they present evidence of the increased responsiveness of school officials to parents. Sharp suggests that morality policy issues present challenges for intergovernmental cooperation in decentralized political systems. Previous studies of policing in structurally decentralized metropolitan areas suggest that cooperative or coordinated problem solving often occurs through joint efforts among local governments (Ostrom, Parks, and Whitaker 1978). This was not the case with regard to sex-industry regulation. Sharp reports little effort at cooperation or coordination in this policy arena.

Much work remains to be done to more fully elaborate the institutional collective action framework. Institutional collective action shares many of the characteristics of individual collective action, but it differs in important ways. Local government officials who participate in cooperative agreements are agents. As such, they may have different preferences for, and payoffs from, cooperation than the average resident or median voter (Feiock 2002). This may create selective incentives for political entrepreneurs (Schneider, Teske, and Mintrom 1995), but it also may introduce agency problems that complicate the calculus of cooperation. Local government officials' political careers are linked to the characteristics of political constituencies, and their strategies are constrained by local political opportunities and institutions.

The characteristics of constituencies and the diversity of preferences within government units need to be examined more systematically. Clingermayer and Feiock (2001) found that council members with racially and economically diverse districts focused attention outside their district and built citywide electoral coalitions. The extension of this logic to the metropolitan level might suggest that a diverse constituency leads city officials to seek alliances with other jurisdictions that could provide sources of political capital. The institutional structure of local governments and powers of office also come into play as they influence the ability of bargainers to credibly commit their city government to collective action.

THE ROLE OF STATE GOVERNMENT

The idea that higher-level governments can create incentives to promote regional governance and encourage cooperation among local governments has gained considerable currency (Weir 2000). In particular, Orfield's (1997, 2002) work argues that state legislatures have the potential to facilitate regional policy when local cooperative action and self-governance prove difficult or impossible. Orfield contends that, because older suburbs share the problems of central cities, representatives of central cities and close-in suburbs will form a legislative alliance to impose regional institutions.

The work reported in this volume suggests that intervention to promote regional governance and institutional collective action poses challenging dilemmas for states, even if these legislative alliances emerge. Nevertheless, state actions that constrain local choices and reduce uncertainty may be valuable because regional policy problems are characterized by strategic interaction, multiple equilibria, and analytic uncertainty. Efforts to promote regional governance and cooperation must be able to influence the strategic actions of jurisdictions with competing interests. This strategic element underlines the fact that local governments make choices *dependent* on the choices of other governments.

POLITICAL SCIENCE AND THE STUDY
OF DECENTRALIZED GOVERNANCE

The relationship between competition and cooperation in governance institutions is an issue of general interest in political science. The conceptual and theoretical tools developed by political scientists to address these questions promise to provide new insights and give researchers more leverage when they think about problems of cooperation and competition in regional governance arrangements.

Through the study of regional governance, the urban subfield has an opportunity to make important contributions to the larger discipline of political science. To do so, however, urban scholars must be willing to adopt the conceptual and theoretical tools developed by political scientists working in other subfields. For example, theories of collaboration developed in the study of international relations and common-pool resources situations might be applied to issues of service delivery in metropolitan areas. Moreover, the methods and techniques applied in those fields, such as social network analysis, might provide useful analytic tools for the study of governance in metropolitan areas.

The work of Ostrom and others on cooperative institutions provides a parallel to local actors in a metropolitan area seeking to solve regional problems of development, inequality, urban sprawl, and so on. The more serious the underlying problem, the larger the aggregate gains from resolving it, and the greater the likelihood of a cooperative arrangement to do so. This condition has most often been noted in the resolution of common-pool resource problems. As losses from overconsumption increase, it is more likely that all parties involved will seek some agreement to restrict use (Lipecap 1989; Lubell et al. 2002; Ostrom 1990; Ostrom, Gardner, and Walker 1994). Work on public goods provision also notes the necessity for aggregate gains to exceed the aggregate costs of provision, with the greater the margin, the greater the ability of the collective to provide selective incentives or attract a political entrepreneur to organize the group (Olson 1971). Unlike the common-pool resource situations, the welfare losses resulting from sprawl and other metropolitan problems may not be dramatic, and inaction may not have catastrophic consequences. Given uncertainty and multiple equilibria, doing nothing (i.e., no cooperation or coordination) remains a likely result, even if every jurisdiction is made worse off.

A consistent finding in the institutional analysis and development work has been the importance of contextual factors. Cooperative solutions to common-property resource problems are possible if specific boundary and transaction costs conditions are met (Ostrom 1990). Lipecap and other new institutionalist scholars argue that the homogeneity of the actors involved will affect the resolution of certain competitive situations (Lipecap 1989, 1996).

The study of the institutional supply of cooperative agreements to manage watersheds has directed attention not only to the characteristics of stakeholders but also to the importance of networks of interaction among them (Lubell et al. 2002). Additional theoretical work is needed to build on these ideas to explain how networks of policy and communication among governmental and nongovernmental actors might establish the credibility of commitments, build social capital, and foster organizational learning. Such work could significantly enhance our understanding of competition and cooperation in decentralized systems.

EMPIRICAL RESEARCH

The empirical studies presented in this volume begin to fill an important lacuna in our understanding of how decentralized systems of government work in practice. Nevertheless, much additional work needs to be done.

The study of decentralized governance in metropolitan areas also promises to advance the study of institutions. Much of the institutional work in other subfields is constrained by the limited number of cases available for analysis. The large number of metropolitan areas and the wide variety of institutional arrangements that they exhibit make urban areas the ideal laboratory for testing general propositions about institutions and governance arrangements.

The theoretical approaches described here view local governance and policy as resulting from the strategic interactions of a variety of governmental and civic organizations that encompass both competition and cooperation. The empirical study of local governance confronts several research design issues that make testing propositions based in these theories difficult. This is particularly true where empirical work seeks to test formal models, such as those presented by Annette Steinacker in chapter 3.

Despite the obvious policy spillover effects within metropolitan areas, the study of urban and regional politics has neglected strategic interaction. With the exception of Breuckner's (1998) study of interactions among California cities' growth management programs, empirical analysis that incorporates strategic interaction is conspicuous by its absence. Several factors may contribute to this gap. First is the reluctance of much of the urban politics subfield to embrace formal models of politics, as was discussed in chapter 1. Second, a number of statistical estimation problems are associated with estimating the jurisdictional reaction functions necessary to capture strategic interaction. These include the endogeneity of the choice variables of other jurisdictions, which are used to estimate a jurisdiction's reaction function, spatial dependence, and correlation between community characteristics and the error term.

Several empirical studies at the state level have successfully addressed these concerns. For example, Case, Rosen, and Hines (1993) estimated reaction functions for state per capita spending decisions where states benefit from expenditures in neighboring states. Fredriksson and Millimet (2001) estimate pollution abatement reaction functions among states.

The process of policy and institutional learning that results from the interaction of local actors also needs to be studied more systematically. Network analysis provides a powerful analytic tool to examine patterns of interaction and their consequences. Recent works on collaborative approaches to environmental management identify how the supply of institutions in unstructured settings is shaped by patterns of communication and the structure of networks among stakeholders (Lubell et al. 2002). Similar designs applied to issues of metropolitan governance would allow us to identify how cooperation in one policy arena influences other issues and the role of information and communication networks in facilitating institutional collective action.

REFERENCES

Bickers, Kenneth N., and Robert M. Stein. 2002. Inter-Local Cooperation and the Distribution of Federal Grant Awards. Paper presented at a Devoe L. Moore Center conference, Decentralized Governance: The Implications of Government Organization in Metropolitan Areas, Tallahassee, Fla., October 4–6.

Brueckner, Jan K. 1998. Testing for Strategic Interaction among Local Governments: The Case of Growth Controls. *Journal of Urban Economics* 44: 438–67.

Carr, Jered B., and Feiock, Richard C., eds. 2003. *City–County Consolidation and Its Alternatives*. Armonk, N.Y.: M. E. Sharpe.

Case, A. C., Hines Rosen, and J. C. Hines. 1993. Budget Spillovers and Fiscal Policy Interdependence: Evidence from the States. *Journal of Public Economics* 52: 285–307.

Clingermayer, James C., and Richard C. Feiock. 2001. *Institutional Constraints and Policy Choice: An Exploration of Local Governance*. Albany: State University of New York Press.

Feiock, Richard C. 2002. A Quasi-Market Framework for Local Economic Development Competition. *Journal of Urban Affairs* 24: 123–42.

Feiock, Richard C., and Jered B. Carr. 2001. Incentives, Entrepreneurs, and Boundary Change: A Collective Action Framework. *Urban Affairs Review* 36: 382–405.

Fredriksson, Per G., and Daniel Millimet. 2001. Strategic Interaction and the Determination of Environmental Policy Across U.S. States. *Journal of Urban Economics* 51: 101–22.

Heckathorn, Douglas D., and Steven M. Maser. 1987. Bargaining and Constitutional Contracts. *American Journal of Political Science* 31: 142–68.

Lipecap, Gary. 1989. *Contracting for Property Rights*. New York: Cambridge University Press.

————. 1996. Economic Variables and the Development of the Law: The Case of Western Mineral Rights. In *Empirical Studies in Institutional Change*, ed. Lee J. Alston, Thrainn Eggertsson, and Douglas North. New York: Cambridge University Press.

Lubell, Mark, Mark Schneider, John Scholz, and Mihriye Mete. 2002. Watershed Partnerships and the Emergence of Collective Action Institutions. *American Journal of Political Science* 46, no. 1: 148–63.

Olson, Mancur. 1971. *The Logic of Collective Action*. Cambridge, Mass.: Harvard University Press.

Orfield, Myron. 1997. *Metropolitics: A Regional Agenda for Community and Stability*. Washington, D.C.: Brookings Institution.

————. 2002. *American Metropolitics: The New Suburban Reality*. Washington, D.C.: Brookings Institution Press.

Ostrom, Elinor. 1990. *Governing the Commons*. New York: Cambridge University Press.

Ostrom, Elinor, Roy Gardner, and James Walker. 1994. *Rules, Games, and Common-Pool Resources*. Ann Arbor: University of Michigan Press.

Ostrom, Elinor, Roger Parks, and Gordon Whitaker. 1978. *Patterns of Metropolitan Policing*. Cambridge, Mass.: Ballinger.

Post, Stephanie. 2002. Local Government Cooperation: The Relationship between Metropolitan Area Government and Service Provision. Paper presented at a Devoe L. Moore Center conference, Decentralized Governance: The Implications of Government Organization in Metropolitan Areas, Tallahassee, Fla., October 4–6.

Schneider, Mark, Paul Teske, and Michael Mintrom. 1995. *Public Entrepreneurs: Agents for Change in American Government*. Princeton, N.J.: Princeton University Press.

Weir, Margaret. 2000. Coalitions for Regionalism. In *Reflections on Regionalism*, ed. Bruce Katz. Washington D.C.: Brookings Institution Press.

CONTRIBUTORS

JACK BUCKLEY is an assistant professor of education at Boston College. He received his Ph.D. in political science at the State University of New York, Stony Brook. His interests are in political economy and statistical methodology. He has forthcoming articles in *Political Analysis, Education Evaluation and Policy Analysis,* and *Social Science Policy Review*.

JERED B. CARR is an assistant professor of political science and urban affairs at Wayne State University. He received his Ph.D. from the Askew School of Public Administration and Policy at Florida State University, and his dissertation on local boundary competition was the recipient of the 2001 American Political Science Association's Leonard White Award for the best dissertation in public administration. He has published in *Urban Affairs Review, State and Local Government Review,* and *Political Research Quarterly*. He is the editor of a forthcoming book on city–county consolidation.

RICHARD C. FEIOCK is a professor of public administration, affiliate faculty, in the Department of Political Science and the DeVoe Moore Center at Florida

State University, where he directs the Program in Local Governance. His work on local governance has appeared in a number of scholarly journals, and he also coauthored *Institutional Constraints and Local Government: An Exploration of Local Governance.*

LINDA JOHNSON is completing her Ph.D. at the Askew School of Public Administration at Florida State University. Her interests are in local institutions, governance, and environmental policy. Her research on city–county consolidation has appeared in the *Journal of Political Science,* and she has contributed chapters to several edited volumes.

MARTIN JOHNSON is an assistant professor of political science at the University of California, Riverside. His research and teaching interests focus on American political behavior and public policy. He is currently studying how social context and other sources of information shape public opinion and the policy choices governments make. His research has appeared in the *American Journal of Political Science, Electoral Studies,* the *Legislative Studies Quarterly, Political Analysis,* and the *State Politics and Policy Quarterly.*

PAUL G. LEWIS is a research fellow at the Public Policy Institute of California and currently also directs its program on governance and public finance. He is the author of *Shaping Suburbia: How Political Institutions Organize Urban Development,* which examines the influence of metropolitan governmental structure on patterns of urban growth. His work on local government, land use, and urban policy has also appeared in numerous academic journals and in several monographs for the Public Policy Institute of California. He received a Ph.D. in politics from Princeton University.

MAX NEIMAN is associate dean and director of the Center for Social and Behavioral Science at the University of California, Riverside. His major interests include urban political economy, as well as public policy and land use politics. In addition to articles published in the *American Political Science Review, Western Political Quarterly, Social Science Quarterly,* and *Urban Affairs Quarterly,* he is the coauthor (with Nicholas P. Lovrich) of *Public Choice Theory in Public Administration.* His most recent book is *Defending Government.*

RONALD J. OAKERSON is a professor of political science at Houghton College, where he is also academic vice president and dean of the college. He has written ten numerous articles on local governance, and his most recent book is *Governing Local Public Economies: Creating the Civic Metropolis.*

STEPHANIE SHIRLEY POST is a political consultant and researcher in Houston, Texas. She received her Ph.D. in political science from Rice University, where she held a one-year postdoctoral fellow position in the School of Social Sciences. Her research interests focus on metropolitan area government service provision and cooperation among local governments. Her work has appeared in *Urban Affairs Review, Political Research Quarterly,* and *Legislative Studies Quarterly.*

MARK SCHNEIDER is a professor of political science at the State University of New York, Stony Brook. He is the author or coauthor of six books and fifty-seven articles on local government and competition among cities and schools in the leading urban and political science journals.

ELAINE B. SHARP is a professor of political science at the University of Kansas. She has written numerous books and articles on local government, including *Culture Wars and Local Politics, The Dilemma of Drug Policy in the United States, The Some Time Connection: Public Opinion and Social Policy,* and *Citizen Demand-Making in the Urban Context.*

ANNETTE STEINACKER is an assistant professor of political science at Claremont Graduate University. Her work has focused on economic development issues and changes in local government structure. The use of bargaining models to explain location incentives provided to businesses is the focus of both her forthcoming article for *Policy Studies Review* and of a research project funded by the National Science Foundation that she is undertaking with Richard Feiock. She is also currently working on the relationship between the growth of infill development in cities and their level of affordable housing.

JILL TAO is an assistant professor of political science at the University of Oklahoma, Norman. Her areas of research and teaching interests include comparative and development administration, community and economic development policy, implementation theory, policy analysis, and urban politics and administration.

INDEX